Colours In The Sky

The History of Autair
and
Court Line Aviation

Graham M Simons

Pen & Sword
AVIATION

First Published in Great Britain in 1997 by
GMS Enterprises

Revised and re-printed in Great Britain in 2018 by
Pen & Sword Aviation
an imprint of
Pen & Sword Books Ltd
47 Church Street, Barnsley, South Yorkshire S70 2AS

Typeset in 10/11 Times
by GMS Enterprises

Printed and bound in India by Replika Press Pvt. Ltd.

Pen & Sword Books Ltd incorporates the Imprints of Pen & Sword
Aviation, Pen & Sword Family History, Pen & Sword Maritime, Pen & Sword
Military, Pen & Sword Discovery, Wharncliffe Local History, Wharncliffe
True Crime, Wharncliffe Transport, Pen & Sword Select, Pen & Sword
Military Classics, Leo Cooper, The Praetorian Press, Remember When,
Seaforth Publishing and Frontline Publishing.

For a complete list of Pen & Sword titles please contact
PEN & SWORD BOOKS LIMITED

47 Church Street, Barnsley, South Yorkshire, S70 2AS, England
E-mail: enquiries@pen-and-sword.co.uk
Website: www.pen-and-sword.co.uk.

Index

Foreword

Bill Armstrong
Chairman Autair.

Of all that there was, Court Line Helicopters of Cape Town is still trading successfully. It is the one aspect that continues to keep the 'Colours in the sky'. From the remains of Court Line Aviation there were plansto revive the business making use of a small number of One-Elevens, but nothing came of the project. Instead, myself, Bill Buxton and others created Autair Engineering a company that continues to this day, still involved with aircraft, still with a set—up at Luton, but also with a successful Miami, USA operation as well. The current Managing Director is Peter Jackson, a Court old timer, ably assisted until very recently by Bob Innes, another Court man.

I cannot let this moment pass without tendering my compliments to Graham Simons who, instead of going to the 'leaders' for their ego-laden stories of '...of course I got them to do this, and at my instigation they did that...' found his way directly to those who did the real work, then enthusiastically wove their words into the factual story behind this airline's great success.

These are the people that deserve our ultimate tribute.

And please have no doubt, for despite what happened in 1974, it was a great success - and I use these words with care...

In a venture which has it's hazards, and over a period of fifteen years, every single worker can be immensely proud of one thing - we carried some five million passengers to many distant places. We took them out, we brought them back - all and every one came safely home.

Bill Armstrong
1st August 1997

Edward Posey
Managing Director Court Line Aviation.
Director, Court Line Group.

The curtain finally came down for Court Line at midnight on Thursday 15th August 1974. I had spent the previous weeks isolated from the action at Luton Airport, closeted with bankers, accountants, lawyers, civil servants and government representatives. It was an intensive time and, finally, with a heavy heart, I went up to Luton that evening for our last Board Meeting. We confirmed the decision to stop flying operations that same night. We were discussing how to tell our people when our Security Officer, Ken Holmes came into my office to say that a number of colleagues were waiting in the foyer to see me. He led me out to the top of the stairs and, as I looked down, miserably, at that sea of faces I will never forget the next few moments; there erupted a prolonged and sustained round of applause. At the time I could not understand it - only now do I realise it was as the ending of a play.

When Graham Simons first asked me to write this Foreword to his book, my heart sank at the thought of having to re-live this whole traumatic time. It was only as I read the proof copies, and memories flowed back over the period he has written about with such enthusiasm, that I have been able to see all the events in perspective. I am deeply indebted to Graham for recording so vividly what was achieved over those exciting years.

I believe that we had one big advantage from the start - we were in the holiday business. This meant we were dealing with people who were pleased to be going on holiday and, on their return, were relaxed and full of happy memories.Flying was still a thrilling experience for them and the airline naturally picked up this holiday mood. The pilots were proud to be flying the very latest of equipment - the BAC One-Eleven 500 Series and the Lockheed TriStars, the engineers liked working on them and the stewardesses enjoyed their Mary Quant uniforms.

I am now put in mind of Shakespeare's words:
"All the world's a stage,
And all the men and women merely players;
The have their exists and their entrances;
And one man in his time plays many parts..."
(As You Like It; II, vii, 139-142)

In my minds eye I can clearly see the whole episode as a great play, and at last understand the applause - for us all - which spontaneously arose in celebration that last night.

The story of Court Line Aviation, which is the core of this play, has a clear framework. The author was undoubtedly Bill Armstrong, the impresario was John Young (who always wore a bow-tie), I was the director - but nothing could have been achieved without the cast, and this Graham knew. He went to the ground crews, the caterers, the stewardesses, the engineers, the pilots, and heard their stories, and only after that came to Bill, John and myself. For us all, our work was a way of life. We were a happy company, and it felt like being in a large family.

Many of us have found other roles in the intervening years, but Graham Simons has enabled us to be proud of the parts we played in this particular drama of our lives. I hope, and believe that this book will be avidly read by everyone involved with the airline, as well as by all those who have a passion for the aviation business and might feel inspired to produce their own version of 'Colours in the Sky'.

Edward Posey

Edward Posey
1st August 1997

Introduction

The airline aspect to this book really only goes back thirty or so years, but the United Kingdom's airline industry - and the attitude and aspirations of the people that use it - have changed out of all recognition in that time.

Autair and Court Line Aviation as described here were in the public's view for just fifteen years. It began in the dying embers of the staid, formal fifties, grew up and consolidated itself through the 'Swingin' sixties' then, like a newly emerged butterfly, entered the Seventies to arch high in the sky like a multi-coloured comet, before cascading to earth with a crash that shook the country following the biggest energy crisis since the war.

Without doubt Autair's and Court Line's main source of income was Inclusive Tour (IT) passengers - these were (and are) the much derided 'bucket and spade to Benidorm' brigade so loathed and looked down upon by some of the national carriers. But innovators within the airline and the tour companies saw that by putting as many 'bums on seats' as possible, a good deal could be offered to the working man... Unlike today, where many people have at least two 'breaks' a year, back in the sixties it was still unusual to have a holiday abroad - families saved all year for their 'two weeks in the sun'. Previously only the wealthy and privileged could fly, but now the tour companies were falling over themselves to open up the market for the 'common man'.

This is not just a book about an airline, it's routes and equipment - such a work could result in something dry and boring to the extreme.

What I have attempted is to record as accurately as possible the story of the airline from it's formation to demise, and use this as a framework to bring in accounts from as many people as possible 'that were there' thus, hopefully, making the story 'real'. Some photographs are lacking in quality; they were, after all, snapshots taken at the time on domestic cameras, not shot by professional photographers on very expensive equipment. The story is also slightly disjointed, telling the public side of the collapse before going 'back in time' to reveal something of what had been going on 'behind the scenes' and the duplicity of the politicians that became involved...

Bill Armstrong and his Autair companies were, and still are innovators. The Court Line Group of the 1960's and 70's were in the same vein - daring entrepreneurs that were not scared of trying...

I hope this book is a fitting tribute to everyone that worked for the company in a time, as one wag has said, was a time, '...*when sex was safe and flying was dangerous.*'

Graham M Simons
Peterborough
15th August 1997

Update – 2017

With the passing of the years the Autair and Court Line Aviation story seems to have taken on a greater importance, for in hindsight it clearly was a pivotal moment in the story of Great Britain's commercial aviation scene.

When the original version of *'Colours in the Sky'* came out in 1997, it appealed to many different aspects of aviation interests – and many that were not! I got letters from business study academics, airline fans, former customers… all were interested in and intrigued by the story. It also seems that publication of the book was somehow cathartic for many – it was as if it drew a line in the sand, and let people move on.

There was very little criticism, and a lot of praise. Sure, one of Anthony Wedgewood Benn's minions penned a long, rambling tirade to - or was that against? - me, attempting to justify his commissars actions, but that had already been covered in the book.

As always, after a book is published there is always an avalanche of additional material that surfaces – and so it was here. Bill Armstrong, the founder of Autair; Ed Posey, the Managing Director of Court Line Aviation and Peter Murdoch, who had the advertising account for Court Line and commissioned many photographs of the company for the company – were all inspired to go digging through their archives and found even more that could have been used. Advertisement layouts, original colour negatives that had previously been printed in black and white, unused images that were left on the floor for being not quite up to requirements, plus some material that was enbargoed for the first book... I was given permission to use it all, and so gratefully took it, and filed it all away for possible future use.

As the years passed and the original book sold out, I occasionally considered a re-print, but it did not seem that any worthwhile market was out there. Then a number of unfortunate 'incidents' occurred. Woolnoughs, the original printers was sold to a new owner, and suffered a somewhat mysterious fire that destroyed the master negatives for the book. I suffered a computer failure that partially destroyed my own layouts, and finally my working copy of the book, signed by so many former Autair and Court Line employees was stolen.

Around 2012 previously read copies started to appear on a certain well-known web auction site – at ever-increasing prices. At the same time a trickle of emails and letters started to arrive asking if I would consider rc-printing it.

Whatever I did, the book would have to be re-mastered, so I might as well take the opportunity to do a full revision, and uprate all those images, for back in 1996/7 digital image reproduction was, comparatively speaking, in its infancy. Then Pen & Sword - for whom I have written a large number of titles - showed an interest.

The result is what you have in your hands!

Graham M Simons
Peterborough
15 August 2017

Chapter One
Setting The Scene

In order to be able to fully understand the activities of the airline popularly known as Court Line, and the train of events that overtook it during the last few months of its trading career, one first has to take a step or two back in order to see a more wider picture.

Court Line - or to give the airline its correct title of 'Court Line Aviation Limited' - was just one aspect of a much larger trading organisation, the Court Line Group, which was divided into four divisions. They had extensive interests in shipping, shipbuilding, ship-repair and ship engineering, aviation, travel agencies, inclusive tour companies and hotels.

Just how large and varied the Court Line Group of companies was at its peak can be seen from the chart showing the principal main, subsidiary and associated companies.

In order to save repeatedly using the somewhat cumbersome 'Court Line Aviation Limited' and 'Court Line Group' titles

The concerns listed below were the main businesses either fully or part-owned (%) by the Court Line Group. The dates relate to the known ownership periods.

The Court Line Group of Companies

Shipowning Division

Court Line Ltd (100%)	-1974
Court Line ' Ship Management) Ltd (100%)	-1974
Caribbean Tankers Ltd - Bahamas (100%)	-1974
Malcolm Ore Carriers Ltd (51%)	-1974

Shipbuilding, Repair and Engineering Division

Appledore Shipbuilders Ltd (100%)	-1974
A&P Appledore Ltd (50%)	1973-1974
A&P Appledore International Ltd - Bahamas (40%)	1973-1974
Brigham & Cowan Ltd (100%)	1971-1974
Brigham & Cowan (Hull) Ltd (100%)	1971-1971
Doxford & Sunderland Ltd (100%)	1973-1974
Doxford Hawthorn Research Services Ltd (50%)	1973-1974
Elliott Associated Developments Ltd (70%)	-1974
K&L Marine Equipment Ltd (100%)	1971-1974
Mercantile Dry Dock Co. Ltd (100%)	1971-1974
Middle Docks & Engineering Co. Ltd (100%)	1971-1974
North East Coast Contractors Ltd. (100%)	1971-1974
North East Coast Ship Repairers Ltd (100%)	1971-1974
Seemark Switches Ltd (100%)	-1971
Sunderland Forge & Steel Engineering Ltd (100%)	1974
Sunderland Shipbuilders Ltd (100%)	1974
Tyne Tanker Cleaning Co. (32%)	1973-1974
Woldingham Steel Company Ltd (100%)	1974

Aviation Division

Autair Helicopters (Pty) Ltd	1971
Court Line Aviation Ltd (100%)	1970-1974
Leeward Islands Air Transport Ltd - Antigua (100%)	1972-1974
Hillside Coaches Ltd (100%)	1971
Courtair Catering Ltd (100%)	1968-1972
Court Line Catering Ltd (100%)	1973-1974
Court Line Coaches (100%)	1972-1974
Court Line Helicopters (Pty) Ltd - S.A. (100%)	1972-1974
Court Management Services (Pty) Ltd- S.A. (100%)	1971-1974

Leisure Division

Court Leisure Ltd (100%)	1974
Court Line Holidays (100%)	-1972
Court Travel Ltd (100%)	-1973
Halcyon Hotels Ltd - St Lucia (100%)	-1974
Halcyon Hotels (Nassau) Ltd - Bahamas (100%)	1973-1974
Halcyon Hotels (Antigua) Ltd - Antigua (100%)	1974
Halcyon Balmoral Hotel (Nassau)Ltd - Bahamas (100%)	-1973-1974
Durrant House Hotel Ltd (100%)	-1974
Court Line Incorporated New York (100%)	-1973-1974
Halcyon Holidays Ltd (100%)	-1972-1974
Harold Ingham Ltd (100%)	-1972
Court Line Travel Ltd	-1974
Murison Small Ltd (100%)	-1973
Owners Services Ltd (OSL) (100%)	-1974
Associated Travel Leisure & Services Ltd (100%)	-1974
Horizon Holidays Ltd (100%)	-1974
Airfair Ltd (100%)	-1974
Transair Market Development Corporation (51%)	-1972
British Student Travel Centre Ltd (100%)	-1974
Clarkson Holiday Holdings Ltd (100%)	-1974
Clarkson Medivillas Ltd (85%)	-1974
Vacation Tours Ltd (100%)	-1972
Vacation Tours (Dover) Ltd (100%)	-1971
Seagate Hotel Ltd (100%)	-1972
Lingress Ltd (100%)	1970
Clarksons Holidays Ltd (85%)	1974
Sunotel S.A. - Liechtenstein (85%)	1974
Servicios del Sol S.A. - Spain (85%)	1974
Cristaltour S. A. - Spain (42%)	1974

Other organisations

R. Harris & Son (Builders) (100%)	-1973-1974
Van Dyke North Sea Group (10%)	-1974

throughout this book, but at the same time maintaining the individual identities, when referring to the airline, the term 'Court Line' is used. Addition of the word 'Group', predominantly in the 'Aftermath' chapter, refers to the overall parent organisation.

It may also seem strange to the reader for details of shipping and other non aviation-related activities to be included in a history of an airline; however, the fortunes of the airline and all the other aspects of the Court Line Group were so interwoven during the years of operation, it is impossible to tell the story of one without at least touching in part on the other. It is also of use and interest to see the origins of some aviation practices that had been transferred across from the maritime side of the business.

Furthermore, period financial figures (where applicable) have had a more up-to-date conversion - calculated for the mid-1990's - provided in square brackets alongside to bring them into today's context.

Origins

The origins of Court Line Aviation have two distinct beginnings that did not come together until the mid-1960's. Firstly, let us deal with the name, and where it came from.

This can be traced back to 1905, when a small tramp steamer business was founded by 25-year old Philip Edward Haldenstein with £30,000, and the steamer *Arlington Court*. Captain S.H. Jones was the Master for her maiden voyage. All of the ships were named after famous country houses with the first word ending in 'ton' and the suffix 'Court'. Called Court Line after its first steamer, the company prospered, and their ships were seen as far afield as Argentina, the Black Sea and in the ports of Burma, where they became heavily involved in the rice trade.

The company traded from 1 Leadenhall Street as Haldinstein & Co. Ltd. The family came from Norwich but had a German-sounding name and so in 1915, with anti-German feeling sweeping the UK

Obviously sailing empty with derricks stowed fore and aft, the 1929 version of Court Line's 'Bonnington Court' is seen from the air. (World Ship Society Library)

due to the Great War, the Chairman changed his name to Haldin by Royal Licence. Two years earlier Haldenstein had begun business involvements with Richard Phillips (later Lord Milford) and the Phillips family so that by 1922 this working relationship had progressed to the formation of a small company called Haldin and Phillips Ltd, which in turn took over Haldin's Court Line concern in 1929. In order to distribute the assets, Court Line was placed into liquidation and then disposed of to the United British Steamship Company Limited. The name was re-adopted in 1936 to encompass a fleet of nineteen steamers and three motor vessels.

All the vessels during this time carried similar versions of the fleet name. There were numerous versions of *Arlington Court, Dorrington Court, Kensington Court, Sinnington Court, Geddington Court, Barrington Court, Tilsington Court, Framlington Court...*

Court Line found itself in possession of a large fleet just as the 1930s depression was getting under way and as a result a large part of the fleet was laid up for many years – some on the Tyne, some at Sunderland and some at Milford Haven. The company managed to keep going by mothballing most of its ships and through trading with four or five ships at a time.

Philip Haldin served on the Tramp Shipping Subsidy Committee between 1935 and 1937 and was knighted in 1939.

At the outbreak of World War Two some twenty-four vessels were owned, but throughout the conflict thirteen - some sources say eighteen - of these were lost to enemy action. In 1943 Cory and Strick (Steamers) Ltd were acquired and, along with their three vessels, re-named the British Steamship Co. Ltd. During World War Two Court Line both operated its own vessels and managed others belonging to other owners. During the war Court Line vessels played a significant role in the convoys that kept the UK going. Also *Dorrington Court* (1938) became the model for what was known as the Empire Ship building programme and later for the

'Ocean' and 'Liberty' ships.

The British Steamship Co. Ltd took over Court Line in 1946 and the Court Line name disappeared, only to re-surface again in 1952 when a new Court Line took over the British Steamship Co. Ltd! After the war, a rebuilding programme was instituted, but by 1957 with a severe drop in freight rates, this stopped and several of the older ships were sold.

This fourth reincarnation of Court Line went about its business in an inauspicious manner until a softly spoken Yorkshireman called John Young joined the Board on 25 October 1961, the same year that the group posted a record £266,000 net loss. Two years later, John Young became Managing Director, succeeding the Hon. W. S. Phillips, who then became Chairman, and by 1964-65 the group had moved back into the black with a profit of £32,000. Sandhurst-trained John Young had served three years in the jungles of Malaya before leaving the Army and moving to South Africa to learn the fruit canning business. He was soon to marry Tulla Trouton, the daughter of Robert Trouton, the Chairman of Hector Whaling. After he had completed a three year stint in America, Norway and Scotland to learn what shipping was all about he was taken into the family business, '...*I came into the business on the nepotism ticket*' he was often heard to say jovially. After British and Commonweath took over Hector Whaling he left to join Court Line.

John R Young, the Managing Director of the Court Line Group of companies from 1963, and later Chairman, seen in his trademark bow tie. [Autair-Court Collection]

The 1952-built 'Framlington Court' seen at Rotterdam, date unknown. [Autair-Court Collection]

From Tramps to Tankers.

By the 1960s, the company's ship-owning activity was steadily declining and it was starting to diversify. A bulk carrier called *Hector Halcyon* was purchased in 1961 and renamed *Cressington Court*. There was then a switch to larger ships and the smaller tramps sold off. Court Line also moved into tankers with a number being purchased and given the hallmark *'Halcyon'* prefix.

Between 1963 and 1966 a programme of modernisation was undertaken, Court Line - at John Young's instigation - gradually disposing of all its fleet of ageing tramp steamers to an Indian company, replacing them with a growing fleet of oil tankers. Somewhat remarkably, the money owing to the company, nearly £500,000, from the sale of these five vessels in a complex financial arrangement - known in the accounts as 'The Jayanti Debt' - was listed as still outstanding in the published 1973 accounts!

The first of these tankers, the 20,205 dead weight tons (dwt) *Halcyon Days* arrived second-hand in 1963 at a cost of £1,385,000 and was operated on a time charter to Shell. It was followed by the 67,112 dwt *Halcyon Breeze,* built for the Court Group in Japan and delivered to one of it's subsidiary organisations, Caribbean Tankers Ltd in April 1964. This vessel was operated on a bareboat charter with the Ministry of Defence from July 1967 to August 1974 under the name of *Derwentdale*. Eventually six tankers and two bulk carriers were operated by Court Line or its subsidiaries, the largest of which was the 226,692 dwt *Halcyon The Great*, delivered to the company from its builders in 1971.

The vessels were operated on two types of charters - long-term 'time' charters that brought advantages of a fixed, predicable income

The largest tanker in the Court Line fleet - the 226,692 dwt 'Halcyon The Great' [Autair-Court Collection]

and 'spot' charters, where a ship was provided for single voyages which could be highly profitable. The entire Court Line tanker fleet was predominantly operated on time charters to numerous oil companies.

Diversification

Moves into other spheres first came in November 1963 when John Young and James Venus formed Appledore, a company that acquired a small North Devon shipbuilding business that was then in liquidation. In turn this concern was acquired by Court Line following independent accountant valuation in July 1965 as Appledore Shipbuilders Ltd.

The origins of Appledore date back to 1855 on the estuary of the River Torridge. The Richmond Dry Dock was built in 1856 by William Yeo and named after Richmond Bay in Prince Edward Island, where the Yeo family's shipping fleet was based.

The business was led by Philip Kelly Harris during the early part of the 20th century and known as P.K. Harris & Sons until 1963 when it became Appledore Shipbuilders.

The vendors were John Young, Mr Robert de B. Trouton (John Young's father-in-law), Shipbuilding Services Ltd (at that time a company owned by James Venus), Malcolm Ore Carriers Ltd (a Court Line subsidiary), J. W. Chapman, and C. Rawson, each of whom owned 10% of the shares. This transaction introduced James Venus and Wyn Chapman to the Court Line Main Board.

Appledore operated a number of ship-building and repairing docks in North Devon, all of which prospered in Court Line's hands. There was the Richmond Dry Dock (built in 1855) and the Middle Dock (the former Newquay dry dock built in 1860), but it was their Bidna Dock that was a considerable success, for this, aided with

The Court Line group operated numerous ship-building facilities in the North-East of England. (Autair Court Collection)

The Appledore covered dock in North Devon. (Autair Court Collection)

Government loans, pioneered the first covered-in shipyard concept in the United Kingdom. This enabled work to be undertaken on vessels in the 3,000 to 4,000 dwt range in all weather conditions in a similar manner to a factory production line. This new shipyard, built on a greenfield site in Appledore at a cost of about £4m, opened in 1970. Appledore proved to be a very sound investment for Court Line across the entire period of its ownership.

From 1966 the scale of Court Line's shipping and ship-repairing interests increased with further acquisitions and the expansion of Appledore. By January 1970 this involved the acquisition of North East Coast Ship Repairers Ltd, itself an amalgamation of the Middle Docks and Engineering Co. Ltd. and Brigham and Cowan Ltd, both of which were dry dock owners and ship-repairers on Tyneside, and the Mercantile Dry Dock Co. Ltd. of Jarrow.

In June 1972 the Court Line Group's ship-building expansion was complete with the acquisition of Doxford and Sunderland Ltd and all of its subsidiaries which included ship-building and ship-repair yards and engineering works.

The advantages of being able to work 'under cover, in the dry' can be seen from this picture taken inside Appledore's Bidna Dock. (Autair Court Collection)

Mention should also be made of Court Line Group's investment in a 10% share of Van Dyke North Sea Group, a speculative Oil and Gas consortium exploring the North Sea. Court Line ultimately invested £679,000 in the consortium, but no oil or gas was discovered during the period this book covers.

Two holding companies became involved in these arrangements - Court Line Shipbuilders Ltd, acting as the ultimate divisional holdings company, and Burngreen Securities Ltd, an intermediate holdings company

Part of the Middle Dock & Engineering Co. Ltd complex of eleven dry docks in South Shields. [Autair-Court Collection]

established by Court Line. Neither company traded as such, although both were used in exceedingly complex processes to raise finances for the Group, predominantly to fund the Group's expansion into the Caribbean hotel market.

Both Court Line Shipbuilders and Burngreen Securities continued in their duties until some - but not all - of their operating subsidiaries were formally acquired by Her Majesty's Government on 19 September 1974, just over a month after the Group had been placed into liquidation. The financial difficulties in which the Group found itself forced the sell off - the background to this can be found in a later chapter.

Chapter Two

From An Idea...

The aeronautical origins of what is possibly one of Europe's best-remembered holiday airlines, Court Line Aviation, can be traced back through several stages to 1953 when, after three years working privately, a new organisation called Autair was formed as a London - based helicopter operating company. W. H. Armstrong was its Chairman and Managing Director.

Early days of the founder...
In order to grasp the background into the formation of the airline, it is beneficial to look briefly at the aeronautical career of its founder.

Squadron Leader (Retd) William Henry ('Bill') Armstrong F.RAeS started his aerial involvement in 1941 when, after induction into the Royal Air Force at the Aircrew Recruitment Centre, Regent's Park - inductees were mustered on Lords Cricket Ground and fed at London Zoo - he passed through various training units and qualified as a Navigator, being entrusted to take a new Bristol Beaufort torpedo bomber to 39 Squadron, then based under siege on the Mediterranean island of Malta.

In January 1943, after a variety of strike operations, Bill and other members of 39 Squadron took a handful of Beaufighters to Marrakesh to protect Winston Churchill and other Allied leaders at a pre-invasion conference there from a possible long-range German attack.

Following a further six months hitting mainland European targets and short spell with 153 Squadron (passing his night intruder knowledge on to others) Bill found himself on a ship heading for home. On arrival he was greeted with the news that a V-2 rocket had arrived in the garden of his parents home in London - luckily without permanent injury to the family - so then it was some long-outstanding leave and then onto instructional duties at East Fortune in Scotland.

Immediate post-war Europe was a very fragmented and disjointed place and Bill, who can speak fluent German, found himself working on Missing Research duties at the Allied Forces Headquarters, Berlin, working with the Russians in Eastern occupied

William 'Bill' Armstrong, founder of Autair and his new wife Doreen at their marriage in Nice in 1952. Doreen was to become a future co-director, business partner and secretary.
(W. Armstrong archive)

Germany, but after 'incompatible activities' they were expelled by the Soviets. He was then posted as Squadron Leader commanding No. 22 Missing Research and Enquiry Service locating crash sites of downed Allied airmen until leaving the Air Force in 1949.

A new decade saw Bill involved in a number of tasks; working with Dušan 'Duško' Popov OBE. Popov was a Serbian triple agent working for MI.6 during World War Two under the code name 'Tricycle' and the Abwehr code name 'Ivan'. Popov is said by many to be one of the inspirations for Ian Fleming's James Bond character. Indeed, Fleming knew Popov during the war, and, it is said, followed him in Lisbon, Portugal as an escort appointed by the MI6, witnessing an event in the Estoril Casino where Popov placed a bet of $40,000 in order to cause a rival to withdraw from a baccarat table: Fleming used this episode as the basis for *Casino Royale*.

Bill worked with Popov and his associated companies establishing a

An entrepreneur and his efforts!

Above: Ronnie Myhill in a jovial mood by one of the light aircraft he sold to American officers.

Above right: R. M. Overseas Motors GmbH's skywriting AT-6F Harvard D-IDOK in an undignified position.

Right: Perhaps not the best sight to encourage financial institutions to back aviation projects, nor a good way to create passenger confidence! The ex-BEA Rapide G-AGUR following its accident at Rhein-Main airport, Frankfurt. [all via Bill Armstrong]

Left to right: John 'Jock' Cameron of BEA's Helicopter Experimental Unit, a member of the Henkel family, Ronnie Myhill and Bill Armstrong at the point purchasing the first Sikorsky S.51 G-AJOR.
[via Bill Armstrong]

technical and commercial network in Germany; also as a consultant for aviation activities, but it did not take him long to join up with another great aviation innovator of the post war years, Ronald 'Ronnie' Myhill.

Bill and Ronnie had served together in the Royal Air Force, where Myhill had also been on one of Churchill's Special Flights and with MRES, so it was natural for them to work in co-operation in civilian life. Bill joined his Frankfurt office, where Ronnie seemed to have the proverbial Midas touch; he sold insurance to the Allied Forces in Germany, where he also had the exclusive Jaguar dealership under his company name of R.M. Overseas Motors. But both were still intrigued by aviation, as Bill explained...

'Ronnie and I were also trying to get something going in aviation in Germany on a loose, but close relationship. The Germans were totally banned from all aeronautical activities from the end of the war, so there was scope for us to try a number of things; we sold light aircraft to members of the American Forces for instance. Ronnie also introduced 'skywriting' - for which I did the back-up research in England - using North American Harvards, injecting light oil into the exhaust to produce smoke to form letters. On one occasion Ronnie bribed the pilot to display my WELbeck telephone number high in the sky over London - the phone never stopped ringing for days afterwards!

Aerial Advertising - S.51 G-AJOR, resplendent with Persil and Henkel logos...

At nighttime a framework of lights (inset) could be switched on...
[via Bill Armstrong]

20

The culprit was our friend, ex Sqn. Ldr. Tommy Thompson, Dieppe Raider with 3 Squadron on Hurricanes and later with 33 Squadron on Spitfires and Tempests - still flying, still selling executive turbo-props, and still not quite forgiven!

British European Airways Helicopter Experimental Unit had three Sikorsky S.51 helicopters up for disposal, and just at that time Persil - which was a great German product and part of the Henkel family chemical empire - were looking for ways of promoting their soap products all over Germany. Ronnie nailed them down and, being ex-Air Force, it was assumed that he knew all about aviation, and as helicopters then had a great novelty value, Henkel were 'on'!

Autair's S.51 G-AJHW deposits drilling equipment in an underslung cargo net up to the site of the Malta Dam, some 6,000 feet up, high in the Austrian Alps.

I must pay tribute to Jock Cameron and his BEA Experimental Helicopter Unit. When they gave us contractual assistance to bring the S.51s into service, they happily topped their obligation in every way, and were unstinting in their advice. I am also happy to say that I took the opportunity with Jock and his training section to convert my limited RAF flying experience into that of a fully-fledged solo helicopter pilot. This was on their very early Bell 47B3 - sometimes sold on wheels, sometimes on skids and even one version with an open cockpit, and was the forerunner to the famous Bell 47 series.

An Autair S.51 with three oil drums underslung on a cable in Antarctica [both via Bill Armstrong]

It was very clear to me that the helicopter would be an unbelievably useful piece of transportation equipment for operations in more remote areas where no other form of transport was available. It was not a big leap of the imagination then to see that a potential client field consisted of oil, mining and survey companies, and construction and electrical power organisations and other such resource-based concerns, I was ready to move from 'Soap to Survey and Seismic'!

I soon formed my own company in London, the name Autair was the simple amalgamation of AUTomobiles (we were still assisting with the export of cars to Ronnie's company in Germany) and

The first Antarctic survey expedition aboard the Olaf Sven, with Autair's Sikorsky S.51 - G-AJOR on the helideck. The vessel is surrounded by typically dramatic Antarctic scenery. Working conditions aboard for the ground crews were 'primitive' to say the least, as can be seen from the view of 'JOR undergoing maintenance on the deck. The rotorblade supports - although appearing to be an afterthought, hanging out into space above the safety nets - was in fact a good example for forward planning for the helideck was not wide enough! [via Bill Armstrong]

AIRcraft (my own activities). The first - and longest serving co-shareholder was my wife Doreen, without whose help and support things would have never happened - she was also our first permanent secretary, for she knew what invoices and credit notes were! Doreen had been one of the Auxiliary Territorial Service 'warriors' who served in active foreign theatres of war and worked in the Headquarters of General Alexander, Commander in Chief of Central Mediterranean Forces.

Autair tackled various jobs around Europe - we did crowd control, carried surveying and drilling equipment up mountains and one machine was used as an overhead commentary position during the 1954 German Grand Prix at the Nurburgring! Also momentary fame in helping film the Riviera chase scenes in Alfred Hitchcock's 'To Catch a Thief' starring Grace Kelly. The

After the first Antarctic season Autair's S.51 helicopters were required at the other end of the globe, so after undergoing modification by Eagle Aviation Services at Blackbushe, they were transported to Southend Airport to be airfreighted to Greenland by a Bristol Freighter belonging to Air Charter. [via Bill Armstrong]

flying was done by John Crewdson, who realised the potential and later established his own concern, Film Flight Services. He was one of four close aviation friends and, along with Tim Clutterbuck was later to work on the Daryl Zanuck and Steve McQueen movie 'The War Lover' using a number of Boeing B-17s filmed at Bovingdon. Sadly, John was later to perish in a helicopter accident not of his making in the North Sea.

Worldwide Helicopters were demonstrating their uses with early and lucrative mine-clearing contracts in the African western desert and it was time for us to look elsewhere'.

To the ends of the earth...

In 1955 the company gained the contract - along with some useful publicity - to operate a pair of S.51's with Huntings on behalf of the Falkland Islands Dependencies Aerial Survey Expedition from a vessel, the *Olaf Sven*, going deep into the floating ice of Antarctica for a survey of the Graham Land Peninsular. The vessel had been specially equipped for helicopter operations with an 80 ft by 30 ft flight deck built above her foredeck. This was the first time that civilian helicopters had been operated in these regions and under such conditions.

Here Autair's Sikorsky S.51 G-AJHW, fitted with floats at Eagle Aviation Services at Blackbushe, is loaded aboard the Air Charter Freighter from the back of an Aviation Traders wagon for the flight to northern climes. [Autair Collection]

With completion of the contract, hardly a month had passed since their return to the UK before they were off to cold climates again, this time to the 'other end of the world' for a mineralogical survey of East Greenland on behalf of a Danish company! Bill takes up the story again...

'By now Ronnie was getting involved with the formation of a new post-war German airline called Luft-Transport Union. A quick flick of the financial wrist and he put up the capital of 30,000 Marks, with Bernard Dromgoole, and two German businessmen handling the local formalities. Autair assisted with staff from London - but I was really interested in the larger prospects of helicopter operations in the great wide world!

Because of my current views on independent aviation I backed off, and later Ronnie did also, but the airline went ahead, and prospered greatly during the German 'economic miracle'. This was LTU and on my last count had no less than nine TriStars, twenty-two other airliners and a staff of 4,000. No dare, no win it seems, but other chances were to come!

Ronnie went on to form another airline. Overseas Aviation, initially based at Southend, but later at Gatwick with a fleet of Vickers Vikings, Canadair Argonauts and North Star airliners. Till now the S.51s had been held in Ronnie's 'Overseas' companies and leased to Autair as required. However, they were now transferred to our first foreign associate, Autair Helicopter Services Ltd - with our new partner, Doug Connor, an ex-RCAF Wing Commander and postwar champion 'Cresta Run' rider. We later withdrew, leaving it as a self-contained company which was soon Canada's third-largest rotary-winged operator.

At the end of the brief Arctic summer, personnel and equipment returned to the UK for a rest before being invited to participate in a second Antarctic expedition and so more aircraft were needed. A pair of Swedish-registered Bell 47D1s were obtained for use in the second season aboard the *Olaf Sven*. These machines were smaller than the S.51, and could be serviced in relative comfort 'below decks' being moved around between decks on an improvised lift.

The newly independent international company rapidly gained the reputation of being one of the country's leading helicopter operators, and was soon operating a fleet of Bell 47s abroad on pest control, aerial photography, geophysical surveys and construction work, transporting both men and equipment.

To cater for 'hot and high' conditions in Africa, the new associate Autair Helicopters (Africa) Ltd with Lincoln 'Linc' Lord as the Managing Director, obtained a Bell 47G2, and later 47G3Bs also. Based at Salisbury, Rhodesia, they soon operated the Central African headquarters and maintenance base, and later agencies for Bell

Helicopter and other manufacturers.

Bill Armstrong employed one particular person who was to have a great impact on the company's fortunes about this time...

I appointed one Edward J. ('Ed') Posey for a 'Position to be nominated at a salary to be determined'! After a quick spin around all our African units, we rewarded him with the management of our worst station at Dum Dum airport, Calcutta, where he did the very best of jobs. This unit did a myriad of tasks, amongst other things working for Standard Oil and hauling explosives into remote areas for seismic surveys.

Ed Posey recalls the time clearly....

I had recently graduated from the London School of Economics, and wanted a career in aviation. Having previously written to Freddie Laker at Air Charter, Gerry Freeman at Transair and Harold Bamberg at British Eagle, I was intrigued by Autair's helicopter operation and so I wrote to them also, and got a job!

I joined Autair on 1 February 1957, as Personal Assistant to Bill Armstrong. Soon after I went for a quick trip around Africa - first to Nairobi in an Eagle Airways Auro York from Heathrow with Linc Lord and a Bell 47. At Nairobi we offloaded the Bell, and were assisted in the task by Jimmy Harper, the

Helicopter to Africa!

One of Autair's Bell 47's is off-loaded by Coles crane from G-AMUU, a Hunting- Clan Avro York at Nairobi. It was not unusual to find help being offered by your competition, as Ed Posey discovered! [Autair Collection]

For the second season in the Antarctic Bell 47's were used. Flying conditions could be and were hazardous. Left is a 'wipe-out' after a 'white-out', but luckily the pilot, Capt Jacques escaped without Injury. SE-HAD crashed at 0900hrs on 10th December 1956 at Tower Island, Graham Land.

Below: Capt Patcha brings SE-HAK (with Falklands Islands Dependencies Aerial Survey Expedition (FIDASE) lettering prominent) into land on the slipway at Deception Island, immediately prior to packing up for the journey back home. [both Autair Collection]

Fisons Managing Director, our main competitor!

On my return Bill then needed an Expediter to fulfil a Standard Oil contract in India. I did not know what the job entailed and had just got married but I arranged with Bill to go out to India for six weeks, my new wife June helping to set up the office there; soon after I was appointed Manager. It took two years before we were back in the UK for two weeks leave and then we were off again for another year!

The Indian operation made use of a trio of Bell 47Ds and a single Bell 47G on oil survey work in the Bay of Bengal and maintained a base at Dum Dum, Calcutta. The Indian subsidiary was also involved in the route survey for a 720 mile pipeline from Assam to Digboi, in the north of India, and surveying the route for a new road from Rangoon to Mandalay in Burma. This particular survey was not without its incidents. The whole thing was flown under very tight security as the area was in turmoil, and there was some shooting, although the only Autair casualty was one of their guards - who somehow managed to shoot himself in the foot! Also run from the Calcutta office were operations in Iran, Pakistan and Nepal.

Soon a number of bases and subsidiaries were established around the world, Bill followed the well-tried principal of not keeping all his

Autair around the world... left: a Bell 47 carries seismic equipment into remote sites for the survey teams in India... ...or below: spraying the cotton crop with insecticides at the Chombwa settlement near Mumba in Zambia.
[Autair - Court Collection]

eggs in one basket, setting up companies, providing them with staff revenue capacity and general back-up, but with the pace of expansion, often being forced to leave them to get on with it. In fact, a well-defined reporting system to London was in place. Here the administration and financial affairs were in the capable hands of Laurie Chandler, who could quickly pass on to Bill any critical issues wherever he happened to be - often as not 'living in aeroplanes' (or living with them) in some obscure part of the world.

This 'modus operandi' became even more vital for some limited periods in the nineteen fifties as Bill describes...

'...quite unbeknown to my family, friends and colleagues, I was temporarily 'recalled to the colours' so to speak, to organise certain covert flights into remote and confined areas for Her Majesty's Government. This was, - and still is - subject to a tight security block, but at the time passed by quite unnoticed as we were always involved with commercial operations at short notice in strange places!

By now we had also strengthened our structure by the appointment of a roving director in Africa - one Tim Clutterbuck - an ex wartime Squadron Leader and Photo-Reconnaissance Unit ace who was quite at home anywhere in our wide geography. In addition to Ed Posey in the Far East, we also made other regional appointments such as Linc Lord (a former 144 Squadron Hampden pilot) as Managing Director of our Central African company.

Shortly waiting in the wings would be Ted Spreadbury (an ex carrier pilot) to take over as Managing Director of our South African company, and later Freddie Wilcox, also ex Fleet Air Arm and Queen's Flight helicopters - he was destined to assume command of Autair East Africa - a company which he would eventually acquire and manage to this very day.

For the UK, Europe and the Middle East we now had a new M.D, at Luton, Jimmy Harper, with staff expanded to include two young Luton ladies, Pat Mould and Hazel Light, who between them were to serve for over sixty years. Jimmy had unique RAF experience on the first Sikorsky R4 military helicopters and was later boss of the Fison Airwork Helicopter wing.

As the decade came to a close we were still trying to elbow our way into Australia, and were set to acquire a substantial interest in Woods Aviation, whose Managing director was Jimmy Woods, veteran of the 1934 MacRobertson Air Race from the UK to Australia. This company, along with other associates, we converted into helicopter ways, with two other managers coming in to assist - Andy Neal (also ex Fison Airwork) based at Darwin, with Captain 'Paddy' Jones - later to become a rare 20,000 hour pilot - succeeding Jimmy Woods at Perth.

We grew in bursts, so different waves of people joined our ranks. In the early 1960s, prompted by our new link with Australia we sent the press-gang down to Earls Court (ANZACLAND London SW5) and returned with many long-term stalwarts, like senior secretaries Merle McGarry from Brisbane, Pam Baker from NZ and Graham Broadbridge who was ex-Ansett and our first Manager in the Argentine.

Next arrival was a band of French pilots led by Chris Lallemande, and all with valuable field experience, some acquired in French Indo-China. I also 'raided' the Austrian Air Force, where I had learned that their expertly trained pilots were only held on six weeks notice. Five first class young pilots promptly joined, including Walter Hugel, then even Swiss recruits like Ueli Eisenhut. All were to fly in our many distant operations.

In the various regions maintenance was controlled by such dedicated engineers as Fred Coates, Roy Neep, Dennis Cox, John Bourne (all ex-UK) Danny Patel (ex India) Bill Schoeman (ex South Africa) and Carl Timm (ex Sweden). These, along with many other supporters who go un-named here formed an international brigade who kept our machines in the air in more than fifty countries around the world.

Soon to join the company was a unique personality whom I first met with Ronnie Myhill in Germany - Captain Maurice Rose, who would fly our DC3 aircraft carrying dismantled helicopters and company crews to dozens of different destinations - even as far as the Philippines and Australia – and that's a long way in a Dak! Before joining us he

Autair's Calcutta office assisted in bringing to the world the news that Sir Edmund Hillary had discovered the remains of the scalp of a Yeti', the so-called 'Abominable Snowman'. One of Autair's Bell 47s was used to bring the 'artifact' - which later turned out to be a goat's skull - down from the High Himalayas. [Autair – Court Collection]

had been an early RAF jet pilot, then flown Hastings troopers, and later formed part of a special calibration flight, visiting various civil airfields to test their landing facilities. He had already flown in most parts of the world and so was to continue for many years with us.

If I was to walk in with a contract for some obscure place, even without being asked he would start drafting the route clearance applications and calculating loads and distances. Even after we closed our live operations he would still continue to move helicopters and materials which we bought and sold all over the world.

Autair helpd Agip with oil exploration in the North African Deserts. Here Bell 47 G-ARXH is seen 'on the ground' in typical terrain
[Autair Collection]

An upsurge of interest in Saharan oil well demonstrated Autair's 'rapid response' capability, for when asked to send one helicopter with crew to the Spanish Sahara, Malayan-born Gerald Threlfall - who had recently joined the company from World Wide Helicopters - and a Bell 47G were loaded aboard a Douglas C-47 in the UK for the positioning flight. First stop was Madrid to pick up American oil and geophysical survey personnel and then on to Las Palmas in the Canary Islands to drop off some of the personnel before flying across to the African mainland to unload the helicopter and begin the ten-day search.

The entire operation was successfully completed within two weeks with both aircraft back in the UK. Bill Armstrong:

''Threllers' (as he was often known) was later to play a most important role in our formal entry into the fixed-wing world. Alas, he is no longer with us to make his own personal contribution to the story'.

Chapter Three
In The Beginning...

Autair had been chartering and using fixed wing aircraft for a number of years to support and supplement their helicopter operations - it was now time to expand and consolidate the entire operation and it made good sense to create some form of fixed wing set-up. This came into being during the spring of 1960 when Bill Armstrong made the decision to create the airline associate...

'Prior to our formal entry into the UK airline industry, we had maintained a relatively low profile and kept clear of early 'spin doctors'. We had no wish to attract the competition to those opportunities we had created and where we were rapidly gaining ground. As a result, many of our activities were relatively unknown to the world at large.

It may therefore have appeared to some that our airline came to life as a sudden commercial example of immaculate conception. This was certainly not the case, as the various Autair companies had already enjoyed a steady growth in helicopters, but we had frequently diverted into fixed wing operations, with STOL projects and operation of DC3 aircraft for carriage of our own cargoes. There had also been specialist survey work, and on occasions, leasing out to other carriers.

I had looked carefully at the 'UK independent airline' scene on and off for a number of years. We had seen it boosted fortuitously by the major and minor Berlin Airlifts, and also watched it being helped on its way by the hand-out of a number of trooping contracts to favoured companies, but by and large it seemed a very hazardous form of business to be in on a 'stand alone' basis.

However, by the end of the fifties we had a reasonable financial safety buffer - also an effective infrastructure including well run administration and commercial units at our Head Office in Wigmore Street, London (which was to survive for some forty years). We also now owned a small engineering and operating presence at Luton Airport, whose authorities were offering encouragement for airline type operations and provided better scope to us for permanent expansion. It was also to provide a more convenient location for backup of a new addition to our helicopter operations, such as representation in various countries of major manufacturers such as Bell Helicopter, Agusta SpA, De Havilland Canada and Helio Courier. However, that is another significant story yet to be told.

After almost a decade of aviation toil, often in distant and difficult places, we now had a proven track record with a sound reputation, likewise some credibility in financial circles, which was essential for further development. We were now ready for our new airline baby which after a second christening was to become 'AUTAIR INTERNATIONAL AIRWAYS'

Edward Posey, who was to play such a pivotal role in both the development of Autair International and later Court Line Aviation. [Autair-Court Collection]

First priority was the appointment of the right team to run the show under my Chairmanship. Gerald Threlfall formerly employed by one of our competitors Worldwide Helicopters has fairly recently joined Autair with the prospect that he would graduate to a position of senior management. Now armed with a good knowledge of how we worked, he was ready to fill the position Managing Director - a role which he carried out with a meticulous sense of responsibility.

Ed Posey, who was still helping me to retreat from profitable but complex developments in India, was to be our first Commercial Director, which was a vital role for with no business there could be no airline - even with a perfect production unit. Our two other, twelve hour-a-day working directorships went to Captain Maurice Rowan (Operations) and Bill (T S) Buxton (Engineering), both indispensable and extremely loyal members of the team. All these directors took up minority share holdings in the new company, which risk, I am pleased to say, eventually gave them a well deserved reward on the ultimate take over by Court Line.

At this stage further comment from myself is not needed as the following words from Maurice Rowan explain extremely well how the operation moved forward. Seems he handles the pen just as well as the aeroplane and it is a pleasure to recall these pioneering events!'

Autair's first Dakota G-AMGD seen in 1960 after its purchase from British European Airways. [Autair-Court Collection]

Captain Maurice Rowan, the first Operations Director of Autair, seen at the controls of Handley Page Herald G-APWA on its delivery flight to Autair at Luton in April 1963.

Captain Maurice Rowan joined the airline in 1960, specifically to fly Dakota G-AMGD - the first of a number of ubiquitous DC3s - known by all who were in the RAF as Dakotas which became Autair's first fixed wing aircraft. Not that the embryonic airline had much chance to use it; the aircraft and its Autair crews spent most of the summer on 'wet' charter to the Southend-based Continental Air Transport, who then sub-leased it to Arkia of Israel for use on internal flights from May to August. The Dak returned to Luton in November, where by now Autair had set up maintenance facilities to look after the aircraft in its fleet.

'I had previously been a Royal Air Force flying instructor and ferry pilot during the last war, and subsequently operated with Airwork on the North Atlantic in Douglas DC6's, Eagle Airways on Vikings transporting troops to the Middle East and latterly with BOAC Associates in West Africa and the Persian Gulf.

I soon found myself back flying in Africa! During the Nigerian Independence celebrations that took place in October, Autair provided a C-47 for the Sadauna of Sokoto, Premier of the North. As I had flown with the former West African Airways and knew every internal airstrip by heart, I was 'recruited' to fly the trip! We flew on ahead of the royal aircraft containing Princess Alexandra so that the Sadauna could be there to greet her upon arrival.

The Control Tower at Luton - the first operational home for Autair was a room rented here. The airline's 'Engineering Office' was a caravan parked behind the column!

At the end of 1960 I was offered a 10% shareholding in the company and a directorship. Shortly afterwards 'Bill' Buxton - who had been with Field Aircraft Services up at Wymeswold, where our maintenance was initially carried out - joined us as a shareholder director (Engineering).

I doubt whether Autair would have been able to expand quite so rapidly - despite its undoubted commercial acumen - if it had not been for the very solid base aid by 'Bill' Buxton and myself in maintenance and flying operations. We were both perfectionists, demanding the highest engineering and operational standards from our staff as the company expanded. This was to stand us in very good stead in later years.

In December 1960 it was decided that the

airline had to have a base with engineering and handling facilities. Luton Airport was chosen because of a number of very pertinent reasons. With the opening of the nearby M1, the country's first motorway, the airport was within easy reach of London and the Municipal Authorities were willing to offer good aircraft and passenger facilities at their airport, that had recently received a great deal of investment, including the construction of a new 5,432 foot concrete runway that was much expanded later.

We rented a room in the Air Traffic Control Tower as an Operations Centre, the Commercial and Administration departments remaining at the London Office in Wigmore Street. Bill Buxton's Engineering Office at that time was a caravan parked beside the Control Tower and as we only had one telephone, we kept a supply of small stones handy by the window so we could 'call' him by throwing a stone onto the caravan roof!'

For the 1961 season, the first year of 'real' airline operations, two more ex-BEA Dakotas were acquired and, in order to provide ground support for the aircraft, Autair set up a subsidiary, Lutair Handling Services Ltd, which became the airport's official ground handling agent for visiting passenger or cargo aircraft. That summer was a busy time for the airline, for apart from operating its own inclusive tour flights, Autair's Dakotas were flown by Maurice Rowan and Bill Bond on operations for Tradair from Southend and for Skyways out of Lympne.

Business was good enough and Engineering Director Bill Buxton was joined by Maurice Lockhart as his No. 2 - and who subsequently left and joined the airport authorities at Castle Donington when the new East Midlands airport opened. The third engineer was Ernie Ward, who was the radio man. With the arrival of more aircraft John Allen joined the expanding engineering department...

'In the beginning of 1961 Autair were planning to buy G-AJIC from BEA, and that was when I was approached to see if I would be prepared to join them.

G-AJIC operated for a short time in passenger service, but then, in early 1961 Autair had a contract from Hunting Surveys to provide a DC3 to do photographic surveys in Africa. We took the aircraft to Fields, and the aircraft was modified to remove the interior, and cut a 2ft square space in the cabin floor and the fuselage skin behind the wing, and install a big Swiss camera.

An oxygen system was put in with plumbing and tanks and the engines were modified from manual to electric booster pumps to enable the aircraft to operate above 20,000 ft.

We left the UK with Autair Captain Mike Ellis, a co-pilot on loan from British Air Ferries, myself as the engineer, and a photographer and a navigator from Huntings. The aircraft was ferried down in legs to Sierra Leone, where we did a lot of filming on development projects. We were there for about three to four months and then came back to the UK for a short break.

The aircraft had maintenance work carried out, and then we went back again, this time spending four months in Ghana and Nigeria on similar work. I was with the aircraft for the whole of this period,'

Bill Buxton could now start searching around for additional equipment for the fleet. Ronnie Myhill's Overseas Aviation had gone spectacularly bankrupt in late August 1961, and a pair of their Vikings were up for disposal at Gatwick. Sitting in a hangar at Squires Gate Airport Blackpool, 'guarding' three more of these portly Vickers airliners from another company that had just ceased trading was Peter Hart:

G-AHJC awaits another service. (Autair/Court Collection).

A delightful picture of Viking G-AHPL in flight. [Autair Collection]

'I had been employed by Cyril Claydon, a Luton builder (believe it or not!), who also ran a small aviation concern called Pegasus Airlines, We had a fleet of three Vikings, flying initially from Luton, but later from Blackbushe, Gatwick and finally Blackpool. When the company went into receivership after their last commercial flight in October 1961, I was retained to park the aircraft in a hangar at Blackpool on 27 October and 'mothball' them until a buyer could be found. I covered all the bare metal surfaces with inhibiting oil to keep out Blackpool's salty air and then sat around, serviced the car, and did, well, not much!*

One day, out of the blue, this Director from Autair - it was Bill Buxton - came in and inspected them. He came back a few days later, saying he was going to buy them, along with a pair that had been flown by Overseas Aviation until that company collapsed and could I get these three ready for a ferry flight to Luton? Cheekily I asked if there was a job going with the aircraft - that was how I started work with Autair!'

The 1962 inclusive tour season saw a pair of Vickers Vikings in service with the airline, serving many destinations in Europe and the Middle East. At Luton, Engineering Director Bill Buxton surrounded himself with a team of highly qualified engineers who through sheer hard work established a maintenance standard for the airline that was second to none, as Maurice Rowan recalls...

'Our maintenance standards were outstanding - they certainly were the highest I had ever experienced in civil aviation. Throughout our entire history Autair and Court Line never had a serious operational incident involving passengers, which speaks volumes for the quality of our pilots and engineers.

Perhaps the most outstanding example of Bill Buxton's engineering team's efforts was the work done in the rebuilding of the Vikings we acquired from assorted sources to produce a fleet of six, the remaining five being used as spares.

On the flying side, with the employment of Captain C.P.C.

'Pete' Dibley (formerly of West African Airways) as Chief Pilot, it became possible to build a strong team of Training and Check Captains. These included Sqn Ldr. H. Hazelden (former Chief Test Pilot with Handley Page, responsible for Victors and Heralds) Wing Cmdr. 'Dickie' Martin (Test Pilot with Avro's and previously Gloster Aircraft), Len Prudence (RAF and Empire Test Pilots School) and 'Ted' Gordon (also Handley Page Victors and Heralds). This team, with the addition of other experienced Service and civil airline pilots ensured that the later transition from piston engines through turbo-prop to pure turbines was made smoothly, safely and efficiently.

'Team Spirit' also existed in other areas of the airline - Dennis Elsden was a tireless Operations Chief who actually built the Operations Room at Luton with its communications control desk and wall planning boards himself whilst Charles King, the Senior Traffic Officer led an enthusiastic Aircraft Handling Section. Our Accounts Department then consisted of Maurice LeMaitre and his assistant 'Peggy' Tweddle. Maurice was meticulous in his account keeping, and I well remember his delight the day he burst into my office to announce that we had actually made a profit for the first time!

We were flying mostly for Inclusive Tour companies all over Europe and were having difficulties with in-flight catering. A retired Group Captain Athol Forbes and his wife used to make up meals in boxes and deliver them to the airport in his Heinkel three-wheeled 'bubble' car just before each flight. Athol appearing at speed in his little Heinkel, completely surrounded by the catering boxes, was a never-to-be-forgotten sight! The frequency of our flights soon outstripped his capacity and with the new facilities completed, catering was then supplied from a refrigerated van parked alongside the Operations Room. It was Dennis Elsden's job to ensure that it was kept at the right temperature - it only broke down once as I remember, and with

The Vickers Viking became known within the company as 'the Buxton Viking' in deference to the amount of work Bill Buxton put into rebuilding them. Here G-AHPB is seen at Luton.
[Autair Collection]

Returning holidaymakers deplane from Vickers Viking G-AHPI at Luton. [via CPC Dibley]

great presence of mind Dennis contacted Napiers, who had a cold room on the airport we could use whilst the refrigerator unit was repaired'.

Most flights were operated from Luton, but during the year Autair operated a daily freight service from Schiphol Airport, Amsterdam to Tempelhof Airport in Berlin. John Allen takes up the story...

When 'JIC came back from Africa at the end of 1961, there was no work for it, so it was sent to Berlin Templehof, and myself, a Captain Geoff Ball, and another Captain called Imrey, (who I think is now with Monarch), were positioned in Berlin under the control of a German freight agency, and literally told to just sit there and do any work which came up.

For the first couple of weeks we did maybe one flight, but then it started to pick up a little bit, we got a lot of odd-ball work, we were flying explosives into Berlin from Hanover and Frankfurt, and of course we had to fly in the corridors in those days because of the political situation.

Then eventually the agent landed a flower contract, known as the 'Bloomenflug'. This started with the DC3 and involved one flight a day. The aircraft left Berlin at 11.00 in the morning and went to Schiphol. There the flower buyers had already purchased the flowers and were ready to put them straight on board the aeroplane. We left Amsterdam at 2.00 in the afternoon, arrived back in Berlin at 5-5.30 p.m. and the flowers

Hidden 'out back' away from the eyes of the passengers was Bill Buxton's 'boneyard' - a source of spares for the Viking fleet. Here in this snapshot can be seen the remains of a pair of Vikings and the only located picture of Autair's Bristol Freighter.
[John Hepworth]

were taken directly to the distributor; in many cases those flowers were on sale in the German bars and pubs from the old ladies with the flower baskets that same night, flowers that had been growing that morning in Holland!

That work continued and the capacity went up and we then put two Vikings there, and the two Vikings flew together, making a trip every day from Monday to Saturday. Then, on Saturday evening we cleaned the aircraft and installed 36 seats in each.

On Sundays we did two flights with the students. The first flight went to Sylt, an island in the North Sea, then back to Berlin and the second went to Bornholm in Denmark'.

Don Donald was also in Berlin as a pilot. He has a slightly different story to tell...

'Every evening after the day's flying I went into the Airport Manager's office and paid the day's landing and parking fees - in cash. After a while of this I suggested to the officer behind the desk that it would be more convenient all round if I paid them all in one go at the end of the week. He agreed, and so the next day I did not pay the daily charges. The following morning I went out to Templehof to get things organised for a flight, whereby I was greeted by pilots from other airlines with jeers that Autair had gone bust!

Obviously I was shaken, but on being told that the assumption had been made on my non-payment of fees, I angrily stormed round to the Manager's Office. There was a different chap behind the desk to whom I had made the arrangements, but I demanded to know what was going on. Rather haughtily he told me that Autair had not paid its airport charges. I told him of the arrangements, but he replied that his colleague was not authorised to make such things - only he

'Our man in Berlin' Station Manager George Fredrich and two other Autair staff by the glass-topped check in desk. This photograph must have been taken at the weekend - why? Well, during the week Autair 'flew the corridor' from places like Amsterdam. At the weekends they operated to the popular nudist resorts on the island of Sylt, hence the destination board and the knowledge that it must have been the weekend! [via John Hepworth]

could, and that he would not.

I allowed myself to get fired up - after all, I was wearing more gold braid than he and I had learned that this counted for much in the Teutonic mind. Forcefully I told him that his colleague had agreed the arrangements and that I was not to know he had not the authorisation. I told him that if I discovered that the rumours of Autair's 'demise' had emanated from his office, I would advise my company to sue for slander!

The change could not have been more noticeable - he apologised profusely, offering to honour the arrangements. I refused - now it was my turn to be haughty!

By 1963 the Dakota fleet has been almost totally replaced by Vikings, those Dakotas remaining being leased out to other operators. The airline was beginning to branch out into other services, with an application to start vehicle-ferry flights radiating out from Luton to Beauvais, Calais, Cherbourg, Cologne, Dijon, Dusseldorf, Liege, Luxembourg, Maastricht, Ostend and Tours being placed before the Air Transport Licensing Board (ATLB), making use of Bristol 170 Freighters. Many of these destinations were already served by Autair's inclusive tour network.

Two views of the interior of a Viking, the forward cabin (top) and aft cabin (below)

Heralding in changes...

1963 also saw the introduction (albeit temporary) of a new type of aircraft and a new type of powerplant for the airline, when they

One of the ex-Pegasus Airways machines, Viking G-AHOY, parked outside the maintenance hangar at Luton.

Viking G-AHPJ was fitted with a large freight door, and is seen here having crates loaded by fork lift truck.
[Autair Collection]

G-APWA, the first Handley Page Herald used by Autair by the Control Tower at Luton Airport. [Kurt Lang]

leased a pair Handley Page Herald turboprop airliners from the manufacturers. The first was G-APWA, the company demonstrator which was with Autair from May to August, when it was exchanged for G-ASKK, which remained until December.

The arrangement was somewhat convoluted, for Handley Page Aircraft were taking three Airspeed Ambassadors in part exchange from a Swiss outfit called Globe Air, and Globe Air were going to take Heralds.

Autair was all set to take the Ambassadors for the 1963 season but Handley Page were having some manufacturing problems with the Herald, particularly with the structure, and could not deliver to Globe Air, subsequently Globe Air would not release the Ambassadors to Autair!

Autair managed to shuffle aircraft around to cover a lot of the flights, but to make good the shortage of capacity, Herald G-APWA was leased from Handley Page at very favourable terms to cover that summer, because of the continuing non-delivery of the Ambassadors.

The first Ambassador finally arrived late in 1963, followed by the other two. The three machines were completely re-furbished at an approximate cost of £6,000 each. A re-styled interior, designed by Autair, was incorporated by Reeves; new lightweight seats, also to Autair's design, were installed by Flying Services of Chesham. This increased the seating to 55, although a maximum of 65 was possible. Radio equipment was also updated by the fitment of Decca as an addition to the VOR installation.

Because the Ambassadors were very advanced aircraft for their day - they were pressurised and had sleeve-valve engines - it was considered that Autair would have to fly a ground engineer with each aircraft, for the out-stations would not have any experience in handling them. Three engineers were nominated to fly with the aircraft, John Allen, Dick Docherty and Pete Hart. They flew with

Two views of Luton Airport as it was during the summer of 1963. The lower picture shows the apron of the airport seen from the balcony of the control tower, with the roof of the wooden passenger terminal in the foreground. On the ramp are a pair of Euavia Constellations, with G-ARVP closest to the camera. In the background, on the extreme right and parked alongside the McAlpine hangar is Autair's Herald G-APWA. [via CPC Dibley].

Dave Clark (centre) and two other members of the Dave Clark Five pop group pose on the steps of this Autair Viking for publicity photos at Blackpool.

Issue One of the London to Blackpool timetable, effective from 1 October 1963.
[both Autair Collection]

FECTIVE FROM 1st OCTOBER, 1963   ISSUE 1

BLACKPOOL TO
LONDON

DAILY EXCEPT SUNDAYS

TIMETABLE

07.45	Latest Check-in Blackpool Airport
08.00	Depart Blackpool Airport (Continental Breakfast served in Flight)
09.10	Arrive Luton Airport
10.30	Arrive North London Air Terminal (Paddington)

LONDON TO
BLACKPOOL

DAILY EXCEPT SATURDAYS

TIMETABLE

17.20	Latest Check-in North London Air Terminal (Paddington)
17.30	Coach departs North London Air Terminal
18.45	Latest Check-in Luton Airport
19.00	Depart Luton Airport (Coffee, Sandwiches and Bar Service)
20.10	Arrive Blackpool Airport

AUTAIR *International Airways*
75 WIGMORE STREET, LONDON, W.1.

SEE REVERSE FOR FURTHER DETAILS

the aircraft all the time, and being ground engineers, were not limited by crew hours so it was not unusual to operate two or three consecutive flights with the aeroplanes!

Anne Norcross was Bill Buxton's Secretary and knew all the Engineers well...

'I shared the cabin at the foot of the Control Tower with Bill Buxton and Maurice Lockhart, my typewriter sitting on a narrow counter and my feet resting on boxes of aircraft spares!

It was no ordinary secretarial job, for I was also Technical Records Clerk and worked as Ground Receptionist for Lutair at weekends - I even flew as an Air Hostess on the Ambassadors at weekends and odd evening if they needed me! It became a way of life for thirteen years!

I have also worked all night making tea and hot soup for the engineers working in that freezing hangar if they had to get an aircraft servicable for the next morning - everybody was so dedicated!

Not keeping all your eggs in one basket...

In the short time that Autair (the airline) had been in existence, all appeared to be progressing satisfactorily. Bill Armstrong explains his philosophy...

'Despite our apparent success with the helicopters, I was well aware of the somewhat perilous nature of other forms of commercial aviation.

We tried to protect ourselves by diversifying into other types of work and operations and aircraft. Believe it or not for a spell it was our skywriting operations - principally in conjunction with the Nigerian Independence elections - that brought in more profit than any other aspect of our mini-empire! As many were illiterate, the election was conducted by using symbols - one was a palm tree, which our pilots drew all over the sky of Nigeria!

We also got heavily into aircraft agency work, and were on the look-out for any business that could be gained by aircraft leasing.

It was the same with the airline; I did not want to 'specialise' on one particular aspect of fixed-wing flying. So we flew cargo and passengers, on scheduled and charter services. We had our own passenger collection point in the capital, our own maintenance organisation and formed our own aircraft handling service. If one aspect of the business developed a problem, there were always others in the group that could help and support it'.

The Blackpool to London (via Luton Airport) service steadily gained in popularity.

More Staff...

Two people who started work at Luton in 1963, one for Lutair Handling Service, one for Autair, would find that it had lasting consequences for both. June Powell started in the Spring and captures the times perfectly...

'At the time of my joining Lutair, the staff comprised three traffic officers, one ground hostess at Luton, one part time ground hostess called Marion in Autair's North London

Airspeed Ambassador G-ALZZ gets airborne from Luton in 1963. [via PCP Dibley]

Handley Page Herald G-APAW is seen on the proving flight to Lyon. [via PCP Dibley]

Terminal at the Stephen Court Hotel, and two baggage handlers. Brian Davis was Chief Traffic Officer and also in overall charge of the company. The other two Traffic Officers were Don McCarthy and a chap called Andy. Marilyn Black was Chief Ground Hostess at Luton. Besides myself, two other girls were taken on by Marilyn - Sylvia Browning and Kathy Durnford. Marilyn took us through about four weeks of very thorough training - then we were divided up into shifts. Lutair covered the hours 07.30 to 22.30 every day of the week, and if and when aircraft movements occurred outside these hours, shifts had to be rearranged to cover them.

Our offices were in the terminal buildings, which were single story wooden constructions near to the base of the old control tower. For that time, these buildings were in fact, quite comfortable, and adequate for the number of passengers then passing through the airport. There were two passenger reception halls, the lower one being used by Euravia, and the upper one by Autair and Derby Airways.

Our uniforms were typical airline dress of the era, straight navy skirt, short fitted jacket with gold buttons, heavy navy raincoats, forage cap style hats, white blouse, black court

A trio of Airspeed Ambassadors parked between flights on the newly extended apron at Luton.

shoes, black gloves (white in summer), with the indispensable white headscarf to tie over hats! The same uniform was worn by the Autair air hostesses. The uniform was of the very best quality, each girl being individually measured and fitted. Marilyn, always immaculately turned out herself had a strict uniform code. The hat must always be worn with the uniform, we were never to run whilst in uniform, and we were never to eat in public whilst in uniform. It went without saying that the uniform itself must always be in pristine condition. Marilyn told us that as Euravia had the larger, more impressive aircraft, we must impress our passengers by our smart appearance and behaviour. I hope we lived up to her expectations! It was still a novelty for people in airline uniform to be seen in and around the town of Luton itself and I remember quite often being mistaken for a nurse. Perhaps the fact that our raincoats and raincoat hoods were lined in red had something to do with this. I was even asked if I had joined the Wrens.

Our duties for aircraft departures included greeting passengers, checking them and their baggage in, taking passenger manifests to the immigration officers, escorting the passengers through immigration and eventually, when all was ready, escorting them to the aircraft. On check-in each of our passengers was handed a boarding card, which they then handed back to the hostess upon boarding the aircraft. This way the hostess could check that the correct number of

The elegant lines of Airspeed's Ambassador shows up clearly against the sky in this close up of G-ALZZ high above the Bedfordshite countryside.

One of Autair's Ambassadors is captured in the autumn light at Biarritz during October 1963. [via CPC Dibley]

passengers had boarded. On several occasions the count would be 'under', and we would then have to round up the missing passenger from wherever they had strayed to, but on one memorable occasion I was actually handed one more boarding card than the aircraft had seats for!

On arrival we escorted the passengers from the aircraft to the customs and baggage reclaim hall, directed them to the terminal after customs inspection, and finally got them all on to their coaches for the final leg of their journey.

When we were not scheduled for any departures or arrivals, we spent our time typing passenger manifests, writing tickets, and generally making ourselves useful.

As the season got under way, two more trainee traffic officers joined us, Dave Webber and John Hepworth. As the weekends were of course our busiest time, two girls were taken on part time to help us over the weekend period. Anne Norcross was actually Bill Buxton's secretary during the week, but enjoyed helping out at Lutair on busy Saturdays and Sundays. The other part timer was Nicola Waller, who desperately wanted an airline job full time. I heard she eventually fulfilled her dream when she joined Caledonian as an air hostess. Towards the end of the 1963 season another full time ground hostess, Hannah Page joined us.

The arrival that sticks in my mind most was a flight (not Autair), bringing 100 plus Chinese seamen on their way to join a ship in the port of London. It was on a bitterly cold winter night in 1963, and the flight was due to arrive at some ungodly time in the very early hours of the morning. Sylvia Browning was the other ground hostess on duty with me, and a quick look at the passenger list showed more than one Mr Fuk to be amongst them. Sylvia and I agreed that should any one of these so named gentlemen go missing, we were certainly not going to be the ones to tannoy for him!

As the aircraft taxied in (late of course!), Sylvia and I took up our positions at the foot of the steps, the heavens opened and we were caught in a torrential downpour. The aircraft doors opened, and the seamen came hurtling down the steps, all clutching large white bundles, and all chattering away in

John Hunt's colour picture of Ambassador G-ALZZ on the ramp at Luton.

Chinese. On reaching the bottom of the steps, they all zoomed off in a dozen different directions across the apron, with two very harassed, very wet ground hostesses off in hot pursuit!

Shepherds and their flocks spring to mind! I think we were successful in rounding them all up, but to this day I cannot be 100% certain that the number of passengers who got off the aircraft actually tallied with the number who (eventually) left on the coaches to join their ship.

I wonder if anyone from the early days remembers Lumb's Continental Tours? Mr Lumb was a tour operator from the North of England - the Halifax area I believe - and every other Monday Autair transported several Viking loads of his

Left: Chief Ground Hostess Marilyn Black and Nicky Waller walk back into the Terminal having seen off a flight. The white headscarves were very useful to keep hats on heads at a very windy Luton Airport! [via John Hepworth]

The white roof of Viking G-AHPB dissapears into the milky sky in the picture below taken near McAlpine's complex at Luton. The propeller on the right appears to belong to a P-51 Mustang fighter! [John Hunt]

An image that was used to promote Autair - Airspeed Ambassador G-ALZZ high above the clouds.
[Autair-Court Collection]

passengers from Luton to Ostend. The first Viking left early in the morning, other flights being spread throughout the day, and the last leaving at about 18.30 hrs. Mr Lumb was in the habit of sending Lutair one long passenger list, and so it was left to Brian to divide them up onto specific flights. Tickets were written by Lutair, and handed to the passengers on their arrival at Luton. All Mr Lumb's passengers arrived together on coaches at about 7 a.m., having travelled down overnight from the North. Unfortunately, none had been informed of the exact arrangements for their flights, so there was much dismay, consternation and downright anger from the passengers who had to wait for the later flights. I can still picture Brian reaching for his uniform hat to venture out into the terminal to try and restore some sort of calm. Of course these arrangements also worked in reverse, with the early arrivals back to Luton having to wait for the last Viking to arrive from Ostend before their coaches left for home! Brian Davis, our Chief Traffic Officer, pleaded on several occasions with Mr Lumb to be sent specific passenger lists. These never materialised, so on these Mondays, we all knew we would be needing all the charm, patience and diplomacy we could muster. Only now do I realise that some poor, unfortunate handling agency in Ostend must obviously have been having the same problems!

I only worked one year at Lutair, but it is a year I remember with great affection. The work could be hard and tiring, the hours long, especially when waiting for a delayed aircraft to arrive, but, looking back, it was also great fun. In the spring of 1964 Kathy Durnford and I moved over to Autair to become air hostesses. I remember that during my interview for Lutair with Marilyn, she had said that we were not to think *that being a ground hostess was a step towards flying, and in fact Sheila Whitworth, Autair's Chief Air Hostess, only agreed to take Kathy and myself with Marilyn's permission. I would like to believe that Marilyn didn't want to lose us, but as we were so keen, she gave her permission. Kathy and I were just about to find out what hard work was!'*

John Hepworth also joined the company...

'I joined Autair as a sixteen-year old school-leaver as an office junior in the Traffic Department in July 1963. Brian Davis was the General Manager Traffic Handling and his twin brother Ian was in the Commercial Department working under the late Arnold Mearch, who was the licensing and legal man. My time was spent in Traffic, doing Viking and later Ambassador check-in and loadsheets'.

During the next summer, 1964, and subsequent summers, the Ambassadors flew on the European operations, mainly from Luton to the Spanish and French resorts. In order to keep utilization up, during the winter they were used on what were termed 'air cruises' - which in 1964 were fairly novel. The aircraft left Luton with its load of fifty-five passengers and went down into the Middle East for two to three weeks, the aircraft and crew staying with the passengers throughout. The aircraft would land at the first destination on the itinerary, the passengers would go off for two-three days, before rejoining the aircraft for the next destination. There were basically two routes for these cruises, one being Luton-Tripoli-Cairo-Luxor-Aswan-Athens- Luton. John Allen again...

'For their day the cruises were quite expensive, so in general the passengers tended to be quite elderly. However, having witnessed these passengers touring tombs and other archeological places in blazing heat, they must have been some of the fittest elderly people one could wish to meet!'

Scheduled Coach-Air Services

The vehicle-ferry licence application was turned down, but another one, to operate scheduled six - times - a - week services between

Zulu Zulu taxing past an Eagle Britannia at Luton.

Luton and Blackpool (previously flown by British United Airways, using Gatwick as the London Terminal) met with success.

The Luton-to-Blackpool service - aimed at businessmen wishing to reach London from the mid-Lancashire industrial belt - was inaugurated on 1 October when Viking G-AHPL first flew the route.

Autair initially used 36-seater Vikings and, in order to break even, needed to fill seventeen seats on each flight - a 45% load factor. The Viking left Blackpool at 0800hrs, arriving at Luton some 70 minutes later, where it was met by a coach from Hillside Coaches for the onward road journey to the Stephen Court Hotel, near Paddington Station, London. Arrival time here was posted as 10.30. Interestingly, this was advertised as being the 'North London Air Terminal', a description that seems to have been used by the company for a number of different locations! The reverse journey departed London at 17.30, Luton at 19.00, arriving back at Blackpool for 20.10. The fare was £7 4s Blackpool-London return, including the coach segments. After the first three months Autair had made 75 round trips carrying 2227 passengers - a load factor a little over 41%, so the operation was already almost breaking even.

Nevertheless, this was only a very small part of the airline's revenue, for in the same year over two thousand charter and IT flights were made, with a total of nearly 32,000 passengers carried!

It's Dee Time! Another celebrity to use Autair was disc jockey and TV presenter Simon Dee, seen here with a furry friend disembarking from a Herald.

The Blackpool service became very popular, particularly with the celebrities starring in summer season 'upt North'. John Hepworth remembers many stars hurrying to catch the Viking:

'This service was very popular, and not just with businessmen. I well remember one time we got a call from London saying that dancer Lionel Blair - who was one of our regulars - wanted to catch the flight, but that he would be a few minutes late. We tried to hold it as long as possible, but not long enough. When he finally arrived the aircraft had already taxied out and was preparing to take off. I got the O.K. from ATC, bundled Lionel in our Land Rover and tore out up the taxiway after the Viking. Obviously I had no steps with us, so in order to get into the aircraft, he had to climb onto the bonnet and then stretch across... Just then the crotch of his rather tight mohair trousers decided to let go - and in the slipstream as well - I heard later that one of our girls on board - Carol Mundford I think - repaired them whilst airborne so as to save Lionel embarrassment on deplaning at Blackpool!'

Introduction of the Ambassador meant that the airline could consider flying farther afield. In September 1964, at

the behest of the Lord Brothers travel company, a team from Autair made a proving flight out to Funchal in Madiera with Ambassador G-ALZZ, where they spent three days learning the difficult airfield approaches there.

It came to the attention of Captain Rowan that there was a female instructor working with the Luton Flying Club who was helping to turn out qualified pilots with their Commercial Pilot's Licence and Instrument Rating. Such talent could be put to good use with the expanding company. The Instructor was a young Elizabeth Overbury...

'I came into aviation via a marvellous careers teacher who expected her students to think of doing things out of the ordinary. I thought I would like to see what flying was about, so on my next holiday I took a trial lesson in a Tiger Moth - I knew then I was going to be a pilot! On leaving school I worked at three jobs six days a week and took flying lessons on Sundays. By the time I was seventeen, I had my Private Pilot's Licence and went on from there.

Maurice Rowan started my career in the airlines flying with Autair at a time when there was a strong bias against women pilots. It was Maurice's wife Pamela (herself an ex-BOAC Hostess) that came up with a wonderful phrase I have often used since, when coming up against a male pilot that didn't want a woman sitting up at the sharp end - she said with great aplomb 'It is a matter of supreme imbuggerance to me what they think!'.

I have wonderful memories of my ten years with Autair/ Court Line, memories that are indelibly linked in my mind to pieces of music! I never knew whether Captain Peter Dibley's wife Jean was amused or horrified when I said I loved 'buggered Bach' by Jacques Loussier'! Bobby Hebb's 'Sunny' reminds me of Luton Customs for some reason, whilst The Byrds 'Mr Tambourine Man' suggests the Ambassador simulator Autair booked time on over at Kidlington Airport near Oxford with Graeme Percival 's Air Training Services, and hearing 'A

Sunny Day' immediately transports me back to early morning flights back into the UK along Red One Airway.

They were interesting times flying with Autair. On an early qualifying flight aboard the beautiful Airspeed Ambassador I was doing a series of stalls in an area between Luton and Stansted, flying with Captain Jan Szczesiak, when the nose-cone came loose and flipped up against the windshield, totally obscuring his view and much of mine. He was marvellous, briefing me to call directions left; straight ahead, or right and calling out what I thought of height from my view down to the landing, when the cone went down and he could see to control the aircraft on the landing run and taxi.

I had many flights with Jan, and as we both shared a love of animals, he showed me many European zoos when we had stop-overs. I could never understand why he ate so quickly and

Left: Seen arriving in typical smokey fashion at Funchal, on the behest of Lord Brothers Travel, G-ALZZ on 23 September 1964.

Below: The Autair team pose for the Maderian press on 23rd September 1964 (L.to R.) Ken Hunnington. Manuel Guerriro Figueira of the Portugese Aeronautica Civil, Mr. Merrifield, Pete Dibley, Maurice Rowan, Sheila Whitworth, Anne Bolton, Brian Davis, John MacLean-Hall, other Autair personnel, Mike Ellis, Len Prudence and Jim Torrey.
[Autair Collection]

walked so fast until I found he had been a prisoner of war - it must have played hell with his life. He never mentioned these times to me, but otherwise I found him a real joy to fly with and he happily shared a wealth of flying knowledge with me - sadly he is no longer with us.

I never could three-point a Viking, but I did get the knack of feather-bedding the Ambassador and the One-Eleven!'

MAHON

Anne Dobie and another Autair Air Hostess relax between flights at the old Mahon Airport on Menorca.

With the steady expansion, Autair decided to open an air terminal near the Finchley Road Underground Station in London, to be operated by another associate company, the newly created North London Air Terminals Ltd, where passengers could gather before making the journey up the M1 motorway to Luton Airport in conjunction with Hillside Coaches, another company that was formed in 1953. This new air terminal - somewhat appropriately perhaps - hung in space above a large hole excavated for the Underground. Martin Clough was to be the first manager, and he and John Hepworth inspected the building before it was converted to Autair use:

'It had previously been the Universal Health Club site, an old fitness club. When we walked in, there was exercise and fitness equipment strewn everywhere. It opened in 1966 and I remained manager there until 1968, when I moved up to 'Head Office' at Luton'.

Three Ambassadors were employed on IT flights in the 1964 season, the Vikings concentrating on the Blackpool service, which was increased to nine times a week in the summer. 1964 also saw further expansion, with a hangar and administration complex erected at Luton to cope with the extra work.

Further expansion.

Bill Armstrong's rotary winged world - still under the Autair banner - had reached the point whereby its activities were becoming self-generating and, as experts in their own specialist field, the company was picking up good contracts almost everywhere, some of which also benefitted the airline.

In 1964 Autair created a South African helicopter operation based at Halfway House, Transvaal. After initial struggles, Autair Helicopters S.A.Pty. began to 'take-off' under the auspices of Ted Spreadbury, a former Royal Navy helicopter pilot and, with the gaining of a contract to place a pair of Sikorsky S.55 helicopters on a five year contract to service diamond dredging barges operating off South West Africa, things began to improve in a big way.

Contracts were gained to work on the Mombassa-to-Nairobi oil pipeline, on a similar pipeline between Durban and Johannesburg, and ferrying archaeologists around the remote Lake Baringo area in Kenya looking for fossils to aid in the search for the 'Missing Link'. Two machines were involved in fish-spotting for the *Willem Barentz* and *Suiderkruis* factory ships - Autair helicopters were even called in by the British Embassy in South Africa to ferry relief supplies and food to the snow-bound villages and remote cow pastures high in the mountains around Mokhotlong in Lesotho. On almost every contract there was the possibility of being called for an alternate, emergency role - that of casualty evacuation. This was a vital lifeline for organisations operating in the remote bush or desert and provided the reassurance that help - and hospitalisation - could be near at hand despite the location.

Bill Armstrong's African operation was burgeoning; apart from the helicopter operations, he was beginning to create a number of other opportunities. The ownership/management tangle of Bill Armstrong's companies are incredibly difficult to unravel - something I suspected was deliberately so. I questioned him more than once on this, only to have my questioning airily brushed aside with the comment that he had lost count of how many airlines he had created and lost!

The Autair Group was experiencing mixed fortunes; the South African helicopter operation had become very successful and appeared to be heading for a great future. But there were problems;

Two of Autair's helicopters - Sikorsky S.55 ZS-HDG and Bell 206 both fitted with float equipment stand ready at Luqa Airport, Malta for flights to offshore oil rigs.
[Autair Collection]

Bill Armstrong:

'To understand Africa and what happened to us, one must go back to the beginning. It is quite true to say we were often under-capitalised - nevertheless we made fine progress, often with assistance and welcome guidance of Eric Knight, founder and Chairman of Lombard Banking.

In 1956 I negotiated our first contract in Africa - with Rhodesian Selection Trust who wanted to use helicopters for mineral exploration - it was a good one that started with a single Bell 47 and eventually ran for over 20 years incorporating work for their associate, the Sierra Leone Selection Trust. From this toe-hold other activities emerged, including setting up a regional base in Salisbury, Rhodesia, (later known as Harare, Zimbabwe, following independance). Salisbury was an absolute gem of a place, with every facility - both professional and personal - that we and all our staff could wish for!

All was running well, but very soon Macmillan's famous 'Winds of Change' would be blowing in dark clouds with sinister implications.

Rhodesian Prime Minister Ian Smith, (a former RAF officer and pilot, who was politically moderate and locally well-respected) had been locked in talks with UK Prime Minister Harold Wilson regarding independence for Southern Rhodesia.

Wilson was under pressure from the United Nations and other political groupings to repress what was regarded by many - including many of our Foreign Office 'mandarins' - as the aspirations of rabid colonialists. It did not matter that they were wrecking the lives and destroying the loyalty of many thousands of faithful British citizens!

Smith eventually issued the Unilateral Declaration of Independence (UDI) from the UK and years of sanctions, bush-warfare and terrorism followed, including later the atrocity of downing Rhodesia Airways Viscount VP-WAS by a SAM-7

Bechuanaland National Airways Douglas C-54 Skymaster was originally built for the USAF in 1944. It had previously seen service with Alaska Airlines, Transocean, Thai International and Rhodesian Air Services. Seen here at Luton in 1965, it was wrecked in 1969 taking off from an airstrip in Nigeria. [Autair Collection]

*Bell 47J-2 Ranger of
Autair at rest at its
African base.
[Autair Collection]*

*missile that killed most of the holidaymakers aboard. Of the
four crew and fifty-two passengers, seventeen miraculously
survived the missile and the crash, but all except eight were
slaughtered on the ground by so-called 'freedom fighters'.*

*Our helicopter work expanded, and with money in hand in
1964, we found ourselves looking at the fixed-wing field again,
this time taking over from David Butler's Rhodesian Air
Services and forming a successor company, Air Trans Africa -
known as ATA - with Captain Jack Malloch as Managing
Director, and using DC-3s, 4s and 7s.*

*In 1965 I also formed the first national airline of
Bechuanaland, shortly to become Botswana, with Dave
Morgan as the managing director and Johnnie Gibson as
Chief Pilot.*

Bechuanaland National Airways (Pty) Ltd) was established in
Francistown on 1 October 1965 as a regional scheduled service
passenger and freight airline, with two DC-3s transferred from
Autair. Revenue flights started on 15 November linking
Francistown with Bulawayo and Livingstone. Other routes were
started to from Lobatse to Johannesburg, along with Serowe,
Gaborones, Ghansi, Serondellas and Maun. By the end of the year
the new company had taken over Bechuanaland Air Safaris. 1966
saw the airline flying a twice-weekly round trip between
Francistown and Johannesburg. I have never been able to confirm
his exact role, but I do know that Jack Malloch was involved with
BNA as well.

1964 also saw the creation of Autair Helicopters (EA) Ltd in
Nairobi. F W 'Freddie' Wilcox was sent out to manage the concern,
which, apart from flying assorted charters, also acted as the Bell
Distrubutor for Kenya.

Shady Dealings in Darkest Africa.

John McVicar Malloch, known by all as 'Jack', who Bill Armstrong
brought in to manage Air Trans-Africa, was a pioneering aviator

who ran numerous clandestine airlines in Africa in the early post-independent years, where he was involved in gun-running against the encroachment of Communism. He actively fought against the UN, yet was in the pay of both the Central Intelligence Agency and the French Secret Service, the Direction Générale de la Sécurité Extérieure, or DGSE. He became well known as the arch Rhodesian sanctions buster who almost single-handedly kept Rhodesia alive through a steady supply of consumer goods, arms and ammunition throughout the years of Rhodesia's UDI.

There were reports that Jack was an 'arms dealer', but I doubt that in the true sense of the words he was. Yes, certainly he was a mercenary, he would carry anything to anywhere on behalf of some pretty shady characters, and certainly some of his cargoes were of a highly explosive or illegal nature, but no-one I have ever spoken with have said he was involved in actual dealing.

Bill's business partner in Africa on a number of ventures was Jack Malloch , seen here during the Biaflan war. He later managed a complex with Bill Armstrong a sanctions-busting operation in and out of Rhodesia. On 26 March 1982 he was killed while flying his personal Spitfire F22 (PK350) north of Harare. To the left is Chris Dixon, one of his many loyal Rhodesian pilots.

Jack Malloch's aviation career was as complex and convoluted as Bill Armstrong's. Malloch was closely involved with Rhodesia's Special Air Service regiment, including having direct involvement in some of that unit's long-range cross border operations. He also became involved with the British Military at about the time of UDI and was subsequently involved in some military support flights into the Sudan for Whitehall. There were also clandestine military flights into the Aden desert in the early 1960's delivering weapons for the British SAS in their fight against the Communists.

Air Trans-Africa carried mercenaries to the Congo in 1964 to help the government of Moise Tshombe quell the insurgency of a group of Congolese rebels called the Simba.

It seems that most of Air Trans-Africa's expenses were being hidden from the authorities by the simple expedient of being paid from Malloch's own personal Swiss bank account - furthermore all of ATA's aircraft were not owned by them, they were leased from Autair.

ATA acted as a charter carrier to the Biafran Civil War in Nigeria. During the civil war the C-54 was impounded and the crew imprisoned for a time in 1967. They then operated a Lockheed Super Constellation (VP-WAW) under the name of Afro Continental Airways after UDI for a weekly service from Salisbury to Windhoek.

Aircraft came and went through Autair's Luton base, disappearing southwards into darkest Africa. Noticeable was Douglas C-54 G-ASZT, which appeared briefly under Autair ownership from January to August 1965 before heading for Air Trans Africa.

ATA acquired a Lockheed L-1049 Super Constellation from

VARIG of Brazil for use during the Nigerian civil war, in which part of the country declared itself as the independant state of Biafra. Following the secession of Biafra from Nigeria, a group of mercenaries under Captain Hank Wharton were contracted to begin providing night supply flights from São Tomé or Libreville into rebel airstrips. Following the capture of Enugu and Port Harcourt, the principal destination became the airstrip at Uli.

Wharton and Malloch were sometime rivals, and became - as much as they could be, given the nature of their activities - the public face of the Biafran war - Bill Armstrong preferred to operate much more in the shadows.

The story - much of which is still regarded as 'sensitive', especially by those directly involved - has been told by Michael Draper in his book *'Shadows'* and features such characters as Axel Dutch, Keith Sissons, Frederick Forsyth and a couple of other UK pilots I know, who prefer to be known by their initials: 'SS' and 'GB'!

Wharton, like Bill Armstrong was a fascinating character. Trying to piece together his story is like trying to grab a hold of fog. As far as I can tell, Henry Arthur 'Hank' Wharton (occasionally spelt Warton) was born in Gratz, Germany as Heinrich Wartski in 1916. He immigrated to the United States in 1937, joined the US Army in 1941, and became an American citizen. He fought in the Pacific theatre and worked in military intelligence. He was fluent in German and Spanish. In 1947 he earned a commercial pilot's licence. Beginning in the late 1940s Wharton flew for numerous non-mainline airlines throughout Europe and to developing areas of the world, including Israel and India.

Henry 'Hank' Wharton in front of one of the Lockheed Constellations used in the Biafran Airlift.

'The Biafran Job'...

It was during this time that the saga of the liberated banknotes evolved. When Biafra broke away from Nigeria, the Biafran Government 'took possession' - or should that be 'did a bank job' - of a substantial amount of Nigerian currency in the form of bank notes. This money was then used for the purchase of war materials, and to pay for the airlift.

The Nigerians decided to put a halt to this by withdrawing all the currency from use and replacing it with a new issue. This they did in a relatively short period of time, at the end of which all previous Nigerian banknotes were to be declared null and void. A date of 22 January 1968 was set for this. At the beginning of that month the Biafrans had a considerable amount of cash that they needed to put onto the international currency markets as soon as possible. A plan was made for Jack Malloch and Hank Wharton to fly the notes to

Switzerland and lodge then in the Biafran's Swiss bank account. This would effectively be converting Niagian pounds into Swiss francs, which could then be used to continue to fund the war.

Here the story takes a twist, for there are two versions of what happened next. What is known is that on 12 January two aircraft left Biafra with around twenty tons of Nigerian banknotes in sacks. One version, as told be me by Bill says they made it to Switzerland where they cashed in the money. Bill always claimed to have a picture of himself, Jack Malloch and Hank Whardon sitting in the back of one of the DC-7s on the sacks of money but, despite him promising to let me have sight of it, he never did.

The other version of the story is that the aircraft were turned away from Switzerland because they were Rhodesian-registered, and Switzerland had no diplomatic relations with that country. This is wrong, as the aircraft were all registered in Gabon. Legend has it that they then flew to Lisbon hoping to change the money there, but to no avail. This could have been possible, for Hank Wharton did operate a maintenance base there, so he would have been known.

Then a plan was hatched to fly to Lomé in Togo where it would be roaded to Benin and on to Lagos.

At Togo, Jack Malloch and the crew were summarily detained, the money confiscated and the aircraft impounded. They were imprisioned for around five months then, having paid a substantial fine, they were released.

My own view on this episode is that both actually happened, one aircraft made it to Switzerland, and cashed in the money, the other was turned away for some reason, ended up in Togo where those on board were detained.

Through Bill Armstrong, Air Trans Africa also obtained a fleet of Douglas DC-7C and DC-7CF aircraft (with the assistance of the Rhodesian Government) which were registered in Gabon, when the airline became a major part of the Rhodesian sanctions-busting

Douglas C-54B 9J-RBL, the former G-ASZT with Invicta Airways seen at Luton before delivery to Air Trans Africa. (Bill Armstrong/Autair Collection)

operations - and also part of the Biafran Airlift. They flew beef to Gabon, from where it was flown out by aircraft of its associate company Affretair. Essential materiels for the Rhodesian security forces were brought into the country on the return flights. Affretair migrated to Zimbabwe after independence, when it replaced Air Trans Africa.

Bill Armstrong again, talking in 1994:

As the political and commercial pressures on Rhodesia grew so our aviation business went into rapid decline. Helicopter contracts failed to materialise, Air Trans-Africa faced over-flight restrictions to European destinations and spares and logistics became a nightmare! The biggest problem was servicing the debts on aircraft subject to finance - mainly placed outside Rhodesia and mostly against my own personal guarantee. The pressure was building, and something had to go - first was BNA, disposed of to local interests, which brought temporary relief whilst we struggled with the UK Government for compensation. A procession of names from 'Political Who's Who'inexorably filled the file, including Peter Shore, who was also later involved with the Court Line collapse. 'Tiny' Rowland's Lonrho, a similar 'victim', but with excellent London connections, got an 'instant' £324,000 (a large lump in those days) - we got a double zero!

Air Trans-Africa evolved into Affretair and moved under Rhodesian Government control to become, as Ian Smith put it in his book 'The Great Betrayal ', '... one of the main arms of our sanction-busting operation'. More disaster followed as civil unrest erupted in nearby countries.

Afro Continental Airways was formed by Jack Malloch of Air Trans Africa/Affretair based at Salisbury Airport to operate the weekly scheduled route to Windhoek, South West Africa. The service did not last long, this Constellation VP-WAW was in excellent condition and was used during the Biafra airlift throughout that War. It was later retired to being used as a clubhouse.

It is also worth mentioning another machine appeared under the Autair International banner, if only for a few days. In November 1969 Bill Armstrong bought ex-BOAC, ex-Caledonian Airways DC-7C G-AOIE. The intention was that it would be used by one of Bill's other companies, Air Trans-Africa in Rhodesia, but with the

Seen on the rain-soaked apron at Stansted is Douglas DC-7 G-AOIE. The aircraft was placed back on the British register by Autair prior to transferring to Rhodesia. Eventually, it only went as far as Ireland. [Reg Robinson]

political climate of the time created by Ian Smith's Unilaterally Declared Independance with the United Nations blockade and sanctions applied by the British government of the day, the movement of the aircraft to Africa was impossible, as Bill Armstrong explained in 1996...

'...so it was then flown from Stansted to Shannon in Ireland for 'short term storage'. However, the UDI crisis deepened and extended well beyond the aircraft's 'fly-by date' and not one revenue earning hour was flown by the time it was finally abandoned. In purchase and other costs we suffered a tremendous loss of just over one million pounds in today's value.

She still remains in Ireland to this very day - an interesting piece for the vintage aircraft fraternity, but for me a continuing reminder of the perfidy of politicians and the impact of some of my own mis-judgements. Some you win, some you lose!

I suffered no lasting bitterness, as I was confident (correctly so) that there were many 'winners' still to come - however for now this was an omen of even more disaster as the UDI crisis caused continuing chaos with our helicopter and fixed wing operations in Central Africa'.

But with our darkest hour came some silver linings - as we were forced to expand elsewhere, and seek other avenues to profitablity. Eventually we turned more to 'Sales and Support' and formed solid relationships with manufacturer representation over a wide band of countries.

We also concentrated on our long connection with Bell Helicopter Textron, the largest helicopter manufacturer in the world. For over 30 years we represented them in many countries - mainly Africa. The relationship is maintained to this day in helping one of their Agencies to promote the Tilt-Rotor Bell Boeing Model 609, '... the flying machine of the future!'

Another leap forward was made with our De Havilland Canada franchise in Africa. Here we were lucky to have the

A pair of Air Trans Africa Douglas DC7Fs, the nearest being TR-LNZ. These aircraft were registered in Gabon so that they could operate in all countries as at the time Rhodesian registered aircraft were restricted because of sanctions. These particular aircraft operated a weekly flight to Europe, mainly Amsterdam. (Bill Armstrong/Autair Collection)

help of ex-Court Mangagement Trainee Crispin Maunder who went on later to join Ansett Worldwide Aviation Services where he swings around the world as Executive Vice-President Marketing, placing their 180+ fleet of airliners.

But back to 1970... UDI was hurting, and we were at undeclared war with our own people. The UK Government refused to help and the only option was another asset sale. This time I was forced to sell the company with the greatest potential - the jewel in our crown - Autair Helicopters South Africa.

To explain - the mammoth tankers then used by the oil companies (many in excess of 200,000 tons) were not exactly welcome in many ports because of the hazards to installations and other vessels in the event of an accident. The cost of the helicopter airlift could be considerably offset against the savings in sailing time - slowing down and speeding up to cruising speed of these enormous vessels could literally take hours. Even if the Suez Canal was to reopen (which it eventually did) tankers of this size would be unable to pass through, so the route round the Cape was to remain, and with it the need for Autair's helicopter service.

Bill Armstrong's activities, especially in Africa when known - were causing some concern and it became clear that it was time for a partial 'parting of the ways'. He eased off his British-based airline work to concentrate on other things.

A marriage is announced.

Early in 1965 the Viking fleet was reduced to two and then, on 15 April it was announced to the public that the entire share capital of Autair International Airways had been purchased by the Court Line Group.

Autair International had been looking for a partner to share the financial load, for they required the additional financial muscle and support that a public-quoted company could bring in order to gain the required guarantees for more modern aircraft equipment. The

AUTAIR *International Airways* LTD.

OPERATIONAL AND
MAINTENANCE BASE

LUTON AIRPORT,
LUTON, BEDS.

TELS: (STD CODE OLU 2)
COMMERCIAL: LUTON 23628/9
TRAFFIC: LUTON 28331/2
OPERATIONS: LUTON 21347
ENGINEERING: LUTON 21348
ACCOUNTS: LUTON 22312

CABLES: AUTAIRINT LUTON

TELEX: 82220

HEAD OFFICE
75, WIGMORE STREET,
LONDON, W.1

TEL: WELBECK 1132

CABLES: AUTAIRINT LONDON W.1

BLACKPOOL OFFICE
BLACKPOOL AIRPORT, LANCS.

TELS: B'POOL 43135, 43061

CABLES: AUTAIRINT BLACKPOOL

TELEX: 67622

Your Ref:
Please Quote Our Ref: **300/3**

Please reply to: **London Office.**
14th April, 1965.

AUTAIR AND COURT LINE LIMITED

    I am writing on behalf of the Directors of our Company to inform you officially that it has been decided to merge our interests with those of Court Line, and that Court Line are purchasing 100% of the Share Capital of AUTAIR International Airways.

    Court Line are a publicly owned shipping company, whose shares are quoted on the Stock Exchange. They have considerable financial resources, and we feel that it is definitely in the best long term interests of our Company that we should have the type of financial backing that Court Line can provide. In this way we will not only be able to ensure a stable future, but will also have available the necessary finance to further develop the Company in the years ahead and to acquire more modern types of aircraft and equipment when they become available.

    We would like to emphasise that our Company will continue to be run by the same people as it has over the last five years. One of the Court Line Directors will be joining the Board of Autair, which will ensure that there is close co-operation between the two companies, and that future development can take place to the mutual benefit of both sides.

    I would like to take this opportunity of thanking you for the part you have played in the development of our Company over the last five years, and hope that we can count on your continued support and efforts towards an equally successful future ahead.

For the Directors of
AUTAIR International Airways Ltd.

G. Threlfall

G.H.G. THRELFALL.
Managing Director

DIRECTORS: W. H. ARMSTRONG   G. H. G. THRELFALL   E. J. POSEY   CAPT. M. ROWAN   T. S. BUXTON

Court Line Group had recently raised £580,000 by means of a rights issue and were looking at ways of expanding into the air transport market, and thus 'a marriage was announced' when Court used some £220,00 of their rights issue to purchase the entire shareholding of Autair International Airways.

Gerald Threlfall's letter to all members of staff informing them of the changes that were taking place.

Chapter Four
Under New Ownership

Initially operations continued unchanged under the new owners. The five original Autair Directors, Messrs Armstrong, Threlfall, Rowan, Posey and Buxton all became directors of the new company, under the Chairmanship of John Young, with Bill Armstrong filling the position of Deputy Chairman. Visibly, both on the ground and in the air, it was 'situation normal' for a while, with the scheduled services performing well and a large Inclusive Tour programme being flown by the Ambassador fleet.

In order to cope, extra staff were taken on - Susan Aldridge, then Sue Bizley, was employed as cabin staff, in those politically incorrect days called Air Hostesses.

The heading for Autair's news releases - circa 1966. It also formed the heading for the company newsheets, sub-headed 'Britain's fastest developing airline' [John Hepworth/Martin Clough]

'I joined Autair in the spring of 1965. The training we received was very good and it stood me in good stead for when I later joined British Eagle. I remember well the hours of deportment training, walking up the rear steps of an Ambassador, through the main cabin and down the very tiny steps in the front, balancing books on our heads - the instructor, a very formidable lady called Kathy Hanson, prodded and poked us with a stick demanding to know why were were not all wearing figure-shaping girdles as instructed!

As soon as I had completed the training course, I started to fly on Vikings, accompanied in the beginning by a senior hostess. One of my first memories connected with the Viking was before I had been checked out to fly on my own in the cabin. It was to be my check flight, with my former instructress Kathy Hanson, who was also the Deputy Chief Hostess. Kathy was Australian, had been flying many years and seemed as if she had seen and knew it all.

We were taking a group from a local pub on a day's outing - or should I say drinking - to Ostend. It was an all-male party.

LUTON AIRPORT · LUTON · BEDFORDSHIRE

Phone: LUTON 23628/28331   Cables: AUTAIRWAYS, LUTON   Telex: 82220

A snapshot of the 'coming together' between Autair's Viking 'GRW and the Aeromacchi/Lockheed AL60B G-ARZG on the tarmac at Blackpool's Squires Gate Airport on 7 July 1965. Romeo Whiskey was the innocent, lesser of the two injured parties in this altercation, the Macchi suffering a broken wing spar and was written off. [via CPC Dibley]

I'm fairly certain it was the last such outing the company ever did - for reasons that will soon become obvious!

Everything went smoothly on the way out and I remember trying very hard to please in a uniform that did not fit too well!

By the time the flight was ready to depart Ostend in the evening the weather had changed, it was now pouring with rain and blowing a gale. As we started loading the passengers it became obvious that the ones that had been lighting up cigarettes as they walked across the tarmac had somewhat 'over indulged' in the local liquid refreshment. Not only that, I remember we were twelve passengers short. Nowhere to be found apparently. We delayed for a while, not so difficult in those days, but nobody else turned up.

The first big problem was strapping the passengers in. As soon as you thought you had one strapped in he was up and wandering around, it was mayhem, I eventually went up to the flight-deck to give the checks, we were taxiing out - the tiny windscreen wipers of the Viking were working like mad - and not coping - and the Captain, whose name I can't remember now, had his nose up against the windscreen and muttering to himself. After taking off we hit an enormous thunderstorm and then the trouble really started. It was a signal for all our inebriated passengers to be violently sick and not into sick bags either!

All of this didn't stop them smoking though, and there were soon smouldering seats and carpets. It soon became obvious that we were fighting a lost cause; Kathy called me to the galley and said: 'it's up to you but I'm certainly not doing anything more'.

I can't remember whether I joined her or not, but I can remember being very grateful to land at Luton and Kathy did check me out, I suppose she thought if I could survive that I could handle anything!

Another early memory is a scheduled service to Blackpool

One of Autair's Airspeed Ambassadors awaits another load of returning holidaymakers.[via CPC Dibley]

leaving in the early morning. A very cold and dark Luton Airport and just me and a handful of passengers in the cabin. It didn't have to be very turbulent to feel bumpy on a Viking - you didn't reach great heights! They were of course unpressurized and the draught from the door could be quite considerable. The galley also happened to be at the rear of the aircraft, so it was usually pretty chilly. I remember there was some sort of pole behind the last passenger's seat and boy, was this useful for hanging onto that day! I can't remember serving a full breakfast but certainly refreshments were served. On this particular occasion it was very turbulent, we were bouncing all over the place and I was beginning to feel very green indeed. I must have looked it - one of the passengers got out of his seat, put me in it and took over serving the coffees. No mean feat when you had to negotiate the main spar (an up and over step) towards the front of the aircraft.

I thought my flying career could be very short indeed if I had to do a lot of hours on Vikings.

The spring and summer of 1965 must have been good. I remember we often sunbathed outside the main hangar doors in deck chairs, watching the occasional aeroplane arrive and depart (for in those days Luton was not that busy). After the terrors of my initial flight, it was all quite relaxing really!'

Autair's publicity machine did not miss a trick, here seen linking up with the 1965 16th Annual Gift Fair held in Blackpool.

AUTAIR
International Airways

16th INTERNATIONAL
GIFTS FAIR
1965
DAILY AIR SERVICES
Between
LONDON & BLACKPOOL
February 1st to 5th

Changes and new equipment.

By the autumn of 1965, visible changes were taking place within the airline. The Ambassadors were seen more often on the Blackpool run, and during the year the number of passengers on this service had increased by 35%. This healthy increase allowed Autair to think

Gerry Threlfall signs for the first 748 at Woodford, watched by Bill Buxton (standing left) and Maurice Rowan (standing right). The remainder are Hawker Siddeley executives. [HSA]

about further scheduled service route expansion, resulting in an application to the Air Transport Licensing Board (ATLB) to extend the route up to Glasgow. This was approved, and an order was placed in November 1965 for a pair of Hawker Siddeley 748s, the first, G-ATMI arriving at Luton on 30 March 1966, followed by the second machine shortly afterwards. It was the introduction of this second aircraft that allowed some sort of a record to be claimed - Mike Finlay was involved...

'...*Mike Juliet touched down at Luton at 0920hrs at the end of its delivery flight from Hawker Siddeley Aviation in Woodford near Manchester - forty minutes later it took off on its first scheduled service, heading back up north to Blackpool on its first revenue-earning flight*'.

G-ATMJ at rest on the apron at Dublin, parked in front of a BEA Viscount. [Kurt Lang]

OUTE MAP

AUTAIR
*International
Airways*

You are welcome to take this Route Map as a souvenir of your flight

Autair give-away - the ubiquitious on-board map.

G-ATMI is seen being refuelled at an alpine airfield.[Kurt Lang]

April 1966 saw changes occurring. Ed Posey and Gerry Threlfall were appointed as joint Managing Directors on the first of the month. One of these appointments was to have a lasting affect on Elizabeth Hutchinson, known to all in the airline as simply 'Mrs Hutchinson'.

'I had joined Autair at the end of 1964 as secretary to the Operations Director, Capt. Maurice Rowan, and thoroughly enjoyed the busy office life right from the start. Previously I had worked as headmaster's secretary in a Devon boarding school where most days boys were coming in and out of the study with their problems. This job with Maurice Rowan seemed almost a continuation of that, with young pilots presenting their problems - some connected with their work, but mostly domestic.

I then heard that Capt Rowan was moving on, so I made my mind up to leave at the same time. However, that was not to be. I got a call from our London office and a voice said 'I'm Edward Posey and have just been appointed Managing Director of Autair International, and as such I can pick my own secretary - so I've chosen you '.

I started to tell him that I had every intention of leaving at the end of the month, but he did not want to know. I had never even met him, but his reputation as a dynamic perfectionist had long been common knowledge at Luton. So it was with some trepidation that I agreed to give it a try and that was the beginning of nine very exciting years.

Running the airline, as he did on a day-to-day basis, made for a hectic life at the office, but I loved the challenge of being totally involved in this very wide variety of work. One thing he did teach me was how to maximise time. Not only was he an astute businessman, but he was totally immersed in the

AUTAIR International Airways

in association with

HAWKER SIDDELEY AVIATION

Farnborough
Air Show

welcomes

you!

Jet-Prop
Hawker Siddeley HS 748 Series 2

powered by
Rolls Royce Dart engines

AUTAIR International Airways

DISPLAYING TO THE WORLD...

Not long after taking delivery of 748 MJ, the aircraft appeared at the 1966 Farnborough Air Show, showcase to the world for the British aviation industry.

The aircraft formed part of the Hawker Siddeley Aviation exhibit and as such was open to the industry and public alike.

Autair International made sure that all this attention gained them as much publicity as possible for their scheduled services, producing a leaflet that promoted the airline 's domestic scheduled services and IT and charter flights.

However, it was not quite as simple as that - 'Mike Juliet' was still needed on Autair's scheduled services, so each day after the show closed, the aircraft was stripped of promotional material, cleaned and then flown to Luton for the night services. Early next morning it was flown empty, back into Farnborough ready to be put on display!
[Autair via Peter Ward]

whole concept of running an airline - attention to detail and
excellent staff relations were the order of the day'.

Autair had applied for and, despite numerous objections from other
airlines heard at an ATLB hearing on 5 April 1966, was granted
scheduled services out of Hull to Luton. The ATLB reported its
decision to Gerry Threlfall on 16th April and he in turn told all
departments of the airline in an internal memo...

'I am pleased to say that we have heard from the ATLB that we
have been granted the licence for daily scheduled services
between London (Luton Airport) and Hull. This should become
one of our most important routes, and I estimate that we will
be carrying approximately three times the number of
passengers that we carry on the London (Luton Airport) -
Blackpool route.

The question that now has to be resolved is which airport we
will use in the Hull area. This will be either Brough, which
would necessitate our using H.S. 748s or the RAF Station at
Leconfield, which would allow us to use Ambassadors. The
final decision will be made at a later stage, and will depend
on whether the Ministry of Defence allow Leconfield to be used
for civil scheduled services.

The daily air services will operate throughout the year, and
will commence at the beginning of October. I feel that this new
route will be very important in establishing us as a scheduled
airline.'

Ambassador G-ALZS operated the expanded Luton-Blackpool
service up to Glasgow's Abbotsinch Airport on 24 May 1966, where
the flights were handled by Scotia Air Services. The next week the
748 G-ATMJ appeared on the route, which marked the first scheduled
Autair 748 service. Throughout the 1966 summer season IT services
were flown by the Ambassadors and the 748s, whilst the pair of
Vikings, recently converted into freighter configuration, operated ad-
hoc cargo flights out of Luton. Over 25,000 passengers were flown
on scheduled services in 1966; but a massive 81,000 were carried on
Inclusive Tours and charter flights.

To help with the expansion, Autair obtained a number of the
British European Airways Herald fleet that the national carrier were
taking out of service in late 1966, and the first, G-APWD arrived at
Luton on 14 November, rapidly followed by G-APWC and 'PWB.
Over the winter of 1966 the airline's engineers worked on their three
new acquisitions so that on 28 March 1967 Herald G-APWC was
able to fly the first Autair scheduled service for the type, on the daily
Luton - Blackpool - Glasgow route. Introduction of the Heralds on
scheduled services meant that Autair was free to use the 748s for

charter work with many domestic and north European charter flights undertaken by the type, but later the aircraft spent much time out of the country on lease to other airlines.

Working for royalty...
It was not all scheduled route bashing or charter flying to the sunspots however. In 1966, via Bill Armstrong's contacts in Africa, Autair obtained a contract to supply crews and expertise to King Idris I of Libya's Royal Flight, operating a pair of executive Learjet 23s - 5A-DAC and 5A-DAD - out of Benghazi (Benina) under the auspices of Libyan Arab Airlines. Flying for royalty had its moments as John Allen, who ran the detachment with Captain Ted Gordon as Chief Pilot in the early days recalls:

AUTAIR
International Airways

UNITED KINGDOM INTERNAL
SCHEDULED AIR SERVICES

QUICK REFERENCE TIMETABLE
SUMMER 1966
APRIL 1st — OCTOBER 31st

AUTAIR International Airways

'All went well - we picked up the Lears in the USA and flew them on Royal and Diplomatic duties until one of the crews took 'DAD into Damascus. They were there on the ground when the Arab - Israeli Six Day War broke out and the aircraft was destroyed in an Israeli Air Force rocket attack on 5th June 1967. The crew escaped unhurt, but they literally had to hitch-hike back to Benghazi!'

The summer 1966 timetable, showing the London (Luton) - Blackpool - Glasgow route, along with the summer only Blackpool - Isle of Man route flown in conjunction with British United Airways.. The Luton - Hull - Dundee routes were expected, but were not yet flown, being respresented by dotted lines.

To replace the destroyed Learjet, eventually a pair of Dassault Falcon 20s, 5A-DAF and 'DAG, were acquired early in 1968. Things continued normally until the King's family was toppled in a coup by a military junta led by Muammar al Qaddafi in 1969 - then the Autair personnel, by now consisting of six pilots and three engineers, found themselves operating on behalf of Libyan Arab Airlines for the Libyan Government, on call twenty-four hours a day by senior Government officials. This contract continued on well into the 1970s and tended to be beset with behind-the-scenes dramas - both military and political.

Maurice Rowan, apart from being Operations Director, also regularly 'flew the line' and carried out Check-flights and Instrument Rating Checks, including those for the pilots on the Benghazi Detachment...

Herald 'PWC during a turnaround at Leconfield.

Illuminated by the ramp lights at Luton, Herald G-ARWD is prepared for another service. [via CPC Dibley]

'*I flew out to Benghazi to carry out Instrument Ratings and six-month check-flights on the pilots. On arrival at Benina on a Libyan Airways flight I was told my visa was not in order and so I was arrested on the spot and locked up. After two days I was released, after having discreetly mentioned to the Libyan Army Major in charge that the pilots would not be able to continue flying without their check-flights being carried out!*'

Further expansion to the network

For many years Autair had hoped to operate a direct Dundee to London service, but problems with the Scottish airfield held up the introduction of this route. On 18 May 1966 Captain R. F. 'Dickie' Martin with Captain C. P. C. 'Pete' Dibley as P2 flew Autair's 748 'MI on a proving flight from Blackpool to Dundee's Riverside Park airstrip with much local publicity. On board were an Autair team, including Gerald Threlfall and George Merrifield from the Ministry of Aviation Flight Inspectorate. Gerald Threlfall spoke to the Press, giving the company's reason for the visit was...

Despite the changes going on within Autair, the contract flying for the Libyan Arab Airlines continued. Here one of the Dassault Falcon 20s in seen high over the desert from the other.

'*...to assess Dundee Airport for the HS 748. What we are interested*

in doing is starting a daily scheduled service between Dundee and London. We are applying for a direct service which would take one hour 55 minutes, or less. This is a proving flight to assess the practicability of operating a 748 from here'.

Autair continued to make good use of the Ambassadors, this machine being seen in Rotterdam, during the annual exodus to the Dutch bulb fields. [author's collection]

The timing was perfect - only hours before, the Town Council voted to authorise completion of negotiations with British Eagle Airlines for twice-daily flights to Abbotsinch. After meeting with the Autair team, Lord Provost McManus - who only found out about the proving flight the day before - went with the team to the Riverside Airstrip, inspected the 748, and watched it take-off. He told the Press...

'Autair are not seeking a subsidy. They said they expected the service to break even on a basis of 20 passengers per flight. As we are being offered a service direct to London, it must be considered. This is the best type of flight we could have... I have instructed the Town Clerk not to proceed with British Eagle for a day or two until we can clear this matter up'.

Despite the optimism shown to the Press during the proving flight there were problems to be overcome. The grass airfield was prone to water-logging and there were delays in issuing a licence brought about by a battle with British Eagle which created three hearings and an appeal that caused Autair to temporarily shelve the idea. The licence was eavatually granted in the autumn of 1967, along with licences for Dundee - Jersey and Dundee - Isle of Man, possibly to be flown as weekend, summer-only services.

History is often recorded on yellowing newspapers - this being how the press turned out in force to witness the arrival of 'Riverside's biggest plane'!

After talks with the Royal Air Force it was agreed that Autair could use Leuchars airfield for their Dundee services and that the local

Dundee - London air service plan
out of the blue
—on the wings of
Riverside's biggest plane

56-seater airliner yesterday flew in to land at the Dundee airstrip
verside Park with the surprise announcement that an international
ne wants to fly direct scheduled flights between Dundee and London six
a week, starting in October

Herald G-APWC climbs away from Luton on a regular scheduled service flight.

council would provide a grant of £15,000 per year in subsidy. With the formalities sorted out, Autair opened the Leuchars - Luton route on 1 April 1968 and, although some services were flown direct, others were routed via Blackpool or Carlisle.

Not everybody remembers the Heralds with affection. John Begg was a Luton-based Traffic Officer and Flight Despatcher for Autair from 1964 to 1968, but also did 'time' at Carlisle and Dundee...

> 'The Herald reliability left much to be desired and day after day we endured technical problems. I have vivid memories of the time Dundee Football Club flew Autair for a friendly preseason match with Hull F.C.
>
> My father was very friendly with Bobby Ancell, Manager of Dundee FC, and through him I convinced them to travel to Hull via Luton as it was the quickest way between the two points.
>
> The match was programmed for the Monday evening and so the team travelled DND-LTN on the non-stop Herald service

Handley Page Herald G-APWB sits on the tarmac outside the original Autair hangar at Luton on a stormy afternoon. [John Hunt]

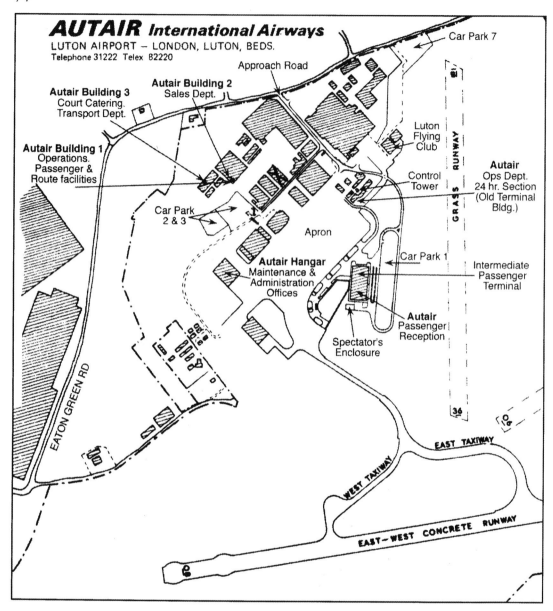

AUTAIR International Airways

LUTON AIRPORT – LONDON, LUTON, BEDS.
Telephone 31222 Telex 82220

Car Park 7

Approach Road

Autair Building 3
Court Catering.
Transport Dept.

Autair Building 2
Sales Dept.

Luton
Flying
Club

Autair Building 1
Operations.
Passenger &
Route facilities

Control
Tower

Autair
Ops Dept.
24 hr. Section
(Old Terminal
Bldg.)

Car Park
2 & 3

Apron

Car Park 1

Intermediate
Passenger
Terminal

Autair Hangar
Maintenance &
Administration
Offices

Autair
Passenger
Reception

Spectator's
Enclosure

36

EATON GREEN RD

GRASS RUNWAY

GRASS

EAST TAXIWAY

WEST TAXIWAY

EAST–WEST CONCRETE RUNWAY

first thing Monday morning, with the same aircraft programmed through to Hull (Brough). An ontime arrival at Hull needless to say was ruined as the aircraft was unserviceable on arrival. The delay at Luton was around three hours, so the team arrived at Hull in the mid-afternoon, thus missing the pre-match practice. I cannot remember the result - it's probably just as well!

Next morning Dundee FC arrived at Brough to be met by a very bemused Hull Station Manager who knew nothing about them - Reservations had 'got it wrong.' To cap it all, Herald performance at Brough was very limited and the flight was

The layout of Luton Airport in September 1966, showing the location of Autair occupied buildings, as portrayed on a map handed to new employees and others seeking directions

Timetable & Fares

SCHEDULED AIR SERVICES

HULL - LONDON

commencing

3rd October 1966

Jet-Prop HAWKER SIDDELEY 748

already pre-booked to capacity - no room for Dundee FC. After some major arguing the Captain eventually took them, although it was a heart-in-mouth take-off. After landing at Luton the Herald was scheduled for a direct Dundee service but, surprise, surprise - tech problems! It was also discovered that there were passengers for both Blackpool and Carlisle - Reservations had quietly slipped those in and not told anybody! Four hours late the aircraft departed Luton, and with the additional stops the flight time to Dundee was 'extended' somewhat. To add insult to injury, the entire British Isles was ravaged by gales that day, and so Dundee FC had to endure three take-offs and three landings in 35-45 kt winds.

Dundee FC arrived at Leuchars at 1630 in the afternoon, instead of 1130 in the morning, and I was unfortunately on duty to meet them. Bobby Ancell was first off and gave me a look that had 'death wish' written all over it and said something unprintable. Surprisingly, we never heard from Dundee FC again!'

Additional expansion occurred to the scheduled services on 1 January 1967 when the airline took over the former B.K.S. Teeside - London route, again making use of Luton as the London terminus. Summer scheduled services were also flown between Hull and Jersey.

Inclusive tour charters continued unchanged from Luton in 1967, but when Treffield International collapsed in June, Autair took over many of their services, including charters from Bristol and Cardiff to many of the Mediterranean sun-spots on behalf of Hourmont Travel.

John Nightingale joined Autair as an aeroplane-mad youth following an introduction to Maurice Rowan by Captain John Handley...

I found myself as tea-boy cum Ops Assistant at the beginning of 1966, the start of an airline career which spanned 23 years.

Within a couple of months I was producing crew rosters which, although not greeted with loud shouts of enthusiasm, were flown with great efficiency and professionalism.

We worked really hard in those days - 16 hour flying duty periods were still then legal and I am pleased to say there was an almost total lack of 'bull' and form-filling! I seem to recall that when I wasn't working (which wasn't often) I was sitting in the jump-seat or standing between pilots! Base checks on Ambassador crews were often carried out on the Saturday night paper run to Dublin - it was an experience, to say the least! A single-engined ILS approach and overshoot, often in the pouring rain and with a crosswind before landing and offloading the Sunday papers... Those were the days! '

Day	STD	Depart	Destination	Arrive	STA	A/C	Capt.	F/O
Extract from Autair International Airways Duty Roster period ending 31st August 1966								
Th 18	18/0645	Luton	Man/Rimini	Luton	18/1955	748	MG Williams	Bradstreet
	18/0900	Luton	Blk/Glasgow	Luton	18/1740	Amb	D.R. White	Willis
	18/1430	Luton	Dusseldorf	Luton	18/1930	Amb	Handley	Letch
	18/1815	Luton	Blackpool	Luton	19/0810	Amb	Hammerton	Browse
	18/2030	Luton	Palma	Luton	19/0650	Amb	Wilson	Love
	18/2100	Luton	Milan	Luton	19/0500	748	Hogg	Varley
	18/2115	Luton	Milan	Luton	19/0515	748	Ellis	B. Hampson
Fri 19	19/0815	Luton	Mahon	Luton	19/2025	748	Cole	Overbury
	19/0900	Luton	Dublin	Luton	19/1300	Amb	DV Hampson	Willcock
	19/1000	Luton	Frankfurt	Luton	19/1610	Amb	Hammerton	Browse
	19/1430	Luton	Dusseldorf	Luton	19/1930	Amb	DV Hampson	Willcock
	19/1815	Luton	Blackpool	Luton	19/2055	Amb	Hammerton	Browse
	19/2045	Luton	Genoa	Luton	20/0545	Amb	Handley	Carter
	19/2100	Luton	Milan	Luton	20/0500	748	Daniel	Lang + MG Williams
	19/2115	Luton	Milan	Luton	20/0515	748	Szozesiak	DE White + Hall
	19/2130	Luton	Palma	Luton	20/0750	Amb	Elliott	Letch
	19/2200	Luton	Barcelona	Luton	20/0650	Amb	Ball	Willis
Sat 20	20/0530	Luton	Kerkyra	Luton	20/2105	748	Dibley	Bradstreet
	20/0800	Luton	Blk/Glasgow	Luton	20/1450	Amb	Prudence	Kingsmill-Moore
	20/0845	Luton	Bastia	Luton	20/1855	Amb	Shedrick	Love
	20/0900	Luton	Calvi	Luton	20/1750	748	Rowan	Varley
	20/0930	Luton	Basle	Luton	20/1555	Amb	Souter/Hogg	Willcock
	20/1600	Luton	Barcelona	Luton	21/0050	Amb	DV Hampson	Browse
	20/2030	Luton	Rimini	Luton	21/0730	Amb	Hammerton	Overbury
	20/2100	Luton	Milan	Luton	21/0500	748	Szozesiak	Lang
	20/2115	Luton	Milan	Luton	21/0515	748	Daniel	D.E. White

Links with the Continent - and tragedy.

The link between the north-east of England and the Netherlands was restored by Autair on 11 July 1967, when a Herald left Tees-side Airport bound for the recently re-opened Schiphol Airport, Amsterdam, with a 25-minute stop at Hull. On board for the 130 minute flight were three passengers, Hull timber merchant C.B. North and his wife, and retired travel agency manager B. S. Dolman, who had been on the first-ever Hull-Amsterdam KLM service back in 1934.

In 1967 over 70,000 passengers were flown on scheduled services and just over 97,000 on IT charters. These figures were a very healthy improvement on the previous year, but 1968 was to be even better; passengers using the scheduled service flights remained fairly static,

Three days of flying schedule in August 1966! The pair of regular 748 overnights to Milan shows up clearly... less obvious is the 15 hour 35 minute duty allocated to Capt Peter Dibley and First Officer Bradstreet for them to take a 748 to Kerkyra (Corfu) in Greece and back!

One of Autair's Ambassadors is 'batted in' to its parking stand at Luton. [Hugh Jampton Collection]

but the numbers flown on IT flights saw a near-trebling to 273,200!

1967, however, ended on a sad note, for during the evening of 23 December Training Capt. Harold G. Dryhurst and First Officer David W. Boothman lost their lives in the crash of HS.125 G-AVGW half a mile west of the end of Runway 26 at Luton Airport. The aircraft - only eight months old and owned by The Beecham Group - was being operated by Autair International on a crew training detail so that David Boothman could complete his conversion onto the 125. A series of flights had been made in the local area, the final being a simulated engine failure on take-off, followed by an asymetric approach and single-engined landing. Witnesses saw the aircraft make a normal take-off and climb to around 300 feet when engine noise ceased.

The aircraft descended and crashed onto the roof of the Vauxhall Motors factory, bursting into flames. Although the cause of the accident was known - almost total reduction of engine power - despite extensive investigations by the Board of Trade's Accidents Investigation Branch, no reason for the accident was ever determined.

Pre-dating the seat-pocket In-Flight magazines was the two-tone blue covered 'Information Book', this being Autair's example for the summer of 1966. [via John Hepworth]

Further changes occurred in the Board on 1 January 1968; Gerry Threlfall was 'moved upstairs' to the post of Deputy Chairman, and Ed Posey became sole Managing Director, Autair International Airways and was also appointed to the Court Line Group board.

April 1968 saw a number of new scheduled services added to Autair's network. Belfast and Dublin from Teesside, Jersey from Carlisle, Dundee and Teesside and the Isle of Man from Hull, Teesside and Dundee. Almost all were flown by the Heralds.

Arrival of the jets!
Much of the improvement in passenger loads during 1968 had been brought about by the introduction of a pair of eighty-nine seat BAC One-Eleven Series 400 jet aircraft in February and March, a third arriving on lease from the manufacturer in May.

Autair's interest in entering the pure-jet field came about as early as

Hawker Siddeley 125 business jet G-AVGW belonging to the Beecham Group which crashed at Luton while crew training. [Hugh Jampton Collection]

The result of selecting 'flaps up' too soon after take-off!

G-APWD sits on the wet runway at Luton as the engineers prepare to move the aircraft. Apart from some damage to the underside of the Herald, both props suffered minor tip-damage. [via CPC Dibley]

January 1967, when Autair had first shown an interest in the new One-Eleven. Indeed, the opening of the Luton - Teesside scheduled service coincided with a demonstration of the type to the airline. This interest evolved via the project-only BAC Two-Eleven, an enlarged One-Eleven design powered by a pair of Rolls-Royce RB2-11 turbofans.

Autair had placed an order with BAC for three examples for delivery in the spring of 1972, just two days before the Labour Government of the day announced that it would not support development of the new type. Autair also demonstrated interest in the 200/294 seat BAC Three-Eleven twin-jet, also powered by the Rolls Royce RB 2-11 engine, but this was yet another 'paper aeroplane' from the British Aircraft Corporation that never left the drawing board.

The airline had studied the Boeing 737 and Douglas DC-9 before placing an order in February 1967 for two series 400 machines (later increased to three) with BAC. As Gerry Threlfall commented in *'Autair News'*, the company newspaper, on the then-£3 million order when it was announced:

'On our assessment the BAC One-Eleven is undoubtably the

An artists impression of the never-to-be-built BAC Two-Eleven in the colours of Autair International Airways [Winged Memories/BAe]

best. We are very happy to buy British. We have closely evaluated not only which aircraft would be best for us in 1968, but also what our jet requirement would be in three or five years time. With the One-Eleven 400 series, which we are ordering initially, we feel that BAC have produced the right combination of aircraft for the next decade.

The -400 series will be initally used on inclusive tour operations. This year the airline will carry approximately 175,000 passengers on scheduled services and inclusive tour flights. That figure is expected to rise to 300,000 in 1968.

John Young also commented to the media...

'The acquisition of these new British jets is a natural step in our plans to develop Autair as a major, independent operator. We are certain they will considerably increase the airline's earning power'.

Ed Posey provides some of the background to the deal that allowed the company 'buy British'...

A team from Boeing Aircraft Corporation came along and gave us a very big presentation on their 'baby Boeing', the 737, but no matter which way we looked at it, the British Aircraft Corporation financing arrangements could not be bettered.

The first time we met with Geoffrey Knight, the Sales Director of BAC at Wisley - where the One-Eleven was being flight-tested - he told us that the One-Eleven was broadly as good as any other of the twinjets. But what they would do is put finance on the tail; their financing was extremely good, based certainly on the contract with Clarksons Holidays. It turned out to be a winning formula'.

The first machine, G-AVOF *'Halcyon Breeze'* arrived at Luton for hand-over on 8 February. 'Oscar Foxtrot', a One-Eleven 416EK, arrived at Luton in the airlines smart light-blue, grey, dark-blue and white colour scheme after meticulous preparation... Two days before the momentous occasion Dennis Elsden, Autair's Senior Operations Officer, instigated the final part of the meticulous planning that included a series of weather checks in order to:

'...ensure that G-AVOF is at Luton by the programmed time of 08/1200 the Duty Operations Officer will carry out the following 'MET' Checks. The aircraft is routeing HURN - WISLEY - LUTON.

A check with the Uxbridge Met Forecaster at the following times 06/ 1200hrs, 07/ 1200hrs,07/2359hrs and 08/ 0800hrs.

In addition to the general situation, particularly ascertain if there is any likelihood of low stratus, fog, snow or crosswinds.

In the event of any adverse conditions, these should be passed to Capt. Prudence, BAC Hurn, BAC Wisley, D. Glasor BAC Chief Pilot or T. Gaitskill or Mr Moore. All movements and /or revised programmes must be processed to all interested

As yet still unnamed, One-Eleven G-AVOF is prepared by BAC engineers on 30 January 1968 for a series of acceptance flights by Capts. Dibley and Ellis of Autair. [via CPC Dibley]

Taken in October 1967, and without any visible registration, this beautiful photograph is supposedly of the first BAC One-Eleven in Autair International colours. There is a suspicion however, that it's really an artists impression.
[via M. Rowan]

parties without delay in order that reception arrangements may 'go off' without a hitch'.

'Oscar Foxtrot' was rapidly placed into service, to be joined a month later by sister machine ''OE. The first Autair crews for the new One-Elevens were given ground and flying training on the type by British United Airways at Gatwick. Once the crews were trained and had the One-Eleven on their licences, experience 'down the route' had to be gained, so the Autair crews flew scheduled services for BUA.

The One-Elevens soon found favour with the travelling public - and it was not long before a further aircraft - G-AVGP - to be named '*Halcyon Cloud*' was leased from BAC.

Elizabeth Overbury was one of the crew members selected for training on the new type by British United...

'I had a really good time, but it was very hard work. I really enjoyed my time with British United before we got down to work flying the One-Eleven for Autair.

I remember one flight when Captain Mike Ellis - our Deputy Chief Pilot - was letting me fly the leg back from Palma to Luton. We were due in during the early afternoon and there was a strong ninety degree crosswind from the south. I elected to land on Runway Zero Eight but was far too high on the approach so we overshot. As Mike Ellis was handling the radios, ATC asked what

The pre-delivery testing of G-AVOF at Hurn.
[via CPC Dibley]

his intentions were for a further approach. His reply I remember to this day .... 'I'm not too sure, but I'll ask the Management!' I then elected to come in on Two Six and the landing was 'smoochy".

The One-Elevens were flown exclusively on Inclusive Tour work. As Ed Posey told the staff in April 1969:

'A year ago we had just started jet operations with BAC One-Elevens. Substantial progress has been made since that time with our first full season successfully behind us, and satisfactory financial results published at the end of our last financial year. We are entering another Summer programme with a much expanded operation requiring five BAC One-Elevens. The Company has reached a size where it is harder to retain personal contact with its staff than it was in the early days. It is, however, essential that you be fully informed of what we are doing and aiming at in Autair, and for you to feel a sense of participation in the activities of the Court Line Group.

The Inclusive Tour side of our business, now operated exclusively with the One-Elevens, continues to expand rapidly. We have had a busy Winter flying in excess of 2,500 hours with four BAC One-Elevens - an enormous growth over previous years. This expansion mainly arose from the special concessions that were granted for Tour Operators allowing them to charge lower minimum prices for Winter

Interior of one of the Autair One-Elevens.

Sandy Keegan (née Smith) at the bottom of a One-Eleven airstairs. The white gloves had to be worn when greeting and saying goodbye to passengers!
[Sandy Keegan]

package holidays. Clarksons Tours took full advantage of these concessions. It is hoped that the Edwards Committee Report will recommend a more liberal policy which will allow us to achieve even higher aircraft utilisation over the forthcoming winter months.

We are now about to operate a very full programme for the five BAC One-Elevens, number four having been delivered on 21 March and number five on a permanent basis on 28 March. A new development for this Summer has been our seat-back catering idea, which has enabled us to increase the seating capacity of the 400 Series by three seats to 89 seats, as well as giving the Air Hostesses more time for attending to the comforts of our passengers. We patented this idea and plan to sell it to other airlines.

Our 1970 programme for Clarksons has been the subject of negotiations for the last few weeks and final agreement has now been reached. An announcement has been made that Autair has increased its order from five to seven BAC One-Eleven 500 Series for delivery by Spring 1970. We will again incorporate seat-back catering which will give capacity of 119 passengers. The 500 Series will replace all but one of the 400 Series and we shall therefore be operating seven BAC One-Eleven 500 Series and one BAC One-Eleven 400 Series - a total of eight in 1970.

Sue Porter in her Autair Air Hostess uniform and at work. Note the white gloves, white-topped hat and skirt length just above the knee - all of this was to drastically change within a few months!

About 75% of the fleet's capacity is contracted to Clarksons on a long term charter, the remaining 25% will be flown for other tour operators and for ad hoc charters.

Having got the first summer season using jets under their belt, Autair embarked on a much-expanded winter programme flying in excess

Holland at bulb time.

Clarksons Famous Short Tours

In The Spring		prices	from
Holland at Tulip Time		1-day	£9
		2-days	15 gns.
		4-days	20 gns.
Paris Champagne Flight		1-day	£9.10
		weekend	20 gns.
		4-days	23 gns.
Ireland, The Emerald Isle		6-days	29 gns.
Copenhagen & Denmark		*1-day	£13.10
		6-days	34 gns.
Switzerland		6-days	30 gns.
Norway		6-days	34 gns.
Austrian Tyrol		6-days	29 gns.
Vienna, Salzburg, Munich		*6-days	32 gns.
Venice, Florence, Pisa		*6-days	31 gns.
Madrid, Segovia, Toledo		*6-days	32 gns.
Rome, Naples, Capri		*6-days	35 gns.

*In Autumn 1969 these tours will also be available.

In The Autumn			
Rhine Valley at Winefest Time		weekend	20 gns.
		4-days	23 gns.
		5-days	26 gns.
Bruges		1-day	£8
Brussels		1-day	£8.10
Burgundy at Vintage Time		4-days	23 gns.
Bordeaux Vineyards		5-days	32 gns.
Heart of France		6-days	.35 gns.

Summer Sun Holidays by Jet

Spain: Costa Brava, Costa Blanca, Majorca, Ibiza, Minorca, Costa del Sol, Canaries 8, 11, 12 and 15 day Holidays from about 27 gns.
Italy: Rimini, Diano Marina, Elba, Lido di Jesolo, Venice. **Jugoslavia, Tunisia, Greece** and **Portugal** 11, 12 and 15 day Holidays from about 29gns.
Also Snowjet Holidays for Skiers, Winter Sunshine Holidays and Motoring Holidays.

Send for coloured brochures on all Tours & Holidays

Clarksons Tours Ltd, Clarksons House, Sun Street, London, EC2.
Telephones 01-247 6575 Reservations
01-283 9711 Administration & Party Liaison

Clarksons
Short air tours by jet
Spring 1969

THE EMERALD ISLE
FAIRY TALE TOUR OF DENMARK
SPRING IN SWITZERLAND
THE AUSTRIAN TYROL
THE FJORDS OF NORWAY

IRELAND
DENMARK
SWITZERLAND
AUSTRIAN TYROL
NORWAY

The cover page of Clarksons Tours Spring 1969 brochure. More and more of Autair's capacity was being taken up by the tour company.

of 2,500 hours with four of the new jets. The turn into the new year saw a further addition to the One-Eleven fleet, when G-AVGP was leased from the manufacturers. The aircraft was in full Autair colours, but was only used by the airline at the weekends - the remainder of the week it returned to Hurn to participate in a UK-based crew training programme for Sadia of Brazil in January and for training crews for Germania and Cambrian.

Alan Smith of BAC was seconded to Autair to gain experience as a One-Eleven Captain as a pre-requisite to becoming a training pilot...

I flew three months in 'OE, OF and G-AWBL. I think the only way I distinguished myself was to have an unscheduled night-stop at Palma with 13 - yes, 13 lady crew on board - Elizabeth Overbury and twelve Hostesses. I remember I did have a First Officer called Clayton to help me out and we had a very pleasant though innocent time!

I rejoined BAC two days later, little knowing that I would be back a few months later to help introduce the 500 series. I subsequently taught pilots all over the world and tried to instil the Autair/ Court Line standards in them'.

One of the One-Elevens was leased to Rolls-Royce for an experimental Spey engine programme at Hucknall, near Derby. Hints were also made by Ed Posey in the April 1969 edition of *Autair International News* of the greater things that were just over the horizon.

Design consultants have now been appointed to advise on the corporate image for all the Group's activities. This will affect our airline as it is planned that a whole new style of livery and uniforms will be adopted to coincide with the introduction of the new BAC One-Eleven 500 Series next spring.

He went on to explain more about the group's other activities that affected the airline.

Autair International's Series 400 BAC 1-11 G-AWBL picks up another load of returning passengers from Alicante Airport in Spain. [Kurt Lang]

A 'new' Company - the Court Travel Group - has now been formed to integrate the activities of Murison Small, Vacation Tours, Harold Ingham and the Court Travel retail agencies. It is planned that the Group will now expand its own tour operating activities, particularly in the specialised travel field.

Our airline and the travel group form two parts of Court Line's plan for the vertical integration of the Group's activities in the leisure field - the third part is the construction of our own hotels. Court Line is developing two hotels on St. Lucia in the Caribbean, the smaller of which will be completed by the coming Winter, and the first phase of the major hotel complex by the winter of 1970.

Our future is tied to that of the Group. We are now studying our aircraft requirements for 1971 and later into the 1970s. The trend for Inclusive Tour holidays to extend further afield, together with the Group's own plans for the Caribbean, indicate that we should introduce long haul aircraft for Spring 1971.

It is probable that DC-8s or Boeing 707s will be used and they will also be operated over the high density short haul routes such as Luton - Palma. Looking even further ahead we must now consider the introduction of airbus equipment in the mid 70s.

With a torch to help with the walkround and Met Information in hand for the return flight Senior First Officer Elizabeth Overbury is seen on the airstairs of an Autair One-Eleven at Palma Airport, Majorca early in 1969. [via Elizabeth Overbury]

The end of scheduled services.

After receiving permission from the ATLB to operate services from Leconsfield instead of Brough to London. Autair transferred its scheduled services from Luton to Heathrow on 1 April 1969 in an effort to improve passenger appeal by offering better connections to international flights. Ed Posey again:

A substantial maintenance programme was planned for the three Heralds this Winter, and as a result of the hard work of all the Engineers concerned, the third Herald recommenced operations to Hull on Monday, 21 April. There were long Governmental delays in obtaining permission to use Leconfield as a replacement airfield for Brough, and a favourable reply was only received at the last moment. The Herald maintenance base will be established at Teesside from 1 May and this together with the re-furbishing of the Herald fleet should lead to a more efficient operation with increased passenger appeal. It is particularly important for all of us to ensure that our scheduled services operate on time. The future for Scheduled Services is also very much bound up with the recommendations of the Edwards Committee Report which it is expected will lead to a national plan for all the various routes now operated by separate airlines.

Our new policy to operate all London services through Heathrow started on 1 April. It is hoped that this will lead to a material increase in the number of passengers using our

AUTAIR INTERNATIONAL AIRWAYS - CORPORATE STRUCTURE

as of 1 January 1969

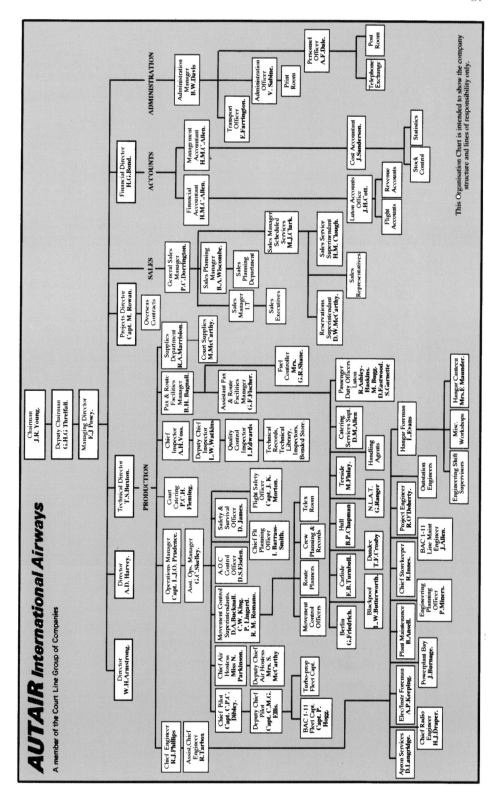

A typical scene at Luton Airport in the late 1960s - Bristol Britannias of Monarch and Britannia Airways and One-Elevens of Autair International. The Passenger Terminal Departure Lounge is on the extreme right of the picture. (Kurt Lang)

services; a sales and advertising campaign has been mounted to achieve this result. Our goal must be to fill every available seat on each sector this Summer.'

These services only operated for a few months before, on 31 July, Autair suddenly announced that at the end of October it was suspending all scheduled services flown by the company. The route system was ideally suited to the Heralds which were giving good service, and they were achieving load factors of 75% in the summer on the Luton - Teesside route, but nevertheless, the reasons for the closures were simple; Autair was losing over £150,000 per year on the scheduled network and the airline could not go on supporting uneconomic routes, although they had

The airline may have been Autair International, but there can be no doubt which holiday company Captain M J Williams, First Officer Henry Pyho and these three Air Hostesses were flying for - the Clarksons logo was very prominent! (Autair/Court Line Collection)

Autair International's Series 400 BAC 1-11 G-AVOE is parked outside the Autair hangar with another company 1-11 parked almost alongside. [Kurt Lang]

never expected to make fantastic profits. The airline had made strenuous efforts to obtain subsidies for serving development areas of Britain, but they had been unable to persuade any local authorities other than Dundee to subsidise the internal scheduled services.

Rumours and Press speculation had been around for a few days, and the airline had hoped to announce the plans privately to scheduled service staff on 1 August before issuing a Press Statement on 4 August. It ended up a public and staff relations disaster, as Ed Posey revealed to the staff:

'I issued an interim News Circular a week ago to those of our staff connected with the scheduled services as I felt that it was right for them to receive information of the latest position in the light of rumours and press reports. I said that we were in very close touch with the Board of Trade and awaited to hear from them by 31 July. We had anticipated that they would comment privately to us today and it had been planned to consider their comments and issue a press release on Monday, 4 August. It was further planned that this would enable us to contact all our staff, and particularly those connected with scheduled services, on 1st August and over the weekend before our comments had been made public.

In the event, the Board of Trade have issued their own press release at mid-day today and we have therefore been forced to re-consider the procedure we would adopt. As you can imagine, a considerable amount of thought has been given by the Court Line Board as well as the Autair Board, to the future of scheduled services and we had made up our minds that unless the Board of Trade could give us some assurances by the end of today that they would be following the recommendations of the Edwards Committee Report, we would have no alternative but to terminate all our scheduled services as at 1 October. In the light of the Board of Trade announcement today, we have therefore no alternative but to implement our decision. It is a decision that has been taken with great reluctance but it is the only one open to us if we are to pay proper regard to the future of Autair and to our responsibility to the Court Line shareholders.

The following is therefore the text of the press release that has been issued at 4 p.m. today:

AUTAIR to discontinue Scheduled Service Network: Will now concentrate on Inclusive Tour Operations.

Autair International Airways, the independent airline within the Court Line Group, is to discontinue its network of domestic scheduled services as from November 1st, it was announced today, Thursday, 31st July.

These scheduled services form only a small part of the airline's operation - this year approximately 12% of total turnover. Autair will now concentrate exclusively on its highly successful and growing Inclusive Tour services, which next year will fly a million passengers in the Company's £12 million fleet of eight One-Eleven jets.

The Scheduled Services - the main ones are London to Tees-side, Hull, Carlisle, Blackpool and Dundee - have collectively been making mounting losses over the last three years. Despite these losses, which have now reached approximately £150,000, Autair on the whole made a net profit last year of £217,000 and a satisfactory increase in profitability for this year has already been forecast.

A statement issued today by Court Line said:

'We do not think it is right that our shareholders should continue to subsidise these services - we feel that it is the Government who should take over this responsibility.

As a Public Company it is our duty to ensure that all ventures give a proper return on capital employed. In our

Autair International's Series 400 BAC 1-11 G-AVOF with a company Ambasssaor and Britannia Airways Britannia in the background.
[John Hunt]

HERALD HEYDAY!

The Handley Page Dart Herald may not have lasted long in Autair service and the ending of scheduled services saw the type enter premature retirement from the airline. Nevertheless, they did not go without leaving their mark - as part of the retirement ceremonies, Autair put up a three-ship formation to overfly the area!

Above: Herald G-APWA overflies the apron at Luton Airport at low level. On the ground can be seen a pair of Britannia Airways' Britannias alongside the Passenger Terminal, another pair belonging to Monarch Airlines and a further example unidentified outside the hangars. Parked in the right foreground alongside the skeletal framework of the new Britannia hangar is a Dan-Air Comet 4. [Kurt Lang]

Below: The three Heralds in loose formation approach the Luton Airport for a final low-level flypast.
[via CPC Dibley]

Right: An artists impression of the Passenger Terminal as planned for Luton in the mid-to-late 1960s.

Below: The Check-In area, Luton in 1969. The Autair desks were at the far end, adjacent to Barclays Bank. Closer to the camera were a number of Britannia desks, then Monarch Airlines and finally, on the extreme right, desks for British Midland Airways.

opinion, adequate profit, related to the capital resources employed, cannot be achieved from the domestic scheduled services in the forseeable future without Government subsidies. The decision to discontinue the network had to be taken as the Government has not accepted the Edward's Committee recommendation that domestic scheduled services to development areas justify financial subsidy.

We informed the Board of Trade about the situation over a year ago and have maintained close contact with them since that date.

A decision on the network's future, already postponed once to allow the Edward's Committee to publish its report at the beginning of May and then again to allow the Government White Paper to be presented, could not be delayed beyond July 31st, if we were to give three months notice of termination to the travelling public, the minimum we consider necessary.

In fact, it would have been reasonable for Autair to have terminated these services a year ago. To expect us to continue them for a further year in the absence of any assurances that favourable decisions would be forthcoming, is quite unreasonable.

We have made every effort over the last three years to improve the economic operation of the domestic scheduled services, including the purchase of the Dart Herald jet-prop fleet, the expense of moving the London base from Luton Airport to Heathrow Airport and establishing a new maintenance base at Tees-side. We have also made every effort to obtain maximum possible financial assistance from the local authorities where we operate.

The seating plan for the Autair BAC 1-11 400 was printed on the rear of the ticket. The forward galley was soon to be replaced by three extra seats with ther introduction of Autair-patented seat-back catering.

PASSENGER TICKET & BAGGAGE CHECK
issued by
C585949

AUTAIR International Airways

LUTON AIRPORT - LONDON

FOR CONDITIONS OF CONTRACT — See Pages 2 & 3
AND IMPORTANT NOTICES on Page 4

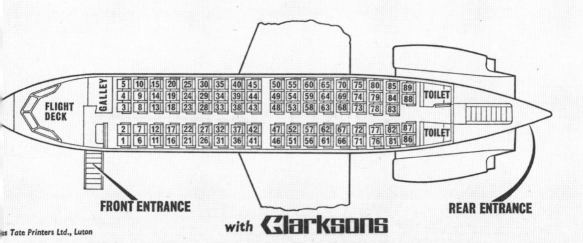

AUTAIR *International Airways*

BAC ONE-ELEVEN SEAT PLAN

FLIGHT DECK — GALLEY

FRONT ENTRANCE

REAR ENTRANCE

with **Clarksons**

Tate Printers Ltd., Luton

The financial results of the scheduled services have been fully budgetted for in the current financial year. By cutting out this loss-making activity, the profits of Autair, and therefore of the Court Line Group will be enhanced for the future.

Autair's decision to concentrate on its profitable Inclusive Tour services is part of Court Line Group's policy of developing its interest in the leisure industry fields of tour operations and holiday hotels.

Every possible assistance will be given to any airline which considers that the integration of any of Autair's routes is a financially viable operation when consolidated into their existing network'.

A busy scene on the ramp at Luton, as G-AVOE loads passengers. As usual for the period, everyone seems dressed in their sunday best!

The Board of Trade were also unable to provide assurances that Governmental support would be forthcoming, so on 31 October 1969 Autair's scheduled services came to a close and the Heralds were put up for sale. After modifications, they flew 'west and south' to La Urraca of Colombia.

During 1969 the number of British Aircraft Corporation One-Elevens was increased from three to five and the number of passengers carried on IT flights rose from a quarter to half a million.

Almost 75% of the total 1-11 utilization was solely for Clarksons Holidays, so it was not surprising that on 11 September 1969 it was

The three Autair One-Elevens on the ground at Luton. [Kurt Lang]

Four of the new One-Elevens for Court Line under construction.

announced that, with effect from 1 January 1970, Autair International Airways would change its name and image. It would become Court Line and the new image was that of Britain's holiday airline; for Autair had already signed contracts for the 1970 season with Clarksons Holidays, Pontinental, Wallace Arnold, Midland Air Tour Operators, Worldwide Air Holidays, Murison Small, Mediterranean Villas, Owners Services Ltd, German Student Travel, Star Villas and Vernon Holidays.

Times of contrasts

Although Bill Armstrong had sold out to John Young and Court Line back in 1965 he still retained a position on the Board of Autair International, for a while initially being the Deputy Chairman.

Inevitably perhaps, given such dynamic characters involved, a number of commercial differences of opinion grew up as to the direction of the airline. Bill had wanted it to continue on a broad, multi-legged base with scheduled and charter flying taking place, carrying both passengers and freight. John Young preferred to concentrate on charter flying, placing great emphasis on the concept of 'time charters'.

Although Autair International continued to work in close co-operation with other Autair Group companies, the change of emphasis meant that Bill Armstrong was able to concentrate again more on operations in Africa, where a new and burgeoning enterprise with great potential was well under way in Cape Town.

'*During my wartime flying in the Med, we were ordered to*

Twenty five years seperate these two pictures. The torpedo strike photo (above) was taken in 1943 after Bill Armstrong's aircraft had 'dropped' on the target and flown at zero feet between the dreaded flak ships, dodging the attention of the fighters. This unique picture aligned to the negative - taken just after the target tanker exploded - shows clouds of smoke and burning debris climbing skywards for thousands of feet.. Sadly it also shows the fate of Bill's wingman's aircraft - downed by flak - burning in the water to the right of the vessel in the top left of the photograph.
[WA Armstrong]

The contrast could not be different as Autair's S.55 ZS-HCN replenishes another oil tanker, with the cargo underslung in a net.

attack the Axis oil tankers supplying Rommel's Afrika Korps operating in the Western Desert - most enemy vessels were heavily escorted, along with fighter top-cover and our HQ were tempted to lose an entire squadron to destroy one sizable tanker. Not the most friendly of environments to fly in!

With fair fortune one beats the statistics and comes through with an optimistic attitude towards survival, which may be good training for the hazards then to follow in a lifetime of commercial aviation! It was this combination of aviation and maritime experience that helped me land the startup contract for ship-borne helicopter operations in the Antarctic; this led on to support of various offshore oil rigs and also work with special vessels dredging the sea-bed for diamonds beyond the massive surf on the Skeleton Coast of South West Africa. We were then well set, following the closure of the Suez Canal in the early summer of 1967, to establish the world's first regular

Oil tankers were not the only African operation! Above: An Autair Bell 47J comes in to land on the heli-pad aboard a diamond dredger off Fernando Po.

Above right: An Autair S.55 comes in to land on the heli-pad offshire Mozambique [both Autair-Court Collection]

Autair Helicopters business was now truly global. Here a Bell 47G is seen high in the Andes... (Autair Collection)

helicopter service for tankers on their long haul around the Cape heading for the European markets.

Autair's helicopter stores and Mail delivery service proved to be a boon to tanker operators and business boomed.

Bringing about changes...

The airline was about to enter a new decade with new equipment and a new name, launched to the media at the Savoy Hotel in London on 11 September 1969. What brought this about? Ed Posey the airline's Managing Director again:

'The decision to change the name from Autair International to Court Line Aviation came about because of the increasing involvement of Court Line Ltd. (the parent company) in the affairs of the airline and the increasing profile of the airline

...while a Bell 206B in Autair markings is seen in Greenland. (Autair Collection)

itself. When the BAC One-Eleven series 400s were introduced in the summer of 1968 they were seen as the airline's first major foray into the mainstream package holiday charter business - a toe in the water so to speak.

With that season's success - mainly in co-operation with Clarksons Holidays and the introduction of additional aircraft for summer 1969, the big decision was taken to switch to a new, all-500 Series fleet for the summer of 1970. We had talks with Geoffrey Knight, the Managing Director of BAC, and John Ferguson, Technical Director, who had from the outset been focused on the possibility of us upgrading to the increased capacity of the 500 Series should all go well - from 89 seats to 119. This was an all-important increase in load of some 34%, as Tom Gullick the MD of Clarksons, and Donald McQueen their Aviation Director were willing to take up the increased load in full, thereby increasing the overall viability of the operation.

Once the decision had been taken to go ahead with this major and exciting new step forward, it was inevitable that thoughts would turn to enlivening the whole image of the airline. At the same time it had been decided to discontinue scheduled services, so that any thoughts concerning the validity of retaining the name became irrelevant. Bill Armstrong, its orginator, had no objection to the name being dropped by the airline - on the contrary, for it allowed clear differentiation between the activities of his Autair group and those of Court Line.

There was much debate about the choice of the name itself but 'Court' seemed so appropriate as, not only did it reflect the ownership as well as the overall support being given to the airline by the Court Line Board, but in itself it was a most suitable word for the service the airline aimed to give - one of 'courting' our passengers with a 'royal' flight. Of course there were those who preferred the old name and livery, but I believe

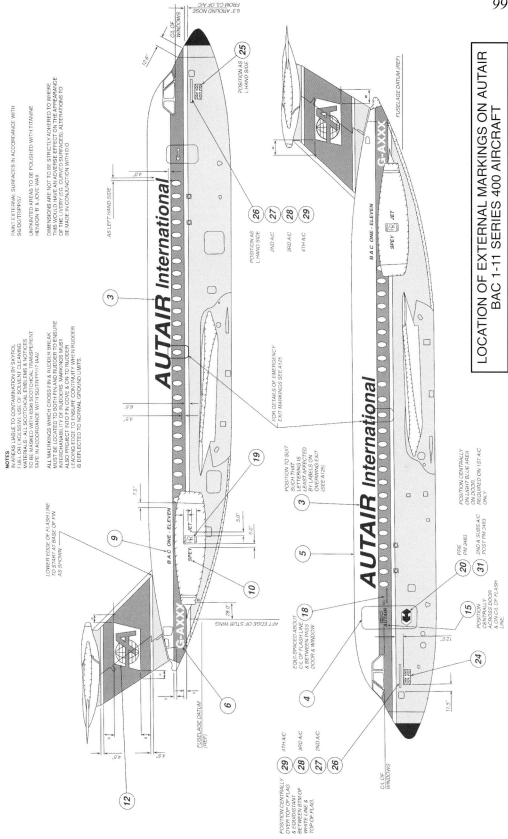

LOCATION OF EXTERNAL MARKINGS ON AUTAIR
BAC 1-11 SERIES 400 AIRCRAFT

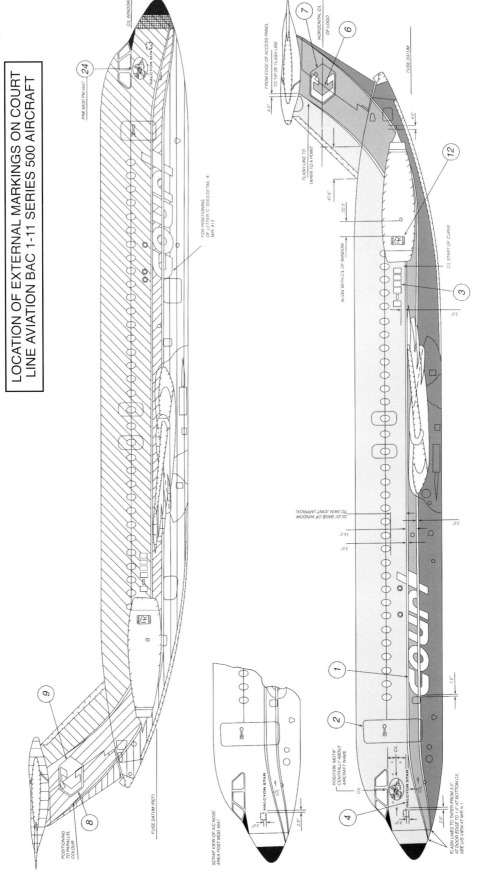

LOCATION OF EXTERNAL MARKINGS ON COURT
LINE AVIATION BAC 1-11 SERIES 500 AIRCRAFT

CL WINDOWS

HALCYON SUN

PRE-MOD PM 4647

FOR POSITIONING
OF LETTER 'C' SEE3 DETAIL 'A'
MIR. A13

HORIZONTAL CL
OF LOGO

FROM EDGE OF ACCESS PANEL
TO TIP OF FLASH LINE

FLASH LINE TO
TAPER TO A POINT

FUSE DATUM

ALIGN WITH CL OF WINDOW

CL START OF CURVE

22.25" BASE OF WINDOW
TO SKIN JOINT (APPROX)

POSITION MOTIF
CENTRALLY ABOUT
AIRCRAFT NAME

HALCYON STAR

FLASH LINES TO TAPER FROM 3.0"
AT DOOR EDGE TO 1.0" AT BOTTOM CL
SEE U/S VIEW AT MIR.N 1.

SCRAP VIEW OF A/C NOSE
AREA POST MOD 4647.

HALCYON STAR

FUSE DATUM (REF)

POSITIONING
TO PARALLEL
COLOUR

Until recently, the only photographs to be located (albiet of less that brilliant quality) of the Savoy Hotel launch of the new image for Court Line Aviation were these two previously printed black and white contact strips. These strips show three fashion models - especially hired for the occasion -posing with Ed Posey and John Young along with a number of large BAC One-Eleven aircraft models, outside the Savoy Hotel in London. The latter part of the filmstrip shows genuine Court Line staff with the same aircraft models inside the Savoy Hotel and posing outside.
[both Peter Murdoch via Joyce Bugge]

Subsequent research discovered one print from each of the filmstrips. The picture above shows the three professional fashion models outside the Savoy Hotel.

The picture of the left is from inside the hotel at the launch, with three 'genuine' Court Line hosties.

that a much larger proportion, and the Court Line Group employees and shareholders as a whole, welcomed the new image. We cultivated the holiday image in the colours, the uniforms, everything we did.

We were a young management, not too set in our ways, but at the same time backed by experience and knowledge; Bill Buxton's wisdom and dedication allowed us to grow and introduce the aircraft in the manner we did and in the air there were the likes of Maurice Rowan, Mike Ellis and Pete Dibley in positions of leadership with Nora Parkinson as our Chief Air Hostess. I was personally supported to an enormous extent by my Secretary Elizabeth Hutchinson, and by Glen Swire, who joined as my PA and became an extremely effective Administration Director.

We also developed a good working relationship with the other users of Luton Airport. I enjoyed a very happy understanding with John Sauvage, MD of Britannia and John Hodgson of Monarch. I must also say a word about Don Harvey, who as Town Clerk of Luton always supported the development of the airport. On his retirement we felt honoured that he accepted our invitation to become a non-executive director of Court Line. Don 's advice was always invaluable!

All our staff were happy to be a part of what we did and what we were to become - the most innovative, swinging 'sixties'airline'.

Chapter Five
Holidays with a 'C'

Autair International Airways' - and later Court Line Aviation's - fortunes were closely linked to those of Clarksons Holidays. The link was so close during the late 1960's and early 1970's that many people, even those inside the industry,

supposed that there must be some form of financial tie-up between the two organisations, but that was not the case - Autair maintained an 'arms-length' relationship with Clarksons, but the very nature of IT operational requirements meant that there had to be a very close day-to-day working relationship.

*Tom Gullick -
Managing Director of
Clarksons Holidays*

The massive increase in Autair International's Inclusive Tour passenger loads was mainly due to the introduction of a fleet of British Aircraft Corporation BAC One Eleven series 400 aircraft, with 70% of the aircraft's capacity being sold to Clarksons Holidays. Much of the remaining capacity went to the Court Line Group's own travel subsidiaries, Vacation Tours, Murison Small, Harold Ingham, Court Line Holidays and Court Travel.

Clarksons itself was a subsidiary of the Shipping and Industrial Holdings conglomerate; their Managing Director, Tom Gullick, had been making use of Autair's aircraft for his inclusive tours for a number of years and, with the arrival of the new aircraft, Autair was now operating almost all of Clarksons' holiday tours from Luton Airport - indeed, the Clarksons 'C' logo appeared on the side of the aircraft - and the same applied to the emergent Court Line, now the 'C' was writ large in shiny silver on the tail!

The competition between inclusive tour operators was becoming increasingly fierce. With almost everyone in the industry expanding, it is not surprising that with expansion came price warfare, particularly to Spain. It was under Gullick's aggressive management that Clarksons Holidays blazed a trail of low-price, short-term holidays to the sun which brought them an apparent bonanza of new customers. Tom Gullick's slogan was volume, and to win it he was prepared to undercut everyone

else's prices and overbid his competitors ruthlessly to tie up accommodation in which to package his new business. His competitors could not see how he could make a profit on the crazy prices that Clarksons were offering in both directions, but they either had to compete or leave the market to him! The apparent money-making key was the travel trade's new buzz-word phrase - 'vertical integration' - a concept designed to ensure that as many aspects as possible of the holidaymakers spending whilst they were in the company's care went to Clarksons Holidays or one or more of its own subsidiaries.

The rise of Clarksons had been meteoric. From 1965 through to 1973 the firm expanded from a small operation carrying 4000 customers a year into a giant providing packages for l.l million. That expansion took place mainly in Spain, where the Franco government was subsidizing the growth of its tourism industry through a system of credits to hotel developers to enable them to build the accommodation needed to cope with ever-increasing demand. When this system ended towards the end of the 1960s, Clarksons kept hotel building ticking over with its own form of financing, advancing so called 'bed deposits' to developers in return for reduced bed prices when the hotel began to receive its customers. The company also bought shares in a variety of holiday projects on the Costas - not just in hotels but in land, beach barbecues, English-style pubs and a local travel agency.

The man driving it all was Tom Gullick. He was born at Westgate-on-Sea in Kent in 1931, was evacuated to North Wales during the war, entered the Royal Naval College at Dartmouth as a 13-year-old cadet, and in 1948, aged 17, joined the Navy as a

A destination for many a Clarksons' sun, sea, sand and sex-seeker - the famous, or infamous - Lloret de Mar on Spain's Costa Brava. In the late 1960s and early 1970s new hotels were being opened up here - and in most of Spain's other Mediterranian resorts - almost weekly, often with the builders going out of the back door just as the first guests were arriving at the front!
[Author]

midshipman. After a spell in submarines he became assistant operations officer with the reserve fleet on the Clyde, where his shooting and management skills on the Scottish grouse moors so impressed his superiors that he was appointed flag officer to the Commander in Chief of the Home Fleet.

After 14 years in the service he left in 1958, using his naval contacts to get a job running a small travel agency called H. Clarkson (Air and Shipping Service), owned by the prosperous London City company Shipping and Industrial Holdings (SIH). It was a business call to the Petrofina oil company that set his mind racing about the possibility of day trips to the continent. The firm wanted to run an outing for its employees to the World's Fair in Brussels, where the symbolic construction of tubes and spheres known as the Atomium had become a huge attraction. That deal failed to materialize, but Gullick organized outings to the exhibition for other groups, charging clients £7 a head to travel from Charing Cross. Realizing that here was a market waiting to be tapped, he set up a group tours department at the agency.

Vertical Integration at it's best! Be they Bar-B-Qs Travel Agencies, Wine Tastings or Baby Bullfights, Clarksons Holidays endevoured to control the spending of their clients as much as possible in order to maximise their profits. [Author]

One of those trips to Brussels was arranged for the Walthamstow Chamber of Commerce. An official of the chamber suggested he should organize similar outings somewhere else. 'What about the tulips in Holland? he wondered. 'I'm sure my people would like to go.' But it proved to be the Women's Institutes of Britain who really wanted to go. So extensive was this network of clubs, so great the

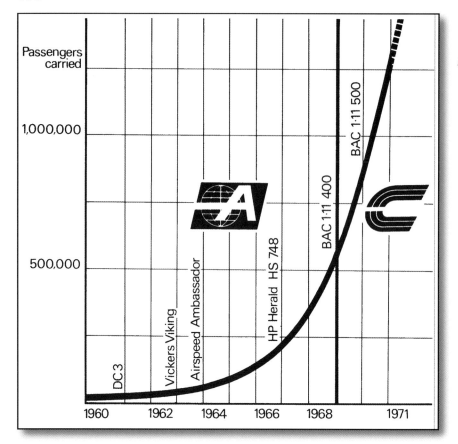

Passengers carried

1,000,000

500,000

DC 3

Vickers Viking

Airspeed Ambassador

HP Herald HS 748

BAC 1·11 400

BAC 1·11 500

1960   1962   1964   1966   1968   1971

A company-provided graphic that aptly demonstrates the incredible growth rate of Autair and later Court Line Aviation, much of which was brought about by the Clarksons charters.

demand to see the Dutch bulb fields, that in the second year of his operation there he chartered some fifty aircraft.

In 1959, Clarksons was hived off as a separate operation. For the next three years it concentrated solely on short breaks, including slightly longer ones lasting three, four and even six days. By now it was offering trips to the Rhine, Copenhagen and the vineyards of Burgundy. In Holland, Gullick displayed an early symptom of the business flair which was to take Clarksons briefly to the stars. The main attraction here during the spring was Keukenhof ('Kitchen garden' in Dutch), also known as the Garden of Europe and, situated near Lisse, the world's largest flower garden. The current garden was established in 1949 by the then-mayor of Lisse. The idea was to present a flower exhibit where growers from all over the Netherlands and Europe could show off their hybrids – and help the Dutch bulb and flower export industry.

Couriers were always trying to divert tour buses to particular souvenir shops, where they could earn commission on the side, rather than get them straight to the bulb fields. He recalls: *'By the time they had taken them round all the places selling Blue Delft pottery, cheese, clogs and whatever, the time they had in which to see the tulips at the Keukenhof was very limited. So we banned shopping diversions and erected what could best be described as a sort of giant aircraft hanger, where we sold all these things ourselves.*

We limited customers to twenty minutes' shopping time. There was a chap with a stopwatch to ensure they didn't linger any longer. It was doing this that we learned about charging businesses for a licence to sell souvenirs to people at our beach barbecues or on our donkey rides later, in Spain.'

Clarksons decided to expand into longer holidays, despite Gullick's doubts that many people would go for anything but the shortest of these tours, and that most would be previous short break customers. Nevertheless, the programme was a sell out.

Two views of Benidorm, about 40 years apart. Prior to the 1960s, Benidorm was a small village. Today it stands out for its hotel industry, beaches and skyscrapers, built as a result of its tourist-oriented economy that was largely fueled by Clarksons in the early 1970s. The village had a long history of fishing which created the myth that before tourism Benidorm was a charming fishing village when in fact it never was. Today Benidorm has three major beaches: Playa de Levante, Playa de Poniente and Playa de Mal Pas; all of them having a blue flag since 1987.

The first brochure offered packages of eight, eleven, twelve or fifteen days - with prices from 26 guineas: *'We realized we could do it more cheaply than anyone already in the market. I think one reason for our success was that we had established tremendous contacts with the Women's Institute groups that included the next generation of younger holidaymakers. We made very few sales through travel agents - virtually all holidays were sold direct following word of mouth recommendations.*

Our prices were probably around 20 to 30 per cent less than other people's, which was partly to do with negotiating better rates with suppliers such as hoteliers, partly down to the intelligent use of charter aircraft, and partly down to the fact that we were paying less commission than our competitors'.

Gullick declared that *'... in a few years time I'll be the biggest operator of them all'* - and within four years of launching into the mainstream summer package business, Clarksons had shot to

Tossa de Mar is a municipality in Catalonia, Spain, located on the Costa Brava, about 103 kilometres north of Barcelona and 100 kilometres south of the French border. It is accessible through Girona Airport, some distance north. Fishing has traditionally been a relatively minor contributor to the village's economy, although it has consistently provided an alternative source of income in times of economic crisis. This is the Platja Gran beach, in front of downtown with the medieval castle at the western end. Tossa was another resort whose expansion was fuelled by Clarksons. (author)

Captain M G Williams and a pair of Autair Hostesses with One-Eleven 'Halcyon Days'. The Clarkson 'C' was noticable on the forward door! [M G Williams]

number one. Gullick's boast was that, while he ran the company, the aircraft it chartered never flew with an average of less than 95 per cent of their seats filled. Never content to sit on its laurels, the firm built on its success by offering potential customers free calls to its reservations centre after 6 p.m.

In 1964 the fledgling Clarksons Holidays carried around 4,000 passengers - by 1967 it was up to 90,000, 1968 saw 175,000, 1969 250,000, 1970 400,000, 1971 750,000, 1972 900,000 and 1973 1,100,000 - an average yearly increase of almost 55%!

By the end of 1969, Clarksons - and Tom Gullick - were marketing themselves as the travel concern 'for the people'. At a speech to travel trade representatives meeting at the Savoy Hotel, London, Tom Gullick announced their plans for 1970, adding that:

> *'...we in Clarksons will never forget that we are handling people, and that these people are enjoying the rewards of hard work and saving. Once any holiday company becomes too preoccupied with size and forgets human responsibilities it may as well pack up'*

More than any other, the firm was responsible for the creation of Benidorm, which became Spain's most popular resort. Clarksons customers took up some six thousand of the total of ten thousand or so beds there in the late 1960s. It singled out hoteliers who had shown good management skills and lent them money over five years to build new properties to its own specifications. But even this system proved inadequate to keep up with its mushroom growth, so Clarksons formed its own development company in Spain and built eight giant hotels, each with 600-800 beds, in major resorts.

When HRH Queen Elizabeth II accompanied by Prince Phillip opened Terminal One at London Heathrow, every airline within the United Kingdom was asked to send representatives. With the white tops to their hats, the four sent by Autair were easily discernible, one of whom was Joyce Henderson, seen in the main picture of the extreme right, just by the lighting man holding up ciné lights and on the left in the photograph below. [both via Joyce Bugge]

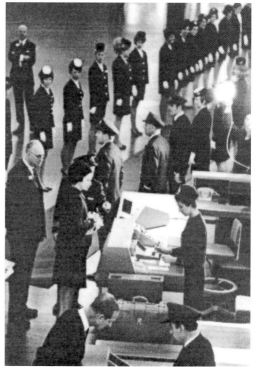

Those who worked for Clarksons were intoxicated by the constant ferment of new ideas. Gullick used Clarksons to pioneer a new business concept into the travel trade: 'vertical integration'. In businessspeak, this was '...when a company expands its business into areas that are at different points on the same production path, such as when a manufacturer owns its supplier and/or distributor. Vertical integration can help companies reduce costs and improve efficiency by decreasing transportation expenses and reducing turnaround time, among other advantages.' In reality, it meant owning and therefore controlling and making a profit - no matter how small a one - from as much as possible. Hence Clarksons involvement in Barbecues, Hotels, Coaches, Excursions, Land Development, Travel Agencies and English-style Pubs and a whole raft of other enterprises.

A vivid example of this was the Clarksons chicken farm. At that time many British holidaymakers were still not entirely happy with Spanish cooking, so Clarksons felt it necessary to provide them with a blander alternative, such as an omelette, on standard hotel dinner menus. It was not long before Gullick began to suspect that somebody was profiteering at his expense, for the egg dishes began to cost more than he knew they should. So a friend of his offered to set up a farm near Benidorm, so that several thousand eggs a day could be supplied at a controlled price. *'We knew that we could always pull down the farm and sell the land at a profit later.'*

Such control was the key. Gullick and his colleagues knew that they could make a lot of money in resorts if they could channel customers' activities, so they set up a department with a self-explanatory label of Resort Development Activities. It acquired nightclubs and barbecues - including one in Benidorm which handled over a thousand holidaymakers every evening. It purchased donkeys in central Spain and imported them to resorts in Majorca and along the Costas, making money from tourists who had their picture taken in the saddle. Squeezing every last penny of revenue from the operation became an art form.

During the 1960's the Spanish Government under Generalissimo Franco subsidised the development of its own tourist industry by a system of credits given to developers to build hotels for the ever-increasing number of holidaymakers that wanted their two weeks in the sun. During the latter part of that decade this practice ceased, as did new hotel development.

Clarksons Holidays therefore had to find a way of obtaining more rooms; they came up with the idea of financing development of hotels themselves in which their own clients would stay by advancing the 'bed deposits' to hotel developers in return for reduced bed prices when the hotels began to trade.

The funds for both bed deposits and other direct investments were fed through a Liechtenstein company, Sunotel S.A. which passed them on to its associated Spanish company Cristaltour S.A., which was owned jointly by Sunotel and a Spanish Bank, the Banco de Noroeste.

The method of funding hotel expansion via the bed deposit scheme forced Clarksons to enter long-term contracts with hoteliers whether or not they provided the clients with the standards required and as described in the brochures. Many hotels were double-booked or overbooked, and hotel building in the Spanish 'Costas', the Costa Brava, Costa Dorada, Costa Blanca, Costa del Sol *et al* was proceeding at a frantic pace, with hotels under construction featured in the brochures that were not ready when the holidaymakers arrived. It was by no means unknown for the builders to be sweeping construction rubbish out of the back door as the holidaymakers arrived at the front! This was the era of the 'artists impression' in the holiday brochures and an archetypal travel trade anecdote of the time reported that Tom Gullick was supposed to have been refused entry into Spain because his passport did not carry the bearer's photograph - there was just an artists impression!

At a fairly early stage a problem arose with the 'bed deposit' scheme. When the time came for the 'repayment' aspect to come into play, a number of hoteliers then claimed that such

Probably the public's main view of Clarksons Holidays - a Reps badge!

advances already received by them had in fact been in breech of the Bank of England's Exchange Control regulations and thus sought to avoid paying back! Although the point was never tested, it carried sufficient weight - allied to the fact that many Hoteliers were not in a financial position to do anything other than make deductions from operating charges - to lead Clarksons Holidays to enter into long-term contracts with Hoteliers regardless of the service provided.

Demand for single rooms outstripped the capacity available, so the firm offered lone customers twin bedded rooms with screens down the middle, even to shares of opposite sexes. Some of them didn't bother to have the partitions sent up from reception. Michael Hooper recalls the inception of the 'hot bed system' in which rooms were used twice in the same night by different clients. One group would leave at midnight and another, having arrived on a night flight, would take its place.

These poor standards provided by some hoteliers, coupled with having holiday clients arriving at unfinished hotels was a public relations disaster, as was the practice of 'switching'. If a particular 'package' in a brochure failed to attract an acceptable load-factor, it was likely to be 'switched' to other resorts, sometimes at the very last minute - and while some clients placidly accepted a change of holiday destination, others did not and complained - long and loud - to the Press.

Working out the rate...

Court Line Managing Director Ed Posey explains how the fares were arrived at, and recalls some of the behind-the-scenes discussions that used to go on to allow Clarksons to set the lowest fares possible:

'Our standard yardstick seat rate, from which all other fares were calculated, was the journey from Luton to Palma on Majorca. It was then up to the Flight Schedulers to work out the time differences and the rate for everywhere else, which was a proportional figure, so it was easy.

All I had to do was to make sure that we got the right price for the seat-rate to Palma. I remember long discussions with Donald McQueen, the Aviation Director of Clarksons, and Tom Gullick the M.D. about the seat-rate - we were arguing about pennies!

Our summer seat rate to Palma was £14.00 return - the winter rate was £8.50! That seat-rate allowed Tom Gullick to market a summer holiday for under £50! Obviously at those prices we were operating at very marginal profits on the seat and so we devised all sorts of incentives to encourage bar and duty-free sales - at that time the mark-up on cigarettes and alcohol was enormous and the on-board sales brought in many hundreds of thousands of pounds during a year. We relied on those sales to increase our overall profit!'

Problems with business...

Clarksons soon found itself in a strange position - they had almost been too successful in attracting business. The rapid growth in the number of clients requiring holidays overtook - almost overwhelmed - the company's ability to administer the operational requirement.

This corporate 'map' of Clarksons set-up in 1973 shows just how the 'vertical integration' concept was established in conjunction with the Spanish bank through a Liechtenstein concern. A similar principal was applied to Italy and would have also been applied to the then opening market of Greece and the Greek islands.

Until 1968 a manual booking, reservation and ticketing system was employed which, although long-winded and slow, was at least accurate. 1969 saw the introduction of the company's then revolutionary computerised booking, reservation and accountancy system, but this was just not flexible enough to cope with even routine changes in holiday bookings, which resulted in amongst other things, incorrect information being presented as to the state of the company, and multiple invoicing to the clients.

For example, if a client changed from a room with a shower to a

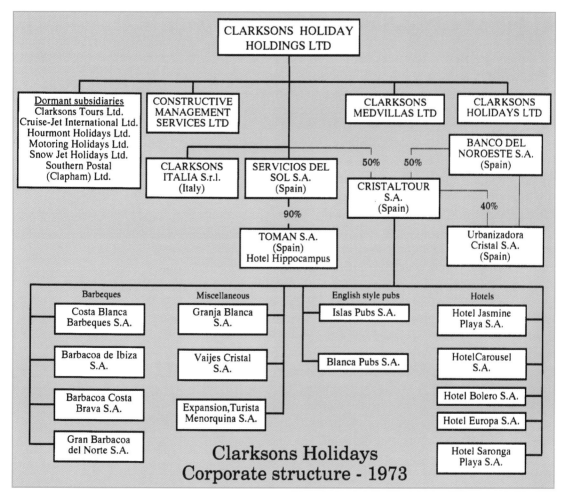

Clarksons Holidays
Corporate structure - 1973

room with a bath, a new invoice had to be raised. This was acceptable if the original invoice was cancelled, but often it was not. Almost certainly the client had already received the original invoice and would now receive a further invoice for the change. If the client paid on the original invoice, or even quoted the original invoice number, then the cash could not be matched against the second (and 'live') invoice, for there was no unique number for each holiday that could be carried across the paperwork. The payment would either cancel the balance on the original invoice if it had not been cancelled or, if it had, be posted to the suspense account - the revised invoice would still be carried on the computer as a debtor. If Clarkson's then queried this with a client who said that they had already paid, the only way that Clarkson's could verify this was to ask the client if they received their cheque back from the bank to tell them - Clarksons - the original invoice number that Clarkson's staff had written on the back. This, of course is from the era when banks returned cashed cheques to their account holders - instead of the current practice where the bank retains them.

Other problems were brought on by the deluge of attracted business. Because of this confusion created by multiple invoicing, flight clerks at the Check-in desks were supposed to check that each client had paid in full. They were so busy that this was often not done until after the flight had departed, thus making it possible to obtain tickets without full payment being made!

Other computerised accountancy problems were created by last-minute fuel or currency surcharges - the only way a client could be billed was by creating another un-cross-referenced invoice with all the inherent problems explained above! All of this led to real administrative difficulties on the accounting side - but there were other problems also.

By 1971, Clarksons Holidays were experiencing another major problem. The capital structure in Spain centred around the fact that the Banco del Noroeste, in addition to subscribing its share of capital to Cristaltour and its subsidiaries, had also advanced substantial amounts to Clarksons Holidays to allow them to finance their own investment which required repayment within seven years. It soon became obvious that this was not possible, so a new agreement was drawn up whereby the hotel-owning Cristaltour leased its hotels to Servicios del Sol. S.A. (its own subsidiary) at rentals sufficient to repay

In 1971 the well-known TV presenter and writer Ernest John 'Johnny' Morris OBE (*b*.20 June 1916 – *d*. 6 May 1999) was commissioned by Clarksons Holidays to record what was known as a 'flexi-disk' of five minutes length. Called 'Welcome to Sunshine '71', the record was given away inside certain brochures and Morris effusively sang the virtues and pleasures of Clarksons holidays in Spain, Tunisia, Italy and Greece, along with the delights of cruising. This was in conjunction with a seven-minute advertising slot - more like a mini-documentary by Clarksons on UK TV.

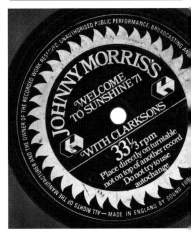

the bank, but which were so high that the subsidiary could not make any profit. All of this meant that Clarksons bore all the operating losses, and the bank, whilst retaining its 50% interest in Cristaltour could recoup its capital with associated interest.

...and passengers.

Not all the problems originated from the company, and not all had a negative outcome. Passengers, in the main, certainly appreciated the value-for-money that most of the Clarksons Holidays offered - but holidaymakers could, and did, come up with the strangest of problems.

Some were more serious than others, as John Hamlin explains:

'I have good reason to remember Clarksons Holidays and the way in which their staff looked after us when we most needed their help. In late May 1972 my wife Sheila and I and two young daughters set off for a Clarksons holiday at the relatively quiet resort of Salou on the Costa Brava. Our flight was in a BAC One-Eleven of Court Line from Luton to the small airfield at Reus, a few miles inland from Salou, but due to the unwillingness of French air traffic controllers to handle more than the minimum number of aircraft at a time, our flight was delayed and was eventually diverted to Barcelona, as Reus had no night-flying facilities.

We spent a very enjoyable two weeks at Salou, but on the morning of the Saturday when we were due to fly back to Luton our elder daughter, then eleven years of age, complained of stomach pains. During the day the pain became more severe, and by the time all the passengers were assembled in the hotel foyer to await the coach to the airport were so alarming that we called the resident doctor. He at once pronounced acute appendicitis and asked what we wanted to do - risk taking her on the flight in the knowledge that she might not survive, or hurry her to hospital in Spain. In our minds there was no contest, and an ambulance was called. Within 45 minutes she and I had arrived at a 'Clinica' in Tarragona, leaving her mother and our younger daughter at the hotel. There the Clarkson representative, Francisco, negotiated a bedroom for them which they could use for as long as necessary, to be paid for by Clarksons pending my making a claim on our holiday insurance. I, meanwhile, stayed at the Clinica with the sick daughter, who had an immediate operation to remove the offending part of her person. Within fifteen hours she was on her feet, but remained in the Clinica for a week, with me as company and looked after by nuns. They spoke Catalan, a cross between French and Spanish, and as I spoke some French, I was able to converse with them a little.

Each day, Francisco made the journey from Salou on his motor-scooter to see how we were, and also visited my wife and younger daughter at the hotel during their enforced extra week's 'holiday'. Nothing was too much trouble for him.

A week later than envisaged, we came together as a family, the invalid now walking although still in some discomfort for an uneventful journey back to Luton'.

Stretched to breaking point...

Throughout the early 1970s there were numerous rumours about Clarksons state of health. Their parent company, Shipping and Industrial Holdings (SIH), were anxious to divest themselves of Clarksons, whose rapid growth and small profitability were over-extending SIH's commitment. SIH was ran by Sandy Glenn (later Sir Alexander and Chairman of the British Tourist Authority) and Peter Parker (later Sir Peter, and head of British Rail).

In mid-1970 an offer of £10 million was made for Clarksons Holidays by W. R Grace, an American Corporation. SIH refused the offer, because their bank, Hambros, valued the concern at £14 million.

By 1971 Clarksons made an operating loss of £2.7 million, which prompted a SIH review. In 1972 SIH and American Express (Amex) entered into negotiations with a view to Amex taking a stake in Clarksons - by the autumn Clarksons forecast losses of £4 million and Amex withdrew from talks.

By October that year Court Line and the Thompson Organisation (owners of numerous travel companies and Britannia Airways) began talks to see if they could take over SIH's holiday interests, with Court's underlying intention of protecting the existing long-term flying contracts with Clarksons.

Terra Firma

The TriStar stands out on the strip,
with idle engines, so, no trip.
The questions asked 'Well, who's to blame ?
why theres now't on clock but makers name?'

There goes that bloody phone again,
another delayed flight to Spain.
Maybe its France or sunny Rome;
why can't the bastards stay at home?

They all arrive outside the door,
with cases, bags and kids galore.
With one accord, they all charge through;
they should be housed in Whipsnade Zoo!

There's fat and thin, there's short and tall,
it's like a flaming Bingo Hall
The Duty Manager slowly nods
He'd like to strangle all the sods.

They've taken over all the bars,
demanding booze and fat cigars!
Complaining of the flight they've missed
and not so slowly getting pissed.

The food stocks vanish in thin air,
as every gannet takes a share.
The Food and Beverage gaze in awe;
just dreading they may ask for more.

The hotel staff all breathe a sigh,
the aircraft now is fit to fly!
The brief night-stop is now replete
they're up at thirty thousand feet.

The havoc that we now survey,
must surely clear come light of day.
A goddamn awful bloody mess;
next year try Brighton - or Skegness!

'Working for an airline - or holiday company - would be great if it wasn't for the Pax.'

How often that call was made when assorted circumstances ganged up against flights getting away. Ground Services and Tour Company reps were in the front line at the airport and took all the flak; occasionally a release had to be found and, as usual, it took the form of black humour, as the above poem penned by 'Pip' once found in Court Ground Services shows!

Numerous schemes were talked around; the first was for Court Line to take over the whole of SIH and then, together with Thompsons and possibly others, restructure the combined companies. Thompsons holiday interests, amongst those the famous 'Skytours' brand, would be combined with Clarksons and Thompson's Britannia Airways would combine with Court Line Aviation to form a new, jointly owned company.

Nothing came of this, or a number of other schemes but rumours were rife.

All of this triggered off an unprecedented level of media attention, which in turn brought forth high levels of client dissatisfaction - real or imagined - and Clarksons was constantly in the headlines for all the wrong reasons.

At the time there was a live, weekly television programme on the BBC called *Braden's Week* hosted by Canadian Bernard Braden and his wife Barbara Kelly.

Bernard Braden, Tom Gullick's potential tormentor and nemesis on the TV Show Braden's Week.

Tom Gullick - who politely, but firmly refused to undergo trial by TV.

This was a successor to a popular consumer affairs television programme called *On the Braden Beat* made for ITV by Associated Television, which ran from 1962 to 1967.

For weeks, every time the programme was broadcast Bernard Braden would point towards an empty chair awaiting the arrival of Tom Gullick to answer the huge volume of customer complaints the programme had received. He never appeared.

Clarksons financial position was deteriorating and creditors were becoming worried about its viability, but Sandy Glenn and Peter Parker had complete faith in Tom

Gullick and his masterplan for virtually cornering the inclusive tour market and then raising prices to provide the first ever profit for his company. The banks started to put pressure on SIH to guarantee all Clarksons Holidays liabilities and obligations.

Then Tom Gullick resigned.

In the autumn of 1972 the Civil Aviation Authority issued draft proposals whereby the granting of operating licences to tour operators would become conditional on their satisfactory financial status - SIH's mere guarantee towards Clarksons Holidays indebtedness would not be enough without their balance sheet being strengthened. Thus, in February 1973 SIH converted part of its inter-company loan account with Clarksons into equity capital by subscribing £5 million for 100 Clarksons Holiday shares.

By now Court Line Aviation was operating a fleet of eleven BAC One-Eleven 500s, nine on twelve year leases which, with their associated spares was costing £17 million. A further two One-Elevens were owned by Court Line Aviation - the purchase of which cost £3,134,000 - but they were in turn subject of a £3.15 million mortgage.

Around the same time Court Line and Horizon entered negotiations with SIH with a view of pooling their holiday interests. These talks reached the stage of drawing up Heads of Agreement and getting clearance from the Department of Trade and Industry, but at the last moment Horizon pulled out, fearing loss of independence.

SIH looked long and hard at their Clarkson Holidays operation, decided it was not worth continuing with, and threatened to pull the plug. With a five-year flying contract with Clarksons that involved almost all of Court Line's capacity, something had to be done to secure the business - Court Line bought Clarksons.

Chapter Six

A New Name, A New Image

Different versions of the Court corporate 'C' used to denote different aspects of the Groups business.

The 'Halcyon Bird' that was originally intended to appear on the nose of all the aircraft in the fleet - next to the name.

The cover of the launch document for the new image.
[all Peter Murdoch]

As part of a total rationalisation of corporate image, almost every company within the Court Line Group would be renamed 'Court Line' followed by a sub-name; Autair International Airways would become Court Line Aviation, but the public just called it Court Line - within the Group, it was known simply as 'Aviation'. It was also time to introduce a new corporate logo, a themed name scheme, with almost every major item of equipment or facility taking a name that included the word *'Halcyon',* that also made use of a further logo - in the airline's case, just on the nose of the aircraft - from where the name originated.

What's in a name...

'Halcyon' was the ancient Greek name for the European Kingfisher, around which grew many legends, one of which was the belief that the seven days preceeding the shortest days of the year were used by these birds to build their nests, which, it was thought, floated on the water, and the seven days that followed were devoted to hatching their eggs. During this period, known as the 'Halcyon Days' the ancients believed the sea was always calm. Hence 'Halcyon days' to describe any calm and peaceful days. To a company with strong maritime connections, 'Calm and Peaceful' days (and seas) was a

Introducing a new airline

good concept theme to use for all their activities, apart from it being a good marketing ploy to describe the holiday image !

...and why change it?

John Young explained the thinking behind what amounted to a total public re-launch of the company in the first edition of 'Halcyon', the Court Line Group Review, published in the Autumn of 1969 and released to all those involved in the Group...

'On 11th September Court Line, which for almost a century has been exclusively the name of a shipping line, suddenly became an airline as well, thereby replacing the name Autair.

What has been the reasoning behind this? And why all this talk of a new 'image'? Were not the old name and the old image

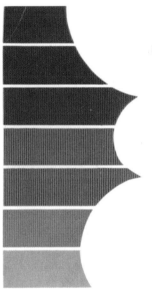

court line

For holidays, and only for holidays

Over the past seven years, the package holiday business has increased by an average of 37 per cent per year. And we're only seeing the start. The potential is enormous.
So we have formed what we believe to be the world's first specialist holiday travel airline. It combines the experience of Autair International with the resources of Autair's parent company, Court Line.
We won't be running any scheduled services. Or any special business flights.

Our aircraft are just for holid makers.
We want to make our passen feel that the flight is an enjo part of their holiday, instead just a boring journey.
So we've done a number of unusual things.

good enough? To ask this question is to ask another; one that, on the face of it, seems too obvious to need answering: what is an airline for? This is, however, a question which we have been asking ourselves, in effect, for the past two or three years, and the answer we arrived at explains quite a lot of what has been happening in the Group this year.

The critical period was 1966-67, when it became apparent that our scheduled air services, from which much was hoped, had little chance of becoming profitable under the existing system, while the charter side showed every sign of growing.

That winter, therefore, we decided to order BAC One-Elevens, to be delivered in the spring of '68; and we did this, very largely, on the strength of our close and thriving

The Aircraft

We're an all-jet airline. And we've painted our jets so that they look different from anything else in the sky.
Our fleet consists of eight BAC One-eleven jets. Seven are the very latest 119-seat 500 series. One is an 89 seat 400 series. They're painted in colours that we borrowed from sunsets and holiday beaches. The sort of thing a person goes away for. Our idea is to put the passenger in a holiday mood literally from the minute he checks in.

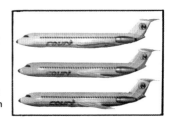

The Cabins

Our aircraft are different on the outside. And different on the inside. Seats, walls and carpets all match the exterior colours. Remember how aircraft used to look inside? Grey. Ours don't and it makes a very pleasant change. (Specially when you're going on holiday).

Us and You

We believe this new airline will be a great success.
It's different. It's been designed for a booming market. And it's backed by years of technical and operational experience gained by Autair International. We want to make it as much fun for our customers as possible. But we're treating it as a very serious business.
Holidays are few and far between. We want to help people make the most of them. And we want them to come back to us, year after year.

We think they will, once they how well we look after them. the more successful we are, th more successful you'll be.

Luton Airport, Be

*a membe
of the
court grou*

association with Clarksons. Put briefly, the demand for jet aircraft for holiday travel was there, if we chose to meet it, while the demand for our scheduled services was not. This is the crux of the matter and the point of the question. The Corporations and the independent scheduled services provide a transport service that is exactly comparable to that provided by trains and buses. All of them leave according to timetable, whether they have any passengers or not. Charter aircraft, on the other hand, are the equivalent of the hire coach which takes a party to a football match or the seaside and which, to be economic, must be full or nearly so.

With the tremendous increase in foreign travel, particularly by means of the package holiday, the 'flying coach' has come into its own; so much so that, as one of our pilots remarked, it is almost like flying a scheduled service. But it is a function which can be exercised more efficiently, more easily, and more cheaply, by an independent airline geared to it than by one whose first concern is to provide a basic transport service.

It was the realisation that this had happened and was going to go on happening on an ever-increasing scale that has led us into tailoring our air fleet, and giving them a livery to match.

Explaining what the holiday concept was about and revealing the logos for the first time. [all Peter Murdoch]

So quick was the colour scheme change over between Autair and Court, that very few pictures were taken showing both together. Series 500 G-AXMF in pink is seen on a snowy Luton apron in front of G-AWBL.

One Eleven G-AXMH
in flight on a publicity
shoot.

The interior of
G-AXMH 'Halcyon
Sun'. The yellow cabin
furnishing matched the
exterior, while the
straw boater-wearing
cabin staff wore
uniforms that were also
cordinated to the
colour schemes. [both
Court Collection]

Holidays, we feel should begin the moment our passengers board their aircraft.

There are certain obvious risks. An airline can look carefree, but it must not suggest frivolity or irresponsibility.' it is a well-known British failing to confuse solemnity with efficiency. All the same, it seemed reasonable to us that aircraft primarily engaged in taking people on holiday should make some attempt to share the holiday spirit, with cheerful colour schemes and uniforms that at least made some acknowledgment to what people actually wear. This is one facet of our new look, but it is only part of an operation designed to give a new look to the Group as a whole. So, while we are, on the one hand, projecting our image' to use the jargon as vigorous and imaginative exponents of the leisure business, we are taking the opportunity of giving meaning and a sense of unity to the Group as a whole.

Thus, variations of the new graphics designed by Peter Murdoch for the airline will be used in connection with all the other companies. This magazine is another aspect of the same purpose. But to return for a moment to the new aircraft livery.

Those who have actually seen one of the new 500 Series One-Elevens in its new colours have been both delighted and impressed. This is what we are aiming for. They are superb aircraft, fast and comfortable; and the organisation behind them is designed to keep them so. The aircraft stores at Luton hold well over £1 million worth of spares; and this, not least, enabled us to get more out of our aircraft last year, more hours in the air, fewer on the ground, than any other BAC One-Eleven operator in the world. It ties in with the engineering side, which is extremely efficient: so much so that we are able to offer its services to other airlines if they need it. And behind the aircraft and their ground and air crews is a sales, operational and project organisation which ensures that, as far as possible, the aircraft are fully employed throughout the twelve months. In this context, a comparison of the figures is

Three Court girls in front of one of the One Elevens parked near the McAlpine Hangar at Luton. [Peter Murdoch Collection]

of interest. In 1966 we carried, all told, 81,000 passengers; in 1967, 97,000, in 1968 with the introduction of the One-Elevens 273,000 This year we shall carry over 500,000; and next year possibly as many as a million.

These developments put Court Line firmly in the leisure business. But not only are more people tending to go abroad on package tours; they are tending to go farther afield. Greece and Cyprus, East Africa, the Aegean Islands and the Canaries are all coming within reach of the mass market; and we believe it will not be long before the same thing is happening in the West Indies. Who knows but that within five years the schnorkelers of Benidorm may not be exploring the Great Barrier Reef, the sightseers exchanging Granada and Knossos for Ankhor Wat or the Mayan ruins in Central America? This pattern of ever farther-flung holidays must affect our airline operations; which is why we are considering augmenting our One-Elevens in the near future by longer-range aircraft such as the 'stretched' DC-8 or the Boeing 707. These will enable us, if things develop as we anticipate, to fly large numbers of people direct to St. Lucia in the West Indies, and so will tie in with another project which we are extremely excited about, the Halcyon Beach Club; and with our own tour business.

To sum it up, the inclusive tour, flown to and from its destination by an independent airline, its low price made possible only by maximum utilisation of

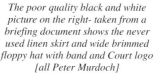

What was - and what was not! In preparation for the launch, models were hired in to display the Air Hostess uniforms. The three colour shots on the left who more or less the final version that the girls wore, with the exception that the staw boater in the pictures were taller in the crown than the ones eventually selected.

The poor quality black and white picture on the right- taken from a briefing document shows the never used linen skirt and wide brimmed floppy hat with band and Court logo [all Peter Murdoch]

the aircraft and hotels, is possibly the fastest growing business in the world today; and it is one in which we have a growing stake. Hence the change of name from Autair to Court Line; hence the new livery - sea colours, sky colours - of our aircraft; hence the new aircraft. And hence the new image.'

The first aircraft to arrive in the new colours and markings was G-AXMF, named *'Halcyon Breeze'* and painted in the new pink colour scheme. - it became an instant talking point and polarised most people's opinions. You either loved it or hated it - but you could not ignore it! 'Pink...,' as the interior decorators say '...is a 'difficult' colour'; and a large pink aeroplane - just like a large pink elephant - took some getting used to. It must be said that there were reservations and much head-shaking.

Then the turquoise-blue version arrived and the reservations began to dissolve; it wasn't so bad after all. With the arrival of the third, in the orange scheme, suddenly things began to drop into place. With all three examples parked on the apron at Luton on a dull dreary day, the intention behind Peter Murdoch's design was obvious - here was gaiety and the lure of foreign parts translated into colour!

'Pink is a difficult colour'! The inside of one of the Court One Elevens, where the ciolour cast a rosy glow over eveything! (Ed Posey/Autair-Court Collection)

But the aircraft were only a part of the overall operation. With the new colours went a matching style of graphics, lay-out and design that involved everything from aircraft towing tractors to letterheads, from office signs to brochures. 'Colour Co-ordination' was the name of the game, and it even extended to issuing boarding cards in the same colours as the aircraft the passenger was about to fly in!

As part of the new corporate image, the cabin staff were similarly equipped with new uniforms designed by Julia Murdoch to match the holiday atmosphere of the new airline.

Part of the uniform - the straw boater, possibly the most inappropriate item of Air Hostess head-wear ever designed for use on a windy, hilltop airfield such as Luton, - was intended to demonstrate that the airline was proud of its links with the town, famed for it's hat-making industry.

Thus the first day of the new decade saw the airline with a new

name and seven new BAC One-Eleven Series 500 aircraft either delivered or being delivered to undertake IT services to numerous Mediterranean resorts from Birmingham, Luton and Bristol.

Ed Posey provides further details':

'...we were, I think you could say, a design aware group, but it was an aspect at that time that had been neglected. We had expanded so fast that it was impossible to do everything at once. The first thing is to make sure you have got a profitable business and that it is moving in the right direction and then it is a sophistication to ensure the image is absolutely right. Murdoch's original brief was a design change for the airline, but it was very quickly appreciated that we could not leave it there. Changing the design or image of the airline had impinged on the parent company and in no time at all his brief was expanded to the group as a whole.'

The distinctive letter C which Murdoch designed for the airline was extended into a complete alphabet which was now in use throughout the Court Line group. As Peter Murdoch said at the time:

'The group has a corporate identity now, not only with the alphabet, but by the use of colour, which I feel very strongly about. Colour can be carried throughout all the companies in

Inside a 'turquoise' - The colour was not as bad as one first imagined! The doors for the seat-back catering are very noticable, as is the continuous line of the overhead hat-racks. This is clearly before the days of the overhead bins! (Ed Posey/Autair-Court Collection)

One Eleven G-AWBL, the only 400 Series aircraft retained from Autair to appear in Court colours. This was known as the 'turquoise' scheme, but many called it 'green'. (Ed Posey/Autair-Court Collection)

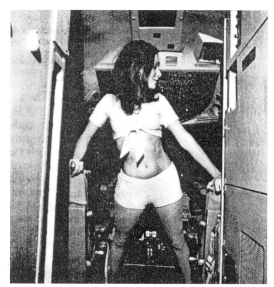

Such was the impact of the new image, Court's One-Elevens were often put to uses very different to which they were designed.

These two pictures - taken from a house newspaper and all that survives from the photo-session - show the flightdeck and wing of 'XMH used as a backdrop and prop for a fashion shoot for the Dorothy Perkins chain of fashion shops.

the group, without necessarily trying to make them all the same, which they are not. What we have designed is a flexible graphic system which can cover all the companies. '

Time Charters...

With the disposal of all the scheduled service aspects of the airline's operation and re-launch with a totally new image, Court Line was now free to turn its entire attention to the charter market. One of the skills that John Young and his shipping company experience brought to the aviation sphere was the long-established concept of 'time charters', whereby an aircraft - or number of aircraft - was allocated for a given period of time to a tour operator, thus providing the certainty of a fixed income over a given period.

This type of contract, so successful in the oil tanker charter market, was recognised by Courts as being a prime requirement for the airline's successful development in the non-scheduled air transport industry. Ed Posey:

'Courts maintained an 'arms-length' relationship with Clarksons as with other clients, but the very nature of Inclusive Tour operations makes indispensable a close day-to-day working relationship. Although a satisfactory time charter agreement is one which runs for a period long enough, and with a substantial enough client, to bring a degree of security to the airline, armed with this agreement, we can go to a manufacturer and obtain finance on advantageous terms for the aircraft needed to fulfil the contract'

It had been long-thought by many in the industry that Autair's, and therefore Court's, close links with Clarksons over the years had led to Clarksons involvement with the financing of the new One-Eleven fleet.

This was not the case for, as Ed Posey told '*Flight*' magazine in March 1970, '*...although the time charter contract with Clarksons was instrumental in financing the jet fleet, it was not used as collateral'.*

Right: Winter Warmth! Hostesses Christine, Cathy and Jacqui in Court Line's winter uniform of capes, hats and gloves 'on the ground' at Munich in January 1971. [via Jaqui Maschira]

Below: Colours for the sky - torquoise, pink and yellow One Elevens on the ground at Luton. [Kurt Lang]

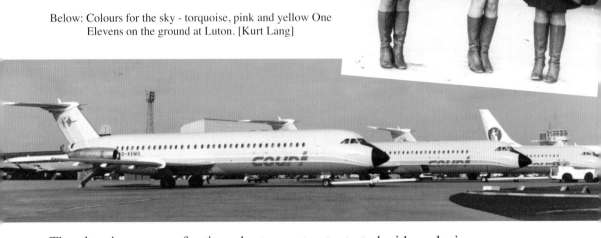

The planning process for time charter contracts started with analysis by the tour operator of its resorts and potential market, together with the type of holiday offered - long or short, with travel by day or by night. The results were written up in terms of aircraft capacity and dispatched to Court, whose sales planning department further analysed the information to arrive at aircraft timings, displaying the data on wall-mounted boards that charted the entire aircraft fleet's movements anything up to a year ahead. Knowing where the aircraft were going to be required at any given time, allowed the company to schedule routine maintenance (each aircraft being allocated 12 hours hangar time a week), training and other essential, but non-revenue earning duties. This type of detailed planning, operating in very close co-operation with Bill Buxton and all the engineering team, allowed Court Line Aviation to claim a world record for One-Eleven operations with 402 hours 36 minutes being flown by one machine in June - an average of over thirteen hours airborne a day!

The five year contract, running from 1969 to 1974 saw 80% of the total capacity sold to Clarksons, falling slightly as the airline grew. '*Flight*' posed the question that was this not dangerously close to putting all one's eggs into one basket? *'Not at all'* replied Ed Posey.

'Charter rates are safeguarded by contract for several years at a time with provisions for revision to account for changes in cost levels'

Joanna Petit, Liz Coventry and another girl in front of a One Eleven, each in different coloured uniforms to complement the aircraft livery, even wearing straw boaters with hat-bands that matched!

...Cabin Staff...

For 1970 Court Line had 45 crews for the One-Eleven fleet - 19 more than the previous year. The all-female cabin staff - it was safe, indeed expected in those pre-politically correct days, to call them Air Hostessses - were maintained at a level of five crews per aircraft, with a 20% over-capacity to allow for sickness, holidays and other reasons of absence.

Sue Bizley had left Autair to fly for British Eagle, but returned when that airline collapsed. Upon her return to the company she was directly involved in the recruitment of additional cabin staff...

'Although not much time had passed, the changes within the company were both considerable and noticeable.

Shortly after this Autair became Court Line and I became the Chief Hostess on the departure of Nora Prudence.

With the increase in fleet, we had to recruit more staff and I decided early on that I would like to hold open interviews in London. Advertisements were duly placed in the leading newspapers and rooms were booked in a London hotel for two days of interviewing. This procedure is not for the faint-hearted or for anyone with a poor memory for faces. Fortunately we had asked all those attending to provide a passport photograph which proved invaluable in remembering just who was who. We were inundated with applicants - they spread themselves all over the hotel, sitting on the floors, stairs, everywhere there was spare space to complete the application forms, but by the time we had short listed and held final interviews back in Luton, it proved to be worthwhile. One of the advertised requirements for the job was the ability to swim. No mention was made that this was required in the event of a ditching, naturally. However this was drawn to the attention of Terry Wogan who at that time was doing his radio Breakfast Show. He made the most of this for some days and we got some very useful additional advertising for our interviews.

According to my notes, the training courses I arranged, each with a maximum of 18 trainees per course, lasted four weeks in total; two weeks in the classroom, one week devoted to Emergency Procedures and the final week on uniform issue, any outstanding vaccinations and at least two supernumerary flights.

We applied strict dress and behaviour codes for all of the cabin staff and this was stressed during the training courses.

Notes for these make interesting reading now...

'...Hair must be neat and worn off the collar; elaborate styles are discouraged. Wigs may be worn, but each wig must have the approval of the Chief Air Hostess or her Deputy.'

'...Tights must never be worn laddered. A spare pair of tights must be carried at all times when on duty. One free pair of tights is issued every 2 months or 15p per month in cash'

'...Gloves and hats are to be worn from 1 November - 1 April.

Boaters are normally worn from April to October'.

'...Jackets and capes should always be worn with buttons fastened'.

There are some lovely general notes about deportment and

Passengers boarding 'MH for another holiday to the sun. The placement of the Halcyon Bird is particularly noticable.

appearance contained in the training papers:

'...Round shoulders are unfortunately accentuated by our present uniform, so please make an effort to pull your shoulders back'.

'...When counting the bar, leaning over to galley and cupboards etc., please do not just bend over from the middle, but bend from the knees, this is much less tiring and much less revealing!'

'...Never walk down the cabin chewing or lean against parts of the aircraft furniture it looks very sloppy'.

No jewelry (this included earrings and sleeper earrings) was allowed to be worn with the uniform, although one small formal ring and/ or wedding ring and a watch was permitted.

The issue of uniform to each hostess was: four winter and two summer blouses, two pinafore dresses (one colour only), two jackets, one cape, one hat- summer (boater), one hat - winter (only for permanent staff), two pairs of shoes, one pair of boots (only for permanent staff), one coverall, one handbag and one pair of gloves (winter only).

Replacement items due to negligence by the owner had to be charged to the individual. The individual had to supply themselves: One pair of black (originally white, but found to be impracticable) flat cabin shoes and one overnight bag.

The overnight case was required to contain:
1 clean and pressed blouse
1 pair of tights
Clean underwear
First aid box
Toilet equipment
Change of clothes (if necessary)
1 pair of flat black plain cabin shoes
1 coverall
1 exchange card
1 ready reckoner

Plonky bag which should hold the following:
1 whistle (Company issue)
Can opener
1 pair of scissors
1 torch
1 sewing kit
1 corkscrew
1 spoon
I knife
1 pair of wire cutters
The latter - seemingly strange to anyone not 'in the know' -

were required to assist in the opening of bottles of 'champagne'. Clarksons Holidays, during my time with Court Line, gave a complimentary glass of 'champagne' to every passenger as part of the on-board presentation. Large numbers of these bottles were often very difficult to open in a small galley area and even using the cutters to remove the wire strands restraining the corks, usually everybody - passengers included - finished up covered in sticky sparkling white wine!

In November 1970 it was proposed that hostesses with one year's service should earn £780 per annum, 2 year's service £840, thereafter going up by £60 yearly increments. I notice that during this time hostesses received 2.5% bar commission on the total sales of the particular flight, paid 2 months in arrears.

Interestingly, I notice that the duty free prices around this time were 1/2 bottle of brandy £1, 1/2 whisky 70p, 1/2 gin 60p. Cigarettes were £1.50 for a carton of 200.

Such was the need for seasonal cabin staff that for the 1971 season I was allowed to engage freelance cabin staff mostly previous members of staff living locally who were unable to work full time.'

The background paperwork and range of items that the cabin staff had to be aware of was enormous. Surprisingly Patricia Knights kept some of the memos sent out by Sue Bizley that fell into her post box,

A girl and her aeroplane! The pose - hanging on to the hat for grim death - became one that was terribly familiar around Luton! This picture also shows to very good effect the 'chrome' Scotchcal 'sticker' used for the Court name.

Hang on to your hats!

Settling the discussion as to what the girls were called. The company dress code booklet, the introduction of which states: 'this booklet is intended for your personal use and all regulations therein must be adhered to at all times whilst on duty, including travelling to and from the airport and especially at outstations'.

twenty-five years on some make strange reading...

'10 August 1970 - Trays & Non-Slip mats. Five large serving trays will now be standard on all flights, plus non-slip mats. Unfortunately these will bear the name 'Monarch' until our own supplies arrive. When using non slip mats please ensure that they are placed face-down - with the plain side upwards!'

'19 August 1970 - Watches. It has been agreed that if a passenger states he bought a watch on his outbound flight and has since found it defective, the watch must be returned with the guarantee to Limit, and not changed by the Hostess on the return flight as this causes difficulties in Bonded Stores when defective watches are returned'.

'26 August 1970 - Aircraft Can Openers. As promised, arrangements are being made for BL to have a can-opener in the galley. Unfortunately, however, it has been found that the present type of can-opener is not strong enough and the galley equipment manufacturers are in the process of designing a stronger model. These will be fitted as soon as possible. Would all girls please make sure to carry their own can-openers in the meantime in case there is not one available on the aircraft'.

'Rimini Flights. The following message has been received from Rimini Airport. Will all Hostesses please comply with this request. 'Upon request of the Airport Health Authorities of Rimini it is imperative that on arrival of each flight, names and first destination in Italy are

AIR HOSTESSES

DRESS & GROOMING

REGULATIONS

court line AVIATION LTD

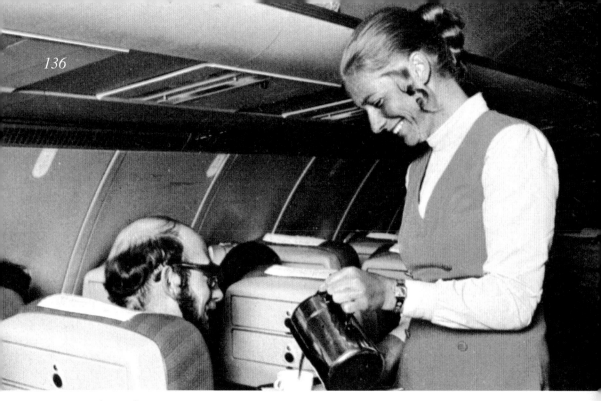

*given by cabin crew to Airport Police of passengers coming
from USSR, Syria, Lebanon, Jordan, Libya and Egypt'.*

**'27 August 1970 Dijon and Bordeaux Flights (OU 557/8
and OU561/2).** *Will all No.1 Hostesses please note that on all
return sectors of the Dijon and Bordeaux series, wine is to be
served to the passengers (one glass per person). The
charterer's representative will deliver the wine to the Handling
Agent who will then ensure that the wine is loaded aboard the
aircraft. Will Air Hostesses please ensure that both wine
glasses and corkscrews are loaded with the catering at Luton.
As a guide, one bottle should serve 6 to 7 glasses'.*

'4 September 1970 - Jacket Coat Pegs. *Although it is in
order for cabin staff jackets to be hung on the pegs in the flight
deck, please do not open the flight deck door immediately prior
to landing to collect jackets etc. The flood of light from the
cabin, especially at night, into the flight deck when an
approach is being made, makes life very difficult for the
Captain and First Officer'.*

'Briefings. *Will all Air Hostesses please ensure that on
flights other than Clarksons, there are no Clarksons brochures
and leaflets in seat pockets. Also, please remember not to
mention Clarksons in your briefings when the pax are Villa
Parties or Owners Services, etc. It sounds obvious, but a few
tour operators had a nasty shock recently when being
welcomed aboard a Clarksons flight!'*

'24 September 1970 - Cabin Service. *In order to try to
overcome the passenger complaints we are receiving re. cabin*

Pat Knights in her new Court Line uniform

service, it has been decided that we revert to the original order of cabin service. i.e Drink service, meal & coffee, Duty-free sales, second drink service if time. However, on short flights (anything under 90 minutes flying time) it is left to the discretion of the No.1 Air Hostess concerned. She must note on her voyage report the order of service adopted'.

All the Hostesses underwent regular assessment to ensure a maintained standard of training and appearance. Patricia Knights endured one such training report by Training Hostess Barbra Chappell on OU731/2 to Alicante...

'Punctuality- 'OK '. Equipment Check - Galley, Bar, Dressing Cabin, Emergencies - 'Satisfactory'. Cabin Checks - Pax Count, Seat Belts, Ships Papers, Co-operation with Ground staff - 'Satisfactory'. PA Announcements - Confidence, Voice Projections, Accuracy of Brief - 'PAs not exactly as per cabin staff manual'. Pax Attention - General Approach, Seating Arrangements, Children - 'Good '. In Flight - Courtesy to crew, Timing, Bar Service, Meal Services, Galley conditions - 'Pax should always be addressed as Sir or Madam! Small trays not used for drink orders or coffee. Advisable to clear away miniatures before making coffee, glasses should have been cleared away first. Miniatures and glasses still out in galley while cabin staff working from trolleys '. Emergencies - 'Checked by Mr Whitten's assistant before take-off

It was common for Courts Air Hostesses to go on courses to learn about the products they were selling in the cabin - here a group are pictured in what appears to be the loading bay of Booths Gin! Some names of those present include June Shipley, Cherry Mason, Sue Porter, Cathy Colebrook, Elaine Lenge, Isabel Castle, Margaret Houseman, Sally-Anne Thompson, Patience Zorn and Elaine Mawe.
[via Sue Farr].

Appearance - Hat, Shoes, Uniform, Hair, Make-Up, Deportment, General appearance - 'Hair too long to be worn down.' Adaptability to Work - 'Worked hard and well - rather trying pax! Pleasant personality and has common sense.'

Shirley Abbott, now Shirley Sosnick of Alberta, Canada has fond memories of Barbra Chapell...

'She was No. 1 on my first flight when I joined Autair in 1969. I was very nervous and worried that I might make some mistakes.

Barbra told me not to worry, she said 'Only you know if you have done something wrong - the passengers are on holiday; as long as it is not too serious, they don't care! '- and they didn't! '

Three Court girls and One Eleven! Patricia Knights (bottom) Celia Wylie and Kathy Brooks on the steps of Mike Juliet during a night turn-around [via Patricia Gill]

It was Shirley Abbott who actually experienced what is regarded by many as an archetypal Air Hostess story...

'One flight over the Pyrenees we experienced moderate turbulence and the passengers started feeling a bit green. I quickly collected up the 'used' sick-bags - the smell only tended to make things worse - and deposited them in one of the toilets at the rear. Just as I was shutting the door one of the call lights

A particularly busy ramp at Luton. This must have been taken not long after Court came into being, for the Autair hangar still is not named 'Court'. [Peter Murdoch]

came on - I went forward to see what was required and found one very perturbed gentleman who mumbled - you 've guessed it - 'I 've loft me teeff' Back to the rear toilet for one of the most unpleasant jobs I ever had to do, but I found them and he gave me a really nice smile after the flight!'

Other Court Line Hostesses have similar stories, many of which have long since passed into airline legend... the Portugese students hell-bent on joining the Mile High Club during a night flight; they were so 'active' the crew did not dare to turn down the lights... the small boy who brought a lizard on board in a paper bag - of course, it escaped!... the group of Tottenham Hotspur supporters who sang *'Nice One Cyril'* all the way to Lisbon and back... the chartered surveyor who went to Tunisia and had one of the girls modelling kaftans for his mistress... the paralytic lady passenger who took off her knickers and waved them around her head... the list goes on.

Coaches, Air Terminals, Catering...

Court Line Coaches..., an eye-catching scheme, even if the first trial versions of the paint-job looked like a squashed slice of Battenberg cake. For the technically minded, the coaches were built on a Ford chassis, powered by the then-new R226 turbo engine, with bodywork by Paxtons of Scarborough.

All were fitted with refinements such as two-way radios, automatic opening doors, PA equipment and individual seat ventilation.
[Peter Murdoch]

As part of the overall vertical integration concept and new image package, Court Line Aviation acquired Hillside Coaches Ltd, re-naming them Court Line Coaches and placing the coaches in a new livery that complimented the scheme worn by the aircraft.

Hillside Coaches (originally known as Diadem Coaches) was formed in 1953 by Ron and Cynthia Keech with just one vehicle. In 1963 they became associated with Autair, carrying holidaymakers and scheduled service passengers from the North London Air Terminal to Luton.

More and more they found the coaching activities matching in to suit the airline. As Autair grew, so did Hillside, making up to eighty coach trips a day to Luton at the summer peak. With the take-over and new identity, the frequency of journeys increased still further, making use of 40 vehicles, also carrying passengers for other airlines, such as Dan-Air Services, so that regularly one hundred trips a day were being made - the multi-coloured coaches became a

familiar sight along both carriageways of the M1!

Under the auspices of Mr Ranger, the Terminal Superintendent, and Duty Officers Chris Simms, Jim Marchant and Peter Seymour, the North London Air Terminal itself was refurbished and expanded at a cost of £30,000 to cater for the increase in passenger traffic - 50% up in 1971. The Terminal handling not only Court Line passengers going to Luton, but also - for a fee - Dan-Air, Aviaco of Spain, Tarom of Romania and, for Stansted Airport, the US charter operators Saturn, Universal and American Flyers.

An indication of the increase in passenger levels can be gained from the fact that in 1966 40,000 people passed through its doors - by 1970 it was over 250,000! As levels of passenger activity fluctuated wildly - although the busiest periods peaked at 0900, 1200 and 1800hrs - it seemed almost a miracle that there was always the right number of coaches on hand - only possible through direct and continuous contact via radio between the coach office, vehicles and terminal. At peak times the whole place buzzed with arriving and

Views in and around the North London Air Terminal operated by Courts. [all via Peter Murdoch]

departing holidaymakers.

Passengers' gastronomic requirements on even the shortest of flights were taken care of by Court Line Catering, initially called Carass Airways Catering Ltd, then Courtair Catering, a wholly-owned associate company based within the confines of Luton Airport.

Court Line Catering provided meals for not just their sister company, but also for Dan-Air, McAlpine's fleet of executive aircraft, Lloyd International at Stansted and any other aircraft that diverted to Luton and required a meal uplift.

Be they a cold meal for a Clarksons party to Malaga or a hot dinner for Lloyd's Middle Eastern run, it was provided by and produced in the Luton kitchens.

The Catering company also bought all the dry goods, all the soft drinks and other kinds that was consumed during a flight.

...a new invention...

One aspect to Court Line's passenger service now that the airline only operated charter flights was the 'invention' by Court Catering back in 1969 of a new method of providing passengers with meals, a method arrived at by studying the requirements of meal presentation. From the airline's point of view, an in-flight meal should be compact, easy to prepare, serve and easy to clear up. For the passenger, it should be palatable and easy to eat in the confines of the seating area. Under existing systems, the cabin staff had the food already prepared in individual trays and stacked in the galley, ready to be heated if required, and then dished out at the appropriate time. This took up a lot of time and a lot of space; it meant endless traffic up the aisle of the cabin, often against the flow of passengers wanting the toilets, and was difficult to do in bumpy weather. It also meant that a passenger might have to wait to be served a revenue-earning drink from the bar.

It seemed to the company that most of these problems could be solved by 're-arranging things'. A long hard look at the aircraft interior revealed the possibility of fitting a small locker with two compartments into the rear of each head-rest that

...E AND INDUSTRIAL CATERERS
Luton Airport Luton Bedfordshire

court line
catering

More vertical integration! Unlike many airlines of today, Court Line had their own catering services division. [all via Peter Murdoch]

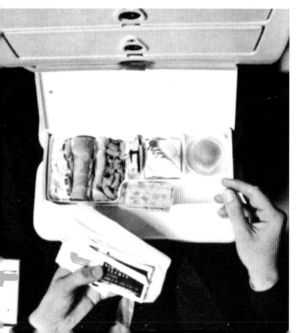

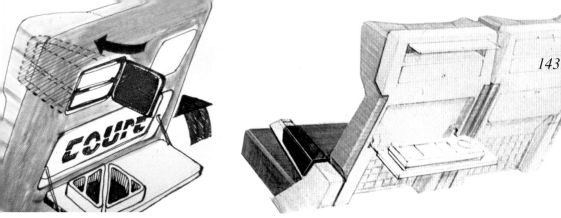

Court developed further the seatback catering idea originally instigated by Autair.

The top two sketches show two versions of the scheme - the versions with the triangular shaped meal trays were not adopted.

The meal tray presentation was totally disposable, as shown by this one on the right used as the standard outbound One-Eleven meal. As Court said: 'We think passengers should be able to eat when they feel hungry. Not just when we want to feed them. So we've designed special seatback meals. They'll be freshly prepared food waiting at each seat. Passengers can tuck in whenever they feel like it. For an idea of what will be on the menu, take a look at our picture. Passengers can also get a little package of souvenirs and goodies to take away at the end of the trip. It's not exactly the Crown Jewels, but it's a nice reminder of what we are: people who take people on holiday'.

was extended to the full width of the seat. Each compartment was designed to take precisely a cold, one tray-meal, appropriate to the time of the flight.

Each breakfast, lunch, evening meal or snack - as appropriate to the time of the flight, both outbound and return - was loaded before the passengers boarded. Thus the passengers could eat when they were hungry, leaving the cabin staff free to sell drinks and duty-frees. It also meant that the galley area could be reduced, allowing an extra three revenue-earning passenger seats to be installed.

After some initial teething troubles - hungry outbound passengers found that they could eat the meal intended for the returning passengers, a problem that was solved by putting a lock on the second compartment - the system worked well for cold meals.

Passengers were encouraged to take away the packaging - tray, cutlery and cup - as a souvenir of the flight, the remainder being removed by the cleaning crew during turn-around.

Seat-back catering failed to live up to its expectation and was certainly not the total success that the airline would have hoped. Kathy Moran (formerly Kathy Lloyd) had first-hand experience:

'Most of the old Court Line hostesses I know would probably agree that this catering system was awful! Even after locks were introduced, outbound passengers would often find ways of opening the inbound locker. As far as I can remember those containers that were left on board at foreign airports were not removed during turn-around and sometimes they fell out on take-off. If delays occurred abroad, the inbound passenger was faced with a horrible curled-up sandwich which had been

The colour schemes on the Court Line aircraft were so radical compared to everything else around it was not surprising that they appeared in all sorts of marketing campaigns. (Ed Posey/Autair-Court Collection)

COURT LINE AVIATION - CORPORATE STRUCTURE

as of 1 April 1970

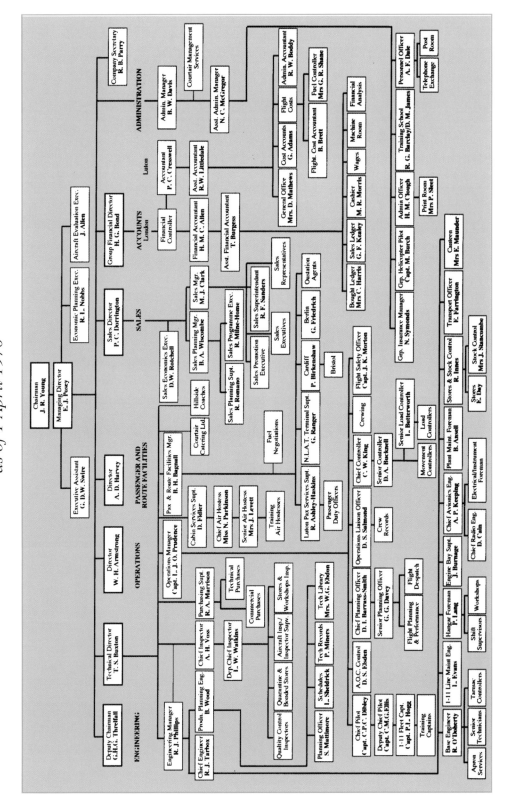

subjected to various temperature changes in the Spanish heat - it really was just the thing to bring out the complaints!'

Patricia Knights also experienced problems with the meals - she filed a written complaint to the company about Flt OU665 LGW-MLA

'Complaint. - LGW catered us for 35 pax on I /B flight as instructed. But we had two extra pax so they had to have sandwiches left from O/ B flight. Wish we had a few extra meals because one gentleman complained bitterly as his meal was eaten and tampered with by an O/B pax (his wife's was as well).

Findings. - 40 meals requested from Aircraft Catering Services, which included 10% on top to cover any problems. Possible short delivery by ACS.'

1971 saw the airline operating numerous IT charters out of Gatwick Airport for a number of tour operators, with IT charters also operated out of Manchester and Castle Donington. Flights from Bristol, however, were suspended in 1972 due to the uneven nature of Lulsgate's main runway and the Clarksons-Hourmont flights from this airport were taken over by British Midland Airways.

...and the passengers.

With all this expansion, it would have been easy to forget about the passengers. Mike Bell of the Duty Office offered a few tips and reminded everyone what it was about in the first edition of 'Court

Behnd the scenes, 'aircraft movements' (as flights were called) were kept track of on the appropriately called 'movement wall'. (Ed Posey/Autair-Court Collection)

Court portrayed itself as a fun airline - the staff had fun too! (Ed Posey/Autair-Court Collection)

Line News' published to all employees at the beginning of 1971...

'What is an airline passenger? , He is that worried individual with a frown on his face, an uneasy feeling in his heart, two cases in his hand, rowdy children on his mind and no place to go but up. And he is unique.

He is the be-all and end-all of our or any other airline's existence.

Yet it is amazing how we in the front-line witness the strange

change that takes over the everyday personality of passengers
once they arrive at an airport.

He may be an easy-going individual in the daily round of
life but show him an airport lounge and he sprouts horns. He
may be realising a dream of authority by making the most noise
over flight delays regardless of the reasons. If he is of this ilk,
then the odds are he will become a ringleader of a threatening
insurrection by passengers against 'the enemy' - anyone in
uniform.

The remedy is to isolate the ringleader from his followers,
when he immediately returns his personality to the normal,
reasonable character that he really is. And the other
passengers tend to dissolve without another word. Strangely
enough, the man who is normally forceful and go-ahead in
everyday life is usually placid, tolerant and understanding.

Another thing you grow used to in the frontline of passenger
services is coping with the 'little boy lost' brigade who appear
totally disorientated when they enter the terminal building and
search eagerly for someone to latch on to. At this point their

*G-AXMG on turn-
around somewhere in
Spain.*

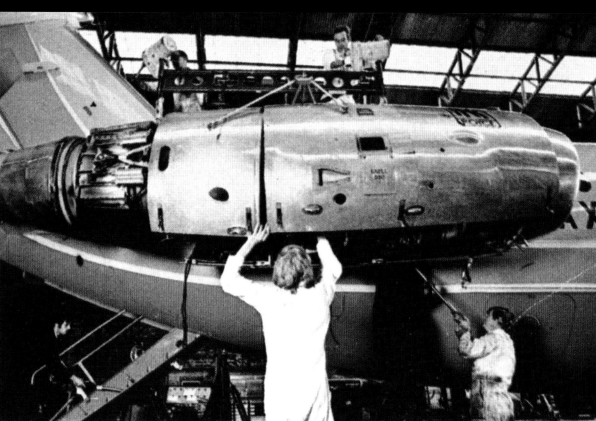

Whether parked outside undergoing day-to day problems that occurred on the ramp, or deeper work that required time in the hangar, the engineers at Luton located and solved all the problems.

eyes catch those of the smiling girls flashing rows of teeth and beckoning them to the fold. After turning round to check that the smiles are not for somebody else, they make for the counter, fumble for tickets, drop passports, and eventually check in.

It is a rare passenger indeed who finds himself at home in an airport. His anxieties normally stay with him until disembarkation at his destination and then new anxieties take their place. To help ease those fears, there is a quiet competence projected by the airline girls. If this breaks down, even for a moment, anxiety rockets to new heights.

Emergencies, on the ground or in flight, if properly handled with calm efficiency are easily accepted by passengers. But if they see someone in uniform running, their imaginations get to work and alarm replaces anxiety. 'What's happened ?' 'Why haven't we been told ?' they wonder.

This is why we make a determined effort to present passengers with all the information possible about delays, bad weather, air traffic control disputes etc. In our experience, the more they are told, the less they worry.

Changes in passenger personalities are common to all, regardless of occupation or religion. Subconscious anxiety is the main factor. If an airline can keep this to a minimum, it will have won that passenger for good.

Even if another carrier is offering the same journey at a cheaper rate, most passengers will stick with the company which gives them confidence whether they are flying for business on scheduled services or heading for a holiday by charter flight.

Confidence and an efficient friendly attitude, coupled with a winning smile will always go a long way to ease passenger fears and add some pleasurable memories of their first steps into flight'.

But this was by no means the end of Court's expansion plans... the Court Line Group were looking to expand again - this time to even further fields...

Chapter Seven
Caribbean Adventures

There has always been something very seductive about thoughts of a tropical paradise; the palm-fringed, sun-drenched tropical island is one of temperate European man's continuing and most enduring dreams, an emotional refuge from monogamy and cold winters.

Jet air travel, holidays with pay, and the inclusive tour holiday concept have brought this dream closer to realisation for more people than ever before. This in essence is what the 'leisure' industry is all about; fitting a reality-that-never-was into a lazy and romantic dream.

It all sounds so appealing, so romantic; like most realised dreams, it is the product of imagination, careful selection, meticulous planning, modern technology - and a great deal of money. One area of the world that attracted the imagination in the 1960s and '70s was the Caribbean - St. Lucia and Antigua in the Leeward Islands, a chain of islands extending roughly North to South for about 600 miles, and Nassau in the Bahamas, which lie to the East of Florida. These islands were the spiritual home of piratical legends about Long John Silver, Captain Henry Morgan, Cap'n Kidd and others which form the tales of the 'Spanish Main'...

This must have been a fascinating attraction for a swash-buckling pair of companies such as Court Line and Clarksons, who at that time were taking on - and apparently beating - all-comers in the Mediterranean. The incursion into the Caribbean, under the direct conception and direction of John Young, followed the normal modus operandi of 'vertical integration' with the acquisition of both hotels and airlines.

Early in 1968 John Young, James Venus and Ken Holmes of Clarksons visited St Lucia, and from this came the original concept

The Halcyon Days Hotel on St Lucia, not long after it had opened for business. [Court Collection]

of Court Line's Caribbean business. This was for Clarksons Holidays and Court Line to jointly build a 'package-holiday' type hotel in St Lucia similar in design and concept to those used in the Mediterranean and fill it to capacity with European holidaymakers, using their own Court fleet of aircraft to carry them there. Clarksons later withdrew from the arrangement, leaving Court to continue with the development on its own, changing the focus of the market from Europe to North America.

Hotel marketing was to be undertaken throughout North America by an organisation built up from a 51% holding in a New York agency, the Transair Marketing Development Corporation, into full subsidiaries with facilities in New York for the USA and Toronto for the Canadian market.

Two hotels were eventually built on St. Lucia - the Halcyon Days hotel came about when in 1968 Halcyon Hotels Ltd, a company incorporated under St Lucian law, obtained a large area of land from the St. Lucian Government near Hewanorra International Airport on a 75 year lease. When complete, the three-story building - the maximum height allowed by local planning regulations - would have 750 rooms and a self-contained leisure complex that included a golf course and stables. To understand how corporately complex things could get in the Court Line Group, Halcyon Hotels Ltd became a subsidiary of Halcyon Hotels (Nassau) Ltd, which itself was a wholly-owned subsidiary of Carribean Tankers Ltd!

The hotel opened for business in June 1971, but with a much lower room occupancy rate than predicted by the North American marketing organisation, resulting in an immediate trading loss. To make the facility more attractive, an aqua-centre was built at the cost of £100,000 but, due to unsatisfactory beach and sea conditions at the Halcyon Days location, this had to be situated a few miles away

The Halcyon Days Hotel on St Lucia, along with the Hotel's promotional leaflet that followed the Court Line corporate principles.
[Court Line Collection]

on the opposite side of the island. Two 65 foot long motor-yachts were purchased to enhance the aqua-centre, the m.v. *Halcyon Breeze* and the m.v. *Sailfish,* but it was soon discovered that the jetty built at the aqua-centre was unsuitable for berthing these vessels!

Occupancy during the high season (December to March) with guests from North America was reasonable, but for the rest of the year the figures were very poor.

In the early days staffing was a problem, for St. Lucia had never experienced a hotel of this size. Court Line therefore established a training school, subsequently training some 800 people during the company's period of tenure, which greatly benefitted the local economy.

Today, in 2017 and after refurbishment, the Halcyon Days Hotel is now the Coconut Bay Resort and Spa. *'It is best described as two resorts in one as there is the 'Harmony' wing which caters to adults only and the 'Splash' wing for families and the young at heart. It is fronted by a fine sandy beach that stretches away in the distance for a mile and offers the opportunity for water sports or simply lounging on a deck chair in the shade of a palm tree'*

Similarly, the more up-market Halcyon Beach Club on St. Lucia and the matching promotional leaflet also followed the corporate identity. [Court Line Collection]

Court Line felt that it could benefit from a second hotel on St. Lucia, so the Halcyon Beach Club project was started in the North of the Island at Choc Bay. A large area of land was purchased near Vigie Airport, about two miles from the capital Castries, much of which was swamp. The land was cheap to buy, but proved expensive to fill. A marine dredger was sent out from the U.K. for an immense amount of in-fill had to be provided. This, along with the construction of a substantial pier instead of the modest beach bar originally planned, the necessity of re-designing all electrical fittings and a strike outside

the control of Court Line and its contractors, meant that the capital outlay was considerably higher than expected.

The Halcyon Beach Club was very different to the Halcyon Days Hotel, being much smaller and designed for 'up-market' customers from North America and, appropriately for a shipping organisation, the decor adopted a maritime theme. Rooms were called 'staterooms', and there were to be models and paintings of Court Line vessels in profusion. The hotel started trading in November 1970 and it too suffered low occupancy rates. Staffing here was also a problem, and expatriate staff were employed who required higher salaries, together with fringe benefits such as cars and accommodation, all of which contributed to the overall loss. Towards the end of 1971 the Hon. W. S. Phillips CBE, Chairman of the Court Line Group reported to shareholders that

> '...for the first time we are marketing a twelve-night holiday in our own hotels, in association with British Overseas Airways Corporation, and starting at £165.00. We believe this gives unrivalled value for money in the Caribbean'.

Both St. Lucian hotels suffered low occupancy rates, and a year later things were still not right, especially with the American marketing organisation. The Chairman of the Group had this to say...

> 'The success of the hotel organisation depends largely on marketing. I am sorry to have to report that the optimistic

Peter Murdoch's colour-co-ordination concept was carried right across the Caribbean, that included the Hotel Balmoral in the Bahamas.

*forecasts produced by our North American office failed to
materialise and a very large programme that it had negotiated
in conjunction with a major U.S. supplemental (known in
Europe as a Charter) airline never operated'.*

During 1972 Court began to market the two hotels in England, where
they began to sell very well. One strong factor in this was that they
were approximately £50 (around US$150) cheaper than any of its
competitors.

The same failure of the American marketing organisation to sell
beds during the low season - April to November - occurred again in
1973. In a further attempt to resolve the situation, these hotels were
aggressively marketed in the U.K. by Clarksons.

In February 1972 a Bahamian subsidiary of Court Line purchased
the Balmoral Hotel (re-named the Halcyon Balmoral) in Nassau that
was later sold to the Bahamian Government in 1974 at a loss.

Also in February 1972 a 32-room hotel at the north end of Antigua,
near the airport was purchased from a liquidator and re-named the
Halcyon Cove. It continued to trade for two months, then closed for
extensive work to be undertaken.

The hotel was at the foot of a hill, its restaurant being located at
the top of the hill, served by a small funicular railway. The original
services were improved to include additional shops, a swimming pool
and other amenities. In addition, a pier was built with full restaurant
facilities that must have been very convenient from the guests point
of view, but duplicated all catering facilities, thus greatly increasing
costs!

These hotels were followed in 1974 by the purchase of a small
hotel in St. Lucia, the Marigot des Roseau.

Interestingly, the Halcyon Beach Club is still around in 2014, but
has dropped the word 'Club' to become part of the Sandals All
Inclusive holiday organisation. *'Sandals Halcyon Beach is surely it.
Here in the midst of a tropical utopia, where majestic palms line a
pristine beach and verdant mountains rise from a turquoise sea, you'll
discover a charming and intimate sanctuary that's the essence of its
name...tranquil, peaceful and calm.*

Eastern Caribbean Airways Limited.
Before we move on to Court Line's other major purchase in the
Caribbean, there is one other little known airline they acquired that
deserves being recorded.

Eastern Caribbean Airways was a Bahamian company owned by
Mr H. Moffat which possessed a single Beechcraft light aircraft used
for ad hoc charters. Court Line Aviation purchased ECA in May 1972
for £3,000, retaining the services of Mr Moffat, for it was thought
that his contacts would be of value when negotiating fare increases

Beechcraft Twin Bonanza VP-LIF of LIAT seen approaching one of the islands.

locally and that the Beechcraft could be used as an 'executive aircraft' by Court Line directors when visiting the area.

Leeward Islands Air Transport Servicess Ltd (LIAT)
Court Line acquired a 75% interest in LIAT in October 1971, and then the remaining 25% on 1 October 1972 (from British West Indian Airways (BWIA), the national airline of Trinidad and Tobago which operated as a scheduled and charter airline throughout the eastern Caribbean) for the total cost of £790,000. At that time LIAT's liabilities exceeded the book value of tangible assets by £1,461,000, so the total cost of LIAT's goodwill was £2,251,000.

Leeward Islands Air Transport Services Ltd had been formed in 1956 by Kittian-born Frank Delisle, who started a modest service between his Montserrat and neighbouring Antigua a sector distance of just thirty-five miles using a twin-engined Piper Apache. His available payload was three passengers and/or some freight, which could only amount to little more than an armful of parcels.

Nevertheless, the service was popular amongst the islanders and the next year the airline's schedule was widened to include St Kitts, St Eustatius and St Maarten; soon the Apache was re-inforced with a twin-engined Beechcraft Bonanza that could carry six passengers.

The same year LIAT became a subsidiary of BWIA. Gradually each island in the chain carved out miniature airports so that they all could become aerially linked - by 1960 the airline had six aircraft, four Bonanza's and a pair of De Havilland Herons, and was flying as far afield as Trinidad. In 1958 LIAT moved its operations base from Montserrat to Antigua and their hangar - a 60ft by 60ft structure erected to accommodate the Herons - was built. Alongside the first

Three postage stamps from the Caribbean, depicting earlier Leeward Islands Air Transport Services aircraft. Top is the Twin Bonanza, middle is the De Havilland Heron and bottom is a De Havilland Canada Twin Otter. [LIAT Collection]

LIAT began operating the Avro 748 in 1965, and it was not long before the design started to feature on a whole range of postards. [Ed Posey/Court Line Collection]

The aircraft always seemed to feature 'down on the deck' as it were, flying over Caribbean islands. [Ed Posey/Court Line Collection]

Another load of passengers board Avro 748 VP-LIV for an inter-island flight.

140:420 0:623:862

liat

Airline of the
Eastern Caribbean

Passenger Ticket
& Baggage Check

Each passenger should carefully examine
this ticket, particularly the conditions of
contract on page 2, the advice on page 3,
the important notice on page 4 and the
check in times detailed on page 5

A member of the Court Line Group

PRINTED IN U.S.A. BY RAND MCNALLY

2 FLIGHT

Above: A LIAT passenger ticket and baggage check

Below: Avro 748 VP-LAJ with a One-Eleven behind. [Kurt Lang]

The setting sun casts long shadows in Jon Charley's snapshot taken at Barbuda of the crew of this LIAT B-N Islander, thought to have been VP-LAF.

hangar was the fuselage of another Heron which was modified to become the office of the Accounting Department! By now the airline was flying scheduled services in a 1,400 mile arc in one direction to San Juan, Puerto Rico (via St Thomas) and to Trinidad (via Guadeloupe, Dominica, Barbados and St Vincent) in the other!

In 1965 Delisle obtained his first turbo-prop, an Avro 748 registered VP-LIK, and a second one a year later, the airline's headquarters moving to Coolige Airport to allow the 748 to be operated. For a time LIAT operated two nineteen-seat Twin Otters, which were replaced in 1970 by five Britten-Norman Islanders. Every winter from 1967 onwards LIAT leased a single 748 from Autair (and later from Court), thus establishing an ongoing link with the company.

Three LIAT B-N Islanders, VP-LAG 'pink' on the left, VP-LAP 'orange' centre and an unitentifiable turquiose machine on the ground at Antigua. [Jon Charley]

The busiest time of the year for tourists in the West Indies was (and still is) from the end of the hurricane season in October through to about April - more or less exactly matching Court Line's quiet European winter time, thus creating a situation where LIAT's possible demand for extra capacity matched Courts possible 'spare'!

LIAT consistently made losses right up to the time of the take-

over. The purchase agreement required BWIA to convert its US$2,500,000 current account with LIAT into a long-term loan. Court Line then guaranteed repayment of this loan, together with guarantees relating to LIAT's aircraft purchase obligations. A further condition of purchase was that LIAT would put into service three additional Court Line aircraft, one One-Eleven and a pair of Avro 748s. A second One-Eleven was flown out to the Caribbean from Luton in 1972, with a further machine scheduled to be flown out later, this one fitted with an extra 350 gallon fuel tank in the forward baggage hold, making the aircraft capable of a 2,200 mile range.

Under new ownership, LIAT underwent more than just equipment changes and a 'new' LIAT emerged. It was intended that LIAT in Antigua and Court Line in Luton would become one company despite the distances involved. There would be constant and regular exchanges of people, equipment, skills and information. Brian Davis was seconded to LIAT as Director and General Manager with Peter Cresswell as Chief Accountant. Captains Ball, Lang, Torrey and Varley with First Officers Hampson, Willis and Walker and Air Hostesses Ute Browse, Isabel Lynn and Aileen Sheehan all went out to set up the One-Eleven operation. Others from Court that moved 'westwards to warmer climes' were Mike Sprule, Ron Hammerton, Scottie Scott, Maurice Lackman and Geoff Cole for the 748, with Engineering support from Eddie Lewis, Trevor Angus, Mike Marchant, Gordon Durber and Fred Kozo, and Operations support from Len Butterworth.

Betsey Johnson, the LIAT uniform designer. In 1978 she started her own label, and created a chain of stand-alone stores across the USA, which went bankrupt in 2012.

The first sign of this at Luton, apart from a One-Eleven so far away from base was the arrival of Captain Ferdie de Gannes and First Officer Duliu for the One-Eleven conversion course, and six LIAT cabin staff for crew training.

In the Caribbean, the girls wore a Betsey Johnson-designed silk mini-dress with a simple canvas belt of the same colour, with a large silver buckle with LIAT engraved large upon it. In Luton, whilst training, the girls wore standard Court uniforms, but with one difference - as they were used to wearing very short dresses, they sought and gained permission to shorten the Court uniform skirt even further, which turned many heads around the airport!

Betsey Johnson is an American fashion designer best known for her feminine and whimsical designs. Many of her designs are considered 'over the top' and embellished. She

became famous for doing a cartwheel at the end of her fashion shows.

The first six Hostesses from LIAT pose at Luton during their training. They are (l to r) Lois Meyer, Rosemarie Trotter, Marie Alfred, Noreen Copland, Judith Ward and Yolande Arthur. [Court Collection],

Johnson's fashion career started after she entered and won the *Mademoiselle* Guest Editor Contest. Within a year, she was the in-house designer for Manhattan boutique *Paraphernalia*. Johnson became part of both the youthquake fashion movement and Andy Warhol's underground scene, along with The Velvet Underground, Edie Sedgwick and Lou Reed. In 1969, she opened a boutique called Betsey Bunky Nini on New York's Upper East Side. Edie Sedgwick was her house model and Johnson designed the clothing Sedgwick wore on her last film, *Ciao Manhattan!*

LIAT's Hostesses were outfitted in sleek and stylish plum-coloured silk mini-dresses, with oblong belts engraved with the airline's name, designed by Betsy Johnson, as worn here by Nalini Dubé. [Jon Charley]

In the 1970s, Johnson took control of the fashion label 'Alley Cat' which was popular with the rock 'n roll musicians of the day. In her first year, her debut collection for Alley Cat reportedly sold $5 million in volume. In 1972 she won the Coty Award.

Former LIAT Air Hostess Rosemarie Trotter (now Fernandez) remembers that uniform with amusement...

> *'When we used to give our Safety Procedure briefing to the passengers before take-off it was almost impossible to maintain our dignity... As we raised our arms to indicate the Emergency Exits behind us, our dress hem would ride up.... you can imagine where all the eyes of the males sitting in the aisle seats went.'*

Lois Meyer, another LIAT Air Hostess, remembers how the silk uniform contour-clung', which created some interesting effects...

> *When landing at Grenada aboard the One-Elevens we had to brief our passengers in advance about the non-standard arrival that was the norm for this island. The runway was so sort there*

our pilots had to use full reverse thrust and hard braking in order to stop. It was perfectly safe as we stressed, but during the process there was a lot of noise and aircraft shook around a lot. Regular passengers would often be spotted watching our err... 'upper foundation wear' move around under the dress during the landing at that airport!

Rough runways were not the only problems that had to be contended with; there was a typhoid epidemic in Grenada, a Polio epidemic in Trinidad and a rumbling volcano on St. Vincent!

As David Price from LIAT Head Office reported:

The BAC One-Eleven 'Jet Express' services, as they became almost 'fondly' known locally, have shown overall load factor increases on a steady basis. We frequently enjoyed a 'full ship' status on the St. Maarten to San Juan sector and our cabin crew, ably assisted by Eileen Sheehan have really refined the techniques of serving light refreshments and a bar to 99 passengers in less than 40 minutes!

An interesting commercial note - we completed a series of twenty successive '748' charters from St. Vincent to Barbados for sugar cane cutters. Our largest single charter group movement to date.

Our big day in March 1972 was no doubt H.R.H. Princess Margaret's travel to Beef Island and Tortola in the British Virgin Islands and return to Antigua by chartered LIAT H.S. 748 on March 7th and 10th respectively. H.R.H. continued on to St. Vincent from Antigua on our regular service '748' on

Four LIAT girls on the airstairs of *'Halcyon Days'*

One of the LIAT One Elevens resting on the ramp at Virgie. (both Kurt Lang)

February 1972, and John Young and Ed Posey visit the Caribbean to inspect the new LIAT operation in the company HS 125 G-AYRG

March 10th and then to Mustique by chartered LIAT B.N. Islander. Thus H.R.H. travelled on three different LIAT aircraft in one day - quite a record for Royalty, we believe!

With the additional equipment LIAT's capacity increased by some 60%, but its income did not rise by a similar figure. Between 1972 and 1973 income only rose by 8%, principally as a result of whatever fare increases could be negotiated.

It was obvious from the start that in order to make the airline viable, fare increases would have to happen, which meant getting approval from the West Indies States Council, a conglomeration of some 20 separate island governments that the airline served.

More fashion shoots - this time with a Caribbean backdrop!

The first application was submitted in April 1972, seven months after LIAT had been purchased, with the expectation that increased fares could be introduced in July. The information supplied to the council was deemed insufficient and more was requested. This was supplied in a report from John Young dated 20 April, but not acknowledged as received by the Council until 27 June, just three days before the date of effective increase. On 13 September local LIAT representatives acknowledged that information supplied to the council was still insufficient. The Council then requested further information direct from John Young on 3 October. He replied in a cable, saying that *'If by 15 October 1972 positive*

steps are not taken to deal with increases, jet services will be suspended'.

No increases were forthcoming, so the One Elevens were withdrawn on 15 October, which in turn brought about an interim 10% price increase secured in January 1973, so flights started up again. On 1 July 1973 a fare increase of 30% was approved by the Council of Ministers, almost a year later, on 30 May 1974 fares again increased, this time by 12%, followed a month later by a 6% increase due to increased fuel costs.

Personnel within LIAT thought these increases were still 'too little, too late' and that heavy losses were inevitable. One-Eleven services continued to operate until April 1974, when they were withdrawn as much as a tactical move in the light of difficulties encountered in negotiating fare increases in a political environment as an effort to reduce losses.

There were other problems also. The West Indies States Council insisted that LIAT's operation's base remained in Antigua, in the middle of the route system. Court Line thought that it should have been at one end, with the central position creating a number of technical operational inefficiencies.

At the take-over, none of the existing directors remained in their

Ground transporation in the Caribbean was also 'different' with Court Line Holidays making use of open topped double-decker 'Bristol' busses with little-to-no sides. Here one such vehicle complete with the ubiquitious Halcyon name and logo is parked beside Avro 748 VP-LAJ 'Halcyon Beach at Hewanorra Airport, St. Lucia. (Kurt Lang)

VP-LAN 'Halcyon Beach' at St Lucia. (Kurt Lang)

The bright colours of the aircraft and the concept of the Halcyon bird worn large on the vertical tail for all to see seemed almost perfectly suited for the Caribbean. (Kurt Lang)

Airline and marketing people meet to discuss the promotional campaign for the One Eleven 'Jet Service' to St. Croix. On the left is John McDonald, Sales Representative, LIAT Antigua. Centre is David Price, General Marketing Manager and on the right is Melvin Black, Marketing Manager, Trinidad [LIAT (1974) Ltd]

posts. John Young and Edward Posey were appointed Chairman and Deputy Chairman respectively with other UK-based Court Line executives filling other appointments. All were heavily committed to UK operations and none had experience in Caribbean airline operations or the type of service that LIAT provided.

The number of employees increased from 550 to 800, many of whom were expatriates, for whom accommodation had to be provided.

LIATs accounting information had been installed onto BWIA's computer in Trinidad before the take-over, and continued to be run from there. Not surprisingly, BWIA had priority, which often resulted in LIAT's accounts returns being late and frequently inaccurate. This meant that current revenue and budget comparison information on which LIAT's management had to base their commercial decisions was also often inaccurate.

On 6 December 1972 LIAT started a new jet service to Kingston

166

Right: Boarding a lilac LIAT One-Eleven at Grenada. Air Hostess Jennifer Aird is at the bottom of the foreward airstairs (Jon Charles)

Below: Given the vivid colours of the aircraft and high fashion styles of the girls uniforms, it is not surprising that everyone wanted their pictures taken - even the crews! Angela de Gannes and two other hostesses pose alongside this LIAT One Eleven.

Jamaica. There were also plans to operate a service to Caracas in Venezuela, but due to the political problems in Grenada, from where the service would operate, it was never started.

Elizabeth Overbury undertook one 'tour of duty' away from the dreariness of the European winter out in the sunny Caribbean...

'I didn't get out to LIAT until 1973 and scheduled flying out there was a totally different kettle of fish to what we were used to flying from the U.K. For one thing, when it rained the baggage handlers disappeared into the holds and would not do their job until the rain stopped, unless you badgered them - a good storm could play havoc with our schedules in more ways than one!

I was based in Antigua flying to the islands North or to the islands South. Vigie (St Lucia) on the One-Eleven you could

LEEWARD ISLANDS AIR TRANSPORT TRADING RESULTS 1970-1973				
	year to 31.12.70	year to 31.12.70	9 months to 30.9.72	year to 30.12.73
Passengers carried on sceduled services	£497,000	£514,000	£406.000	£546,000
Revenue (scheduled and other services)	£2,941,000	£3,300,000	£3,035,000	£4,405,000
Costs	£3,523,000	£3,986,000	£3,583,000	£5,665,000
Loss	£582,000	£686,000	£548,000	£1,260,000

normally only approach over the hill to land towards the harbour. On take-off you had to wait in position at the take-off point for someone to check that no tall-masted yacht was coming across the end of the runway - we could quite easily be low enough to hit it!

Pearls (Grenada) was an unusual approach, again landing and taking off towards the sea, with the approach on a curve. Either southbound from Barbados or northbound from Trinidad, our Outer Marker was a white (or was it a red?) bungalow roof and we flew a curve to another bungalow roof and then a tight turn to the right to land down a steep hill - and you had to land by a white line painted across the runway, otherwise you ran off the runway and into the sea.

The LIAT desk at Coolidge Airport, Antigua. (Peter Murdoch)

During the winter of 1973/4 when I was flying out there, political things were happening in Grenada that we didn't fully appreciate at the time.

On some of the morning flights southbound we had stretcher

Changes in uniorm... Right: Constance Gonsalves (top) Judith Ward and Marlene Meyer pose on the forward airstairs in the long-sleeved silk LIAT uniform for Kurt Lang's camera...

Below: Left to Right: Ute Browse, Lois Meyer, Noreen Copland and Rosemarie Trotter in the short-sleeved cotton dresses. [via Ed Posey]

cases to pick up for Trinidad. On my walk-rounds to check the outside of the aircraft - we didn't need fuel or catering - I noticed badly injured faces and at first thought they were victims of a bad road accident. Ambulances were always readily available and alongside when we landed at Piarco and we hoped that these badly injured people - always men - would get to hospital for care. It was not until the USA invaded Grenada some years later that the world discovered what was going on in that Caribbean paradise.

Quite often we could not get a reply from Pearls when approaching Grenada and our brief then was to continue to Trinidad. On one occasion we made an approach with no radio contact only to find the whole runway blocked with boxes and cars - we continued on to Trinidad and our flight ended. I found out then that this was the normal way of showing us pilots that ATC was not on duty!

Nevertheless, my time with LIAT was great and the help we got in Jamaica when I became involved with our aircraft lease to Jamaica Air Services was superb. On landing we were told to taxi to point PAPA. Ground charts to hand we taxied off the duty runway, but nothing to denote PAPA... Was it my accent, or did I sound a little hesitant? 'I'm frightfully sorry, but this is our first time in Jamaica. Could you give taxi instructions?' In that lovely West Indian lilt the reply came back over the radio - 'Welcome to the best island in the Caribbean, welcome to Jamaica. Follow me

*car will come soon'. 'Soon' was at least five minutes and it
was a shame we had to refuel and return to Antigua within
the hour'.*

The fuel crisis brings about changes...
9 January 1974 saw the first two staff circulars of the year to LIAT
employees. February 1974 saw John Young announce the
appointment of Bill Buxton as Technical Director to LIAT and the
introduction of a third One-Eleven to the Eastern Caribbean. But
1/74 covered eight pages and was, in effect a document for
survival from the Managing Director, Michael Warwick. The
heading - *'1974 - a Crucial year for L.I.A.T'* succinctly set the
scene, but he went on...

*'I am sure you are all concerned at what you read in the
Press and hear on the radio and television about the present*

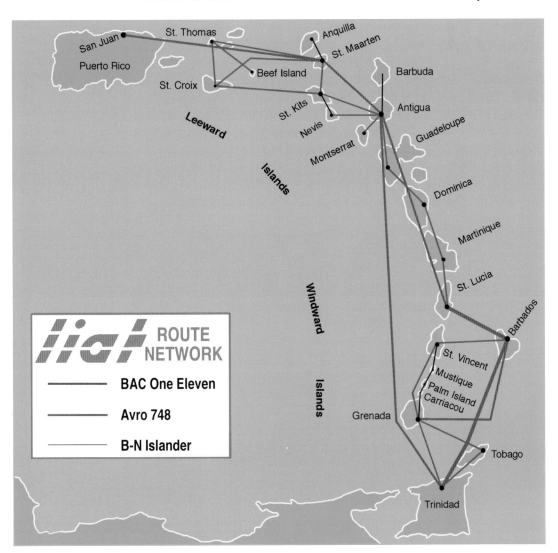

critical fuel situation and the Company's continuing adverse fuel position. The Board of Directors felt it was time to outline in detail to all our staff the facts as we see them, and the steps that must be taken to ensure the Company's continued operation and future financial success.'

The fuel crisis was explained in detail, and this was followed by details of the protracted fare negotiations with the various governments that looked as if they were finally yielding results, with hopefully a completely revised passenger and freight tariff in place by 1 May, but the Accounts - then in preparation - were expected to show a loss of $6 million E.C. or some $10 per passenger carried!

This situation could not continue, so a major departmental review was undertaken with a seven point plan that called for a 10% increase in productivity, reduction in costs, reduce absenteeism, no unrealistic wage claims for at least two years, assess and re-assess the need for new staff, control capital expenditure and encourage business wherever possible. To assist in this the company was re-arranged into six divisions:

The Betsy Johnson uniform was later changed for the Mary Quant version, as worn here by Michaela 'Mickey' Joseph. [Court Collection]

Operations: Joe Mahmood, General Manager, responsible for Aircrew, Ground Operations Control, Air Hostesses and Flight Safety. Ferdie de Gannes appointed Chief Pilot, Richard King as Deputy Chief Pilot and One-Eleven Fleet Captain. Colin Facey 748 Fleet Captain. Phillip Abbott became Ground Operations Manager, with Harry Challenger and Morrison Mack as Movement Control and Flight Despatch Superintendants. Angela de Gannes assumed overall responsibility for all Air Hostesses with Trixie Edwards and Lois Meyer in charge of Operating Standards and Training. Miles McDonalds was in charge of Flight Safety.

From a brochure - LIAT's 1-11 VP-LAK.

Many Caribbean island airports were located in 'interesting' places. These two pictures show Vigie on St Lucia. In one direction pilots had to be aware of yacht's masts crossing the final approach, and a steep climb out was needed on departure!
[both Kurt Lang]

Court Line Aviation's HS-125 G-AVRG seen at London Gatwick. The aircraft gained a Halcyon Bird design on the fin in preparation for a company trip to the Caribbean. [Court Collection]

Engineering: Malcolm Macintyre, General Manager, responsible for Engineering, Technical Supplies, Building and Transport Maintenance. Derek Marcano appointed Production Manager responsible for Hangar, Workshops, Transport and Building Maintenance. Ralph Gissing was appointed Line Maintenance Manager with Dave Burnett as his Deputy, while Eddie Street filled the role of Supplies Manager. John Briggs and Norman Davies were responsible for Technical Planning and Training.

Customer Services: Norman Andrews, General Manager, responsible for Traffic, Catering and In-flight Services, Station Operations including city sales offices and performance of general sales and general handling agents. David Jardine was the Traffic Manager. In order to decentralise aspects of the airline's daily operations, four area managers were appointed. Roddy Grant was Area Manager Windward Islands, responsible for Grenada, St.Vincent, St Lucia, Dominica and the smaller Grenadine islands. Lou Looby as Area Manager Leewards Islands and French Antilles had responsibilities as well for Martinique, Guadeloupe, Antigua, Barbuda, Montserrat, Nevis, St. Kitts and St. Maarten. Keith Scott as Area Manager Barbados and Trinidad also had responsibility for Tobago. Joe Parler as Area Manager Virgin Islands and Puerto Rico was responsible as well for St Thomas, St Croix and the British Virgin Islands.

Finance: Rhidian Griffiths, General Manager, responsible for Accounts, Computer services, Tariffs, Internal Audit, Company Secretarial matters and Insurance. John Macdiarmid was the Chief

Accountant, with Keith Robins as the Cost Accountant, David Attale as the Financial Accountant and Frank Ward as Revenue Accountant. Chris Widdows was responsible for the installation and operation of the company's own IBM System 3 Model 10 computer, expected to be in operation in Antigua by lst April. Ian Calhoun was Tariffs Manager, with Hugh Kersey in charge of the Internal Audit.

Marketing: David Price General Manager, responsible for Sales, Reservations, Communications and Public Relations. Vernon Michael was appointed Sales Manager, Reg Jackson was responsible for Reservations, Sydney Joseph for Communications and Roger Lansley as Sales

Administration: Hugo Ross General Manager, responsible for Personnel, Industrial Relations, Staff Welfare and General Administration matters. Carol Potter was appointed Personnel Manager.

A full study of all projects had been undertaken at the same time, with a number being put 'on the shelf' until the financial situation had improved. Nevertheless, a number of projects was scheduled for 1974.
   a. Introduction of the computer in Antigua to process all accounting and statistical records.
   b. Renovation and introduction of a new image at all LIAT check-in counters and Sales Offices.
   c. Introduction of an on-line computerised reservation system in conjunction with Air Canada as soon as the necessary communications within the region have been installed.
   d. Introduction of new uniforms to all operating personnel.
   e. Renovation of all ground handling equipment.
   f. Continuation of staff training.

As to the future, Michael Warwick finished his Circular on an optimistic note...
   'Providing the financial position of the company shows the necessary improvement, the Management of LIAT in conjunction with the Court Line Group Board is currently evaluating the HS.146 jet aircraft as a replacement for the HS 748 fleet. The aircraft, which it is hoped will be available for commercial operation late 1976/ early 1977, appears to be ideal for the Company's future use and will allow jet operations into airfields at which we are currently restricted.'

Despite everyone at every level involved in the restructured airline working extremely hard, by July 1974 it was obvious that LIAT could not continue as then operated. The introduction of the One-Eleven had been a mistake, for the necessary load-factors never materialised, the fare increases were not approved at the right time and the maintenance costs were much higher than expected.

The Department of Trade and Industry was informed and it was decided that Court Line would dispose of LIAT, but events intervened before this could take place. Perhaps the final word is best left with Angela de Gannes...

'Working for LIAT during the Court Line years was an exciting time, with Courts introducing the jets and bringing in the vibrant new colours. Although everyone worked so hard, we all felt as if it was worth it, for the company was going somewhere.

Looking back now, those days were some of the best in my life - those of us that were around at the time call them our 'Halcyon Days"

Chapter Eight
One Eleven Heyday

Introduction of the new 500-Series BAC One-Elevens into Court Line service proceeded smoothly and the airline soon settled down to the routine - if non-scheduled flying could ever be called that - of it's new task and image.

The original BAC One Eleven 500 Series went into scheduled service with British European Airways on 17 November 1968. BAC then undertook an aggressive development programme that took advantage of the structural stretch the One Eleven airframe afforded to produce a new 500 Series with better all-round performance and greater operational flexibility.

Colours for the sky! Three Court Line BAC One-Elevens on the ramp at Luton. (Kurt Lang)

A very busy ramp at
Luton during the
peak of the holiday
season.

Considerable improvements in aerodynamics had been achieved whilst maintaining the basic geometry and aerofoil simplicity of the BEA 500 Series.

The payload range performance of the new 500 Series was more flexible and thus more useful to operators than that of the BEA 500 Series. The payload range curve showed that the new 500 Series could carry a typical 97 passenger payload up to 1615 nautical miles, that was more than 600 nautical miles further than the BEA 500 Series. A 119 passenger inclusive tour payload can be carried up to 1470 nautical miles - more than twice the range of the BEA 500 Series.

These exceptional improvements in performance were achieved by a number of design changes: the maximum take-off weight increased from 92,500lb. to 104,000 lb; aerodynamic drag reduced by the modification of the wing leading edge and flap track fairings. Fuel capacity was increased by the addition of a 350 Imp. gallon fuselage tank.

The new 500 Series was powered by the Rolls- Royce Spey 25 Mk.12-14DW turbofan with a thrust of 12,550 lb. Rolls-Royce

developed this engine from the BEA 500 Series engine by the use of water injection to give a thrust boost of 550 lb. per engine. Unlike earlier Spey engines the thrust boost from water injection was available even at low temperatures and was not merely a thrust restorer at high temperatures.

The Spey Mk. 512-14DW had been tried and proven in service. In the new 500 Series it provided greatly improved take-off performance.

The Court One-Elevens had been fitted with the new re-contoured wing leading edge and a new range of flap settings that generated greater lift at lower airspeeds. This allowed the airline to carry greater loads out of Luton and other airfields without the use of water injection. The Super One Eleven's operated by Court Line also had interiors which featured face-to-face, non-reclining seating areas over the emergency exit rows to help make best possible use of the space available.

The colours looked good and so very 'right' for a holiday airline, but the paint technology of the day was such that they soon faded in the sun. (Ed Posey/Autair-Court Collection)

In the development of the new image, the airline became increasingly indentified by the holidaying public with Clarksons, which was offering mass travel at the cheap end of the market. In 1972 the airline carried 1.5 million inclusive tour passengers - an increase of 300,000 over the previous year. At one stage over 70% of all flights were for Clarksons, and the tour company was achieving a remarkable 97% load-factor on Court's fleet! Substantial charter work was also being undertaken for Wallace Arnold, Pontinental and others.

The primary concern of Court Line now was simply operating the aircraft, which were all being flown on the long-term charter principal,

so Court's were not overly bothered whether the aircraft flew empty or full - that was the concern of the tour operators, primarily Clarksons.

However, as the aircraft were on long-term charter to Clarksons, it was in Court Line's interests that Clarksons stayed healthy.

Keeping daylight under the wheels...

John Plowman joined Court Line after finishing a Student Apprenticeship at the City University in London, having gained some experience of the One-Eleven while working in the British Aircraft Corporation Service Department at Weybridge...

'I had aspirations of becoming an instant Project Engineer! I was interviewed at Luton in January 1971 by Roy Phillips, who advised me I was probably too young (and inexperienced) to be a Project Engineer and suggested I might be interested in gaining some practical experience as a mechanic, with a view of getting some maintenance qualifications first. After a brief session with Roy

The Court colours and logos were also applied to ground vehicles.

With the introduction of the One-Eleven out in the Caribbean with LIAT Court Line aircraft had to be ferried 'across the pond ' the hard way, for they did not have the range to make the trip direct. This resulted in machines seen in unusual places, as with lilac G-AZEC 'Halcyon Cove', photographed on the snowy ground at Sondrestrom, Greenland by Jon Charley. In the inset are the ferry crew, which included Colin Garner and Dave Anderson on the left and Jim Love on the right. [both Jon Charley].

Phillips I was introduced to the then formidable character of Reggie Tarbox, the Chief Engineer. He proceeded to find out from me everything I knew about the One-Eleven. Just when I thought I did not come up to anywhere near the standard expected for new recruits, Reggie offered me a job as a mechanic in the hangar - starting in a week's time!

I actually began working for Court Line during the most uninteresting part of the year - it was foggy most of the time and there was little flying going on. In fact the whole One-Eleven fleet seemed idle from Monday morning through to Thursday evenings. On that first Monday I reported for work there was not a plane in sight due to fog! Eventually things picked up and I got to work on a 748 during its fleeting return to base between leases - and came into contact with another formidable character, Pete Lang, the Hangar Foreman. I later did a One-Eleven Airframe and Spey Engine course, was transferred to 'The Line' (line maintenance, routine ground checks and fixes out on the apron during aircraft turn-arounds) and finally got my 'A' Licence on the One Eleven.

Strangely, it is 'Fog' that sticks in my mind - I recall one weekend, Stansted, Heathrow and Gatwick were fog-bound, but - unusually - we were open. The airport was inundated with diverted Vanguards, One-Elevens and VC-10s. The Terminal was full and there were even aircraft

parked in the engine running area opposite the Fire Station. Of course, come the morning and the fog started to lift, every crew wanted to start up and leave at exactly the same time, putting much pressure on us working the Line.

Another memorable weekend - in August 1972 I think - it was our turn to be fogged in... for three days! I volunteered during the Friday evening to go up to Castle Donington - East Midlands Airport, where most of our aircraft were going - with Fred Kozo and Jock McCullen to turn-around the One-Elevens.

Passengers were being bussed up the Motorway by our coach company to start their holidays from there. It all worked reasonably normally, although I remember the girls on the check-ins were getting moaned at, and we expected that we would all come home the next day. But the fog didn't lift and later in the day

Court Line engineers - be it in the Engine Shop (top left), Instrument Test Bay (bottom left) or out on the apron at home or abroad (above) life for the staff in engineering department was never easy... [Court Collection]

Passenger ticket and Baggage check
Issued by

D425423

Luton Airport, Bedfordshire

SPECIAL FLIGHT
Passenger Ticket &
Baggage check

court
line

VALID WITH INCLUSIVE
TOUR ARRANGEMENTS ONLY

One of the One-Elevens 'away from home' at Bristol's Lulsgate Airport [Jon Charley]

the same aircraft came back to us and we had to start all over again. By the early hours of Sunday morning we were starting to see most of the fleet for the fourth time that weekend and some aircraft were beginning to need more than just fuel and engine oil. Luckily Fred Kozo had anticipated that some tyres would need replacing and had a few sent up from Luton, along with a number of other spares we were going to need. Finally the fog cleared at Luton and we left Castle Donington late on Sunday afternoon, having missed two night's sleep. I recall going to bed at 7 p.m. and not waking until 7 a.m.

MAXIMISING THE POTENTIAL OF THE BAC ONE-ELEVEN

Court Line Aviation's BAC One-Elevens flew as much, if not more than anyone else. The manufacturers, the British Aircraft Corporation, succeeded by British Aerospace plc and now BAE Systems still have on file the 'monthly returns' for 1973. From these figures it is possible to extrapolate a number of average figures for each month that provide a better idea as to their usage.

The chart below shows the monthly hours flown and the number of landings per aircraft along with the cumulative total of each flown to the start of that year. The last two columns give the total hours for 1973 and the number of flights made. It is clear from these figures that Flight Scheduling were doing a remarkable job, for across the fleet all flew a very similar number of hours and made a similar number of flights!

It should be remembered that the times shown are flying times, not 'chox to chox'. If an average 'on blocks' time is an hour then if G-AXMK was averaging 6.5 flights per day for the whole of August (spending just over 11 hours in the air) then a further six and a half hours are to be added for 'block time'. That did not leave a lot of time for essential maintenance - set at twelve hours a week - or any leeway if things went wrong with the scheduling!

The 'Monthly Returns' - the hours flown and number of landings per aircraft for 1973, as provided by Court Line Aviation to the British Aircraft Corporation, later British Aerospace and even later BAE Systems.

Aircraft	Data to end 72 Hours	Landings	Jan 73 Hours	Landings	Feb 73 Hours	Landings	Mar 73 Hours	Landings	Apr 73 Hours	Landings	May 73 Hours	Landings	Jun 73 Hours	Landings
G-AXMF	8264	4870	175	97	178	98	252	151	260	151	197	112	300	192
G-AXMG	8207	5008	171	96	183	159	228	121	260	152	199	115	243	157
G-AXMH	7880	4629	142	95	139	84	198	97	267	155	237	133	231	133
G-AXMI	7892	4674	172	92	137	74	255	119	270	153	236	133	261	148
G-AXMJ	7806	4442	160	91	153	85	232	125	266	158	227	133	255	142
G-AXMK	7283	5610	147	77	135	78	251	135	274	160	216	117	159	143
G-AXML	7389	4313	148	78	152	83	208	109	272	155	202	114	262	140
G-AYOR	5304	3270	158	111	149	100	219	108	297	164	208	119	279	155
G-AZEB	Leased to LIAT	-	-	-	-	-	-	-	-	-	-	-	-	-
G-AZEC	6581	7530	158	108	155	97	212	115	302	166	182	120	240	142
G-AXLN	7475	5378	134	73	77	43	190	107	293	158	186	122	240	134
VP-LAN	Leased to LIAT	-	-	-	-	-	-	-	-	-	-	-	-	-
G-AXLM	-	-	-	-	-	-	-	-	-	-	-	-	-	-

Aircraft	Jul 73 Hours	Landings	Aug 73 Hours	Landings	Sep 73 Hours	Landings	Oct 73 Hours	Landings	Nov 73 Hours	Landings	Dec 73 Hours	Landings	Tot Flts in 1973	Tot Fh in 197
G-AXMF	331	189	232	152	305	163	236	120	168	89	110	58	2835	1572
G-AXMG	315	180	293	161	283	164	249	118	176	89	150	85	2750	1572
G-AXMH	335	185	276	162	412	168	128	120	185	120	159	87	2709	1539
G-AXMI	310	175	310	177	298	173	219	129	201	97	128	71	2767	154
G-AXMJ	323	186	328	202	296	150	247	130	150	76	166	83	2803	1558
G-AXMK	344	203	335	185	258	149	208	116	207	147	147	78	2781	1578
G-AXML	296	184	330	176	283	158	219	113	166	76	210	108	2744	1494
G-AYOR	298	172	333	190	289	159	156	87	142	108	172	91	2701	1564
G-AZEB	Leased to LIAT	-	-	-	-	-	-	-	-	-	-	-	-	-
G-AZEC	298	169	320	180	317	179	205	115	200	119	To	LIAT	1773	998
G-AXLN	318	180	335	181	Ret to BMA		-	-	-	-	-	-	-	-
VP-LAN	Leased to LIAT	-	-	-	-	-	-	-	-	-	-	-	-	-
G-AXLM	-	-	-	-	9203	6630	224	123	148	71	145	74	517	268

This chart is the extrapolation of the previous data. From the hours flown per month and the number of landings per month it is possible to see that the utilization per month varied, as would be expected given the seasonal nature of the business. It is also possible to see that the average flight time was predominently less than two hours per flight, indicative of the many western Mediterranean destinations. As an indication a Luton-Corfu flight took 3.75 hours, a Luton Gerona flight 1.80 hours.

Furthermore, as 1973 was the year the TriStar was introduced, by understanding that all the One-Elevens G-AXMF - G-AXML were acquired from new in early 1970, it is possible to see if the 1973 utilizations as shown above varied in rough terms from that of previous years by the 'TriStar effect'. This can be done by dividing the previous hours flown by the number of years since new. The figures arrived at are very close to the 1973 ones - therefore it is possible to suggest that the TriStar introduction had little to no effect on individual aircraft usage, although obviously the overall total of One-Elevens in the fleet was reduced to take into account the two 400 seat TriStars.

Key to Chart

FltT = average flight time per sector.　　　　Flts/D = average flights per day
Hrs/D = average flown hours per day.

Aircraft	Data for Jan 73			Data for Feb 73			Data for Mar 73			Data for Apr 73			Data for May 73			Data for Jun 73		
	FltT	Flts/D	Hrs/D	FltT	Flts/D	Hrs/D	FltT	Flts/D	Hrs/D	FltT	Flts/D	Hrs/D	FltT	Flts/D	Hrs/D	FltT	Flts/D	Hrs/D
G-AXMF	1.80	3.13	5.65	1.82	3.50	6.36	1.67	4.87	8.13	1.72	5.03	8.67	1.76	3.61	6.35	1.56	6.4	10.00
G-AXMG	1.78	3.10	5.52	1.15	5.68	6.54	2.35	3.90	7.35	1.71	5.07	8.67	1.73	3.71	6.42	1.77	4.57	8.10
G-AXMH	1.49	3.06	4.58	1.65	5.68	4.96	2.04	3.13	6.39	1.72	5.17	8.90	1.78	4.29	7.65	1.74	4.43	7.70
G-AXMI	1.87	2.97	5.55	1.85	2.64	4.89	1.89	3.84	7.26	1.76	5.10	9.00	1.77	4.29	7.61	1.76	4.93	8.70
G-AXMJ	1.76	2.94	5.16	1.87	2.93	5.46	1.86	4.03	7.48	1.68	5.27	8.87	1.71	4.29	7.32	1.80	4.73	8.50
G-AXMK	1.91	2.48	4.74	1.73	2.79	4.82	2.01	4.03	8.10	1.71	5.33	9.13	1.85	3.77	6.97	1.81	4.77	8.63
G-AXML	1.90	2.52	4.77	1.83	2.96	5.43	1.87	3.52	6.58	1.75	5.17	9.07	1.77	3.68	6.52	1.87	4.67	8.73
G-AYOR	1.42	3.58	5.10	1.49	3.57	5.32	2.03	3.48	7.06	1.82	5.47	9.93	1.75	3.84	6.71	1.80	5.17	9.30
G-AZEB	Leased to LIAT			-	-	-	-	-	-	-	-	-	-	-	-	-	-	-
G-AZEC	1.46	2.35	4.32	1.79	1.54	2.75	1.78	3.45	6.13	1.82	5.53	10.07	1.52	3.87	5.87	1.69	4.47	8.00
G-AXLN	1.84	2.35	4.32	1.79	1.54	2.75	1.78	3.45	6.13	1.85	5.27	9.77	1.52	3.94	6.00	1.79	4.47	8.00
VP-LAN	Leased to LIAT			-	-	-	-	-	-	-	-	-	-	-	-	-	-	-
G-AXLM	-	-	-															
Totals	17.2	29.6	50.5	16.7	34.7	52.1	19.3	38.0	71.3	17.6	52.4	92.3	17.2	43.0	67.4	17.6	48.9	85.7
Average	1.72	2.96	5.05	1.68	3.48	5.21	1.93	3.80	7.13	1.76	5.24	9.23	1.72	4.30	6.74	1.76	4.89	8.57

Aircraft	Data for Jul 73			Data for Aug 73			Data for Sep 73			Data for Oct 73			Data for Nov 73			Data for Dec 73		
	FltT	Flts/D	Hrs/D	FltT	Flts/D	Hrs/D	FltT	Flts/D	Hrs/D	FltT	Flts/D	Hrs/D	FltT	Flts/D	Hrs/D	FltT	Flts/D	Hrs/D
G-AXMF	1.75	6.10	10.68	2.13	4.90	10.42	1.87	5.43	10.17	1.97	3.87	8.03	1.89	2.97	5.60	1.90	1.87	3.55
G-AXMG	1.75	5.81	10.68	1.82	5.19	9.45	1.73	5.47	9.43	2.11	3.81	8.03	1.98	2.97	5.87	1.76	2.74	4.84
G-AXMH	1.81	5.97	10.81	1.70	5.23	8.90	2.45	5.60	13.73	1.07	3.87	4.13	1.54	4.00	6.17	1.83	2.81	5.13
G-AXMI	1.77	5.65	10.00	1.75	5.71	10.00	1.72	5.77	9.93	1.70	4.16	7.06	2.07	3.23	4.70	1.80	2.29	4.13
G-AXMJ	1.74	6.00	10.42	1.62	6.52	10.58	1.97	5.00	9.87	1.90	4.19	7.97	1.97	2.53	5.00	2.00	2.68	5.35
G-AXMK	1.69	6.55	11.10	1.81	5.97	10.81	1.73	4.97	8.61	1.79	3.74	6.71	1.41	4.90	6.90	1.88	2.52	4.74
G-AXML	1.61	5.94	9.55	1.88	5.68	10.65	1.79	5.27	9.43	1.94	3.65	7.06	2.18	2.53	5.53	1.94	3.48	6.77
G-AYOR	1.73	5.55	9.61	1.75	6.13	10.74	1.82	5.30	9.63	1.79	2.81	5.03	1.31	3.60	4.73	1.89	2.94	5.55
G-AZEB	Leased to LIAT			-	-	-	-	-	-	-	-	-	-	-	-	-	-	-
G-AZEC	1.76	5.45	9.61	1.78	5.81	10.32	1.77	5.97	10.57	1.78	3.71	6.61	1.68	3.97	6.67	To		LIAT
G-AXLN	1.77	5.81	10.26	1.85	5.84	10.81	Ret to BMA			-	-	-	-	-	-	-	-	-
VP-LAN	Leased to LIAT			-	-	-	-	-	-	-	-	-	-	-	-	-	-	-
G-AXLM	-	-	-	-	-	-	-	-	-	1.82	3.97	7.23	2.08	2.37	4.93	1.96	2.39	4.68
Totals	17.3	56.9	102.7	18.1	48.8	102.7	16.9	48.8	91.4	17.8	37.7	67.8	18.1	33.1	58.1	17.0	23.8	44.8
Average	1.73	5.69	10.27	1.81	4.88	10.27	1.69	4.88	9.14	1.78	2.77	6.78	1.81	3.31	5.81	1.70	2.38	4.48

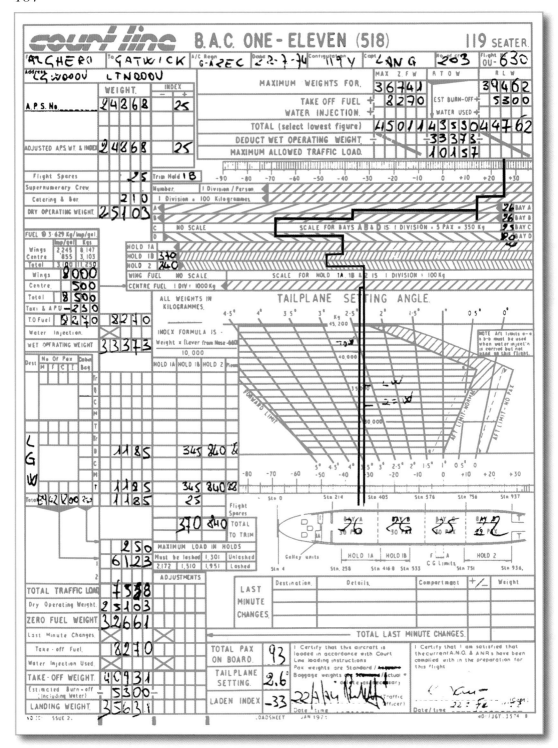

A Court Line Aviation One-Eleven 500 loadsheet for Flight OU630 from Alghero to London Gatwick under the command of Captain Kurt Lang on 22 July 1974, using aircraft G-AZEC.

One Eleven G-AXMH and G-AXMG are seen in slightly different liveries with the 'three Cs' Court logo in place of the Clarksons emblem on the fin. 'MH wearing it in a circle, 'MG wearing it plain!.

Monday morning, still feeling exhausted - and all for one day's overtime!

Incidents and accidents.

Remarkably, througout the entire history of both Autair and Court Line, there were very few accidents, despite the intensity of flying this must say much for the airline's high quality of personnel standards and operating procedures. There were incidents though; Kathy Lloyd remembers 'her' emergency landing..

'I was a No.3, and we had been to Italy to pick up a load of returning holidaymakers. We approached Luton in the evening, and the weather was pretty grim with strong winds and heavy rain. The closer we got to the airport, the more we were thrown around. We touched down, bounced, then landed again. Reverse thrust did not slow us. The No.1 and I sat clutching each other on the forward jump-seat by the galley and we finally turned right around and

AC 1-11 seating plan

Passengers

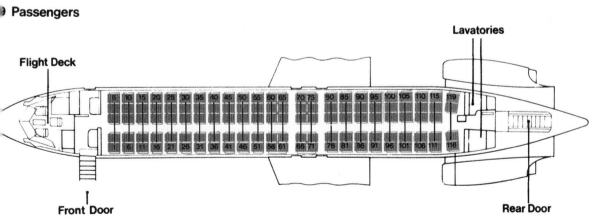

ended up on the grass just a few yards from Vauxhall Motors - it was a close thing!

> *Due to demand, One Eleven G-AXLN was leased from British Midland Airways for a time (author).*

The fire service arrived promptly and we were able to de-plane the passengers onto coaches for the short drive to the terminal. Remarkably, most of the passengers - although elderly - remained perfectly calm and collected throughout, treating the experience of pirouetting down the runway as perfectly normal! As far as I can remember, what happened was that we aquaplaned heavily on landing, then burst all the tyres'.

Sadly, there was another One-Eleven incident which, although causing no injuries to passengers or crew, did incur a fatality. Anthony Nice was a Flight Dispatcher at Luton and vividly remembers the event:

> *'It was early in 1974, One-Eleven G-AXMJ - a green one - was due to take a party of schoolchildren and their teachers for a short ski-break to Munich. Runway 08 was in use, but due to the curvature of the ground it was built on, the 26 end could not be seen from the 08 end. With 'MJ on the runway and turning round on the 08 turning circle, an Aztec - G-AYDE - operated by McAlpine Aviation taxied onto the runway close to the 26 end without Air Traffic clearance. Without a radio call from the Aztec and the bump in the middle of the runway, the crew of 'MJ were not aware of the Aztec until well into their take-off roll. Mike Juliet's pilot tried to lift the port wing over the top of the Aztec, but the wing struck the cockpit, killing the Aztec's pilot, but missing his passenger, who saw the One-Eleven coming at the last moment and ducked.*
>
> *The One-Eleven was brought to a halt amidst a fuel spill brought about by the Aztec's propeller slicing into the wing, and the children were evacuated.'*

The subsiquent inquiry into the accident revealed far greater details. Flight OU95 was from Luton, to Munich-Riem, West Germany. At 15:19 Greenwich Mean Time on 18 April 1974, the One-Eleven received permission to taxi to holding point Delta where it was to await clearance. At 15:24 GMT, permission was granted for the One-Eleven to enter runway 08/26 and backtrack along Runway 08, where the aircraft was to hold at the threshold awaiting permission to take off. The One-Eleven reported it was entering Runway 08/26 between 15:25:14 and 15:25:23. At 15:25:32, the Aztec reported that it was ready to taxi. Information was given to the pilot of the Aztec that the wind was from 300° at 10 knots and the pilot was offered a choice of runway 08 or runway 26 for take-off. He chose to take off from runway 26. At about 15:26, the Aztec was instructed 'Cleared to Alpha Two Six'. This was non-standard phraseology; the correct instruction should have been 'Cleared to holding point Alpha, Runway Two Six'. This was a causal factor in the accident. In the meantime, the One-Eleven had received clearance to take off at 15:25:24 and reported that it was rolling at 15:27:31. At 15:27:49, the Aztec was asked to report when it was ready for take-off, to which the reply was that it would be ready in 30 seconds' time.

The Aztec then entered the active runway. The passenger on board the Aztec, who was a pilot himself, queried the pilot via the intercom as to whether or not the aircraft had been cleared to enter the runway. He did not receive an answer, and by this time the aircraft had entered the runway. At this point, the One-Eleven had reached a speed of 100 knots during its take-off run. The first officer was flying the aircraft at the time. The commander, seeing the Aztec enter the runway from the left and realising it was not going to stop, took control of the aircraft. He fully opened both throttles and steered the aircraft to the right whilst attempting to lift the port wing over the Aztec. The passenger in the Aztec saw the One-Eleven approaching and ducked before the collision occurred, but was unable to warn the pilot of the impending collision. The port wing of the One-Eleven sliced through the cabin of the Aztec, killing the pilot instantly and injuring the passenger. The Aztec lost the top of the cabin and its propellers were damaged, while the outer twenty feet of the One-Eleven's port wing was substantially damaged, resulting in fuel leaking from the tank contained therein. Use of full reverse thrust and maximum braking enabled the take-off to be successfully aborted within the remaining runway length, with the damaged One-Eleven stopping 820 yards beyond the point of collision.

G-AXMJ, the One Eleven that was involved in the accident at Luton. (Simon Peters Collection)

As there was a risk of fire from the leaking fuel, the commander ordered an emergency evacuation of the aircraft. Although the rear doors opened as intended and the evacuation slides deployed, both forward doors required considerable force to open them before all on board could evacuate the aircraft. No injuries were sustained in the evacuation. The investigation subsequently was able to replicate the difficulty in opening both forward doors on the One-Eleven. It was discovered that inadequate guidance from the manufacturer of the escape slides meant that they were incorrectly stowed. Alongside this, one door had an incorrect part fitted.

Keeping the Kids Happy

Even in the 1970s, it was still a time when travelling by air was very much a new experience for many people. The expectant passengers had not yet got out of the habit of dressing up in their 'Sunday best' when turning up at the airport. It was definitely not a time for trainers, demin and hoodies or shell-suits! Parents, let alone their children, used to get excited about the prospect of flying, indeed, many were flying for the first time and so holidaymakers travelling with their children could be a handful, especially in the close confines of a fully-loaded, high-density Court One- Eleven passenger cabin at the peak of the holiday season.

Certainly the duty-free drinks helped keep the parents occupied, but something else was needed to keep the children amused, as Maureen Bone recalls...

'We used to have a children's pack on board that we used to give out to the children when we were in the air to

Right: A montage of images taken from the printed sheets provided in the children 's pack' as recalled by Maureen Bone.

The photograph on the left comes from Peter Murdoch, the packs designer, and shows a young Court Line passenger playing 'dress the Air Hostess'

It was, in the words of the company a way of providing 'Personal service all the way - including a special package of gifts for every child on the return flight.'
(Ed Posey/Court Collection)

Court Line

hopefully keep them amused and keep them from running in the aisle and getting under our feet when serving drinks and duty frees.

It was only a series of push-out figures and planes made out of card; they could dress a hostess figure in winter or summer uniforms, make up a card aeroplane model or play an airport game.

It was all very simple compared to today's computer games, but kept them happy for a while so we could get on with our work'.

Guatemala interlude! Below: G-AXMK in Aviateca markings at Luton before departure.

Below left: Inside 'La Papaya' TG-ARA, alias G-AXMK 'Halcyon Star'. Aviateca Chief Hostess Cristabel Reiche West (left) Eugenie (Sherry) Ponce and Veronica Legrand (right).

Below right: 'La Papaya' TG-ARA with Aviateca hostesses Susie, Lucrecia and Cristabel with Capt Henry Phyo and First Officers Jim Love and Phil Robin. [all Cristabel Reiche West/Sandy Keegan]

A Long Way From Home

During the autumn of 1970 another opportunity arose under somewhat strange circumstances whereby Court Line could temporarily off-load some of their spare winter capacity, when orange One-Eleven, G-AXMK 'Halcyon Star' was wet-leased as TG-ARA to Empresa Guatemalteca de Aviacion SA, known as Aviateca-Guatemala. The lease was a 'stop-gap' until their own aircraft, TG-AZA, arrived in March 1971.

Cristabel Reiche West was the Senior Hostess with Aviateca...

'My airline had an agreement with Lufthansa who were going

Right: When working for any airline friends are often made all around the world. Aviateca Chief Hostess Cristabel Reiche West (left) and Lucrecia - 'Lucky'- Rodriguez Ovando who both flew on Mike Kilo during the lease, visit Court Hostess Maggie Taylor in England a year after the 'La Papaya' lease was over.

Below: TG-ARA 'El Papaya' taxies out onto the runway away from the terminal at the Aeropuerto La Aurora, Guatemala City. The Aqua volcano can be seen in the background. [all Cristabel Reiche West/ Sandy Keegan]

to introduce modern jet equipment to Guatemala. Up to then we had been using DC-3s, DC-6s and Convairs. With great anticipation myself and eleven of our hostesses transferred to Frankfurt, Germany for training on the Boeing 707A/B, but halfway through the training an unfortunate international incident occurred when the German Ambassador to Guatemala was killed, thus ending diplomatic relations and co-operation between the two countries for a while.

Court Line Aviation immediately stepped in, made a careful analysis of the situation and presented a viable plan, which not only changed the lives of our travellers, but also the colours in Guatemalan skies as well!

To go with the new aircraft there were other changes as well, including a new uniform - orange of course! For me, the opportunity of making new friends and exchanging ideas was

a beautiful experience. The crews were professional and refined and I made some life-long friends. It was from them in off duty moments learned to say 'bloody fool' and pick up the habit of drinking tea! At the end of the lease - just before everyone all returned home to the UK we had a big party around my house - a house that is also just memories now, for that was destroyed in the 1976 earthquake!'

The One-Eleven was a generational step up for the Central American airline and caused a stir wherever it appeared. A number of Court staff went out to Guatemala City with the aircraft. One of these was Sandy Keegan (neé Smith)...

'As I remember there was Captains Viv Webster, Henry Phyo, Colin Dawson and John Ditmus, First Officers Jim Love, Phillip Robin and Nick Carter. The Hostesses were myself, Maggie Taylor (neé Houseman) and Jenny Berryman (neé Taylor). Operations Officer Len Butterworth was also with us.

On arrival our aircraft was immediately nicknamed 'La Papaya' by the locals, after the tropical fruit of a similar colour!

We flew scheduled services, mainly to Miami and New Orleans from Guatemala's La Aurora Airport. All our flights were usually late departing from the gate as the check-in never closed while there were still passengers arriving for the flight. The busiest period was around Christmas when the passengers were mainly Guatemalans going to Miami shopping for goods not readily available at affordable prices at home. It was not unusual to see passengers trying to board with a television or other large items of electrical equipment under their arms!

Business diversification and a Simulator Centre.

It was time to launch yet another venture - the Court Line Executive Fleet. Private air charter was a growing market and the company's experience going back into the 1960s placed it in a good position to exploit the need.

Three aircraft were on offer; a 500 mph, 1,000 mile range six-seat HS125 jet G-AVRG, used by (amongst others) Edward Heath during his unsuccessful 1974 election campaign and John Young for his trips home to Devon; a twin-engined, four to six-seat Piper Navajo G-AYEI that was mainly used for crew positioning, and Bell Jet-Ranger Helicopter G-AXMM. A further aerial device used by the company to great effect was G-BAND, the Court Line balloon, used as a promotional item, flying around the country at garden fetes and other events. As the Court Line Aviation brochure said about corporate use:

In the growing field of private aircraft leasing for executive travel, Court Line offer the very compelling advantage that flying is their full-time business.

The executive fleet comprises a range of aircraft selected and

Much of Court Line Aviation's promotional and advertising material revolved around variations of clever use of the corporate 'C' logo, as used in this design for their corporate and executive fleet.

The 'theme' always involved three sections divided by a white line, either vertical of horizontal, sometimes following the design of the complete - or almost complete letter as seen here.
(Ed Posey/Autair-Court Collection)

professionally styled to meet the varying needs of executive use. All are maintained and crewed to the high professional standards on which Court Line Aviation have established their reputation.

For the best in private jet travel, there's the HS 125. Cruising comfortably at over 500 mph, it can carry up to 6 passengers in spacious luxury-non-stop to practically any airport within a 1,450 miles radius.

For intermediate distances and a wider choice of landing strips, Court Line's Piper turbo Navajo B is the 240 mph inter-city express. Ideal for trips of 150 to 500 miles, it has a non-stop cruising range of up to 920 miles if required.

For the shortest travel between two points, the Court Line Jet Ranger flies at up to 115 mph from virtually anywhere to anywhere. The world's most advanced helicopter, it seats up to 4 passengers in quiet comfort.

Any or all of the specialist expertise that goes into the operation of this executive fleet can be made available for privately owned planes. Court Line Aviation's leasing experience includes the provision of trained maintenance men, engineers and pilots to private aircraft owners.

By the summer of 1972 the fleet expanded to twelve One-Elevens, the extra aircraft bringing in a new lilac version of the established colour scheme. Apart from the normal holiday charters, extra business was picked up flying UK Service personnel and their dependants to and from Berlin on behalf of the General Officer Commanding the British Sector of that then partitioned city. Thirty-five One-Eleven round trips in all took place despite angry objections

from British European Airways who complained that their scheduled services would suffer.

With operating such a large fleet and with the imminent introduction of another type due, the company had to consider its aircrew training methods.

Since first taking delivery of the One-Eleven, all flight-deck simulator training had been done in Dublin - the cost and safety benefits of using such training facilities was not lost on the Board, and so it was not surprising that in the autumn of 1972 the company announced that it was building its own complex at Luton. The building housed a single One Eleven and single TriStar simulator, each fitted with a visual attachment to allow crews to practice visual take-offs and landings in both day and night-time conditions.

It was hoped that when complete, the complex would become a focus for other airlines who operated examples of the types - these operators could buy 'time' on Court's machines, thus making the complex even more financially viable.

The One-Eleven simulator was up and working by the end of the year - the TriStar machine working ahead of the introduction of the type in service.

Left: the artist's impression of the new Court Line Flight Simulator complex with One-Eleven on the left and TriStar on the right.

Each device was fitted with projected visual displays, generated by clever optics from the vertical 'map' as shown above.
[Peter Murdoch]

Chapter Nine
Enter The TriStar!

Court Line Aviation established an aircraft evaluation group in the mid-1960s to monitor possible future acquisitions. Membership of the group changed over the years, but it always included representatives of Court Line Aviation and Clarksons Holidays.

By the late 1960s Court Line were contemplating a significant expansion of its airline activities and the Board was told that if the planned growth rate was to be achieved, a fleet of eighteen BAC One-Elevens would be required by 1975. There were serious operating disadvantages in utilising such a large number of aircraft and consequently a larger, and therefore more efficient type was sought.

In February 1969 the evaluation group considered a report from Stratford and Lumb (Aviation Consultants) who had been asked to make a recommendation to meet Court Line Aviation's requirements for a long-range aircraft which could be employed on services to the Caribbean. They suggested the McDonnell Douglas 250-seat DC8-63, but this was rejected.

In January 1970 Lockheed Aircraft submitted proposals for their L-1011 design (known also and spelt in Court Line use as the TriStar) which was then under development, powered by three also undeveloped Rolls-Royce RB.211 engines. In June 1970 the evaluation group presented a detailed study to the Court Line Board,

The concept of Court Line Airbuses reached at least as far as the model stage - the shape of the A300 Airbus seemed to suit the Court Line colour scheme.
[Vince Hemmings]

comparing the TriStar with the Boeing B.720, a four-engined long-range design based on their highly successful B.707 that was only available in small numbers on the second-hand market. Other aircraft types were considered - there are indications that two other Boeing products, the 727-200 of around 170 seats and the 737-200 with around 140 seats were at least tentatively investigated, as was the Airbus Industrie A300B which was looked at but eliminated - it would be available too late, had limited range, and had a 90-minute maximum over-water restriction placed on twin-engined passenger aircraft - these were the days before ETOPS (Extended Twin Operations).

The McDonnell Douglas DC-10 configured for 378 seats was also considered but, Court Line considered, when the perfomance figures were placed alongside the TriStar figures with 400 seats, that the DC-10 was technically inferior for the task required.

The Lockheed L-1011 TriStar, commonly referred to as the L-1011 (pronounced 'Ell-ten-eleven) or TriStar, was a medium-to-long-range, wide-body trijet airliner. It was the third widebody airliner to enter commercial operations, after the Boeing 747 and the McDonnell Douglas DC-10. The aircraft had a seating capacity of up to 400 passengers and a range of over 4,000 nautical miles. Its trijet configuration placed one Rolls-Royce RB211 engine under each wing, with a third, center-mounted RB211 engine with an S-duct air inlet embedded in the tail and the upper fuselage. The aircraft had an

The first two Lockheed L-1011 Tristars fly in formation over Southern California. The first L-1011 (at left) made its maiden flight 16 November 1970 and the second aircraft joined the test program 15 February 1971. Following completion of the test flight series and certification by the U.S. Federal Aviation Administration, Tristars were intended to enter commercial service in 1972. (Lockheed Aircraft Corp)

autoland capability, an automated descent control system, and lower deck galley and lounge facilities.

Therefore the recommendation before the Board was for two TriStars to be ordered for delivery in the Spring of 1972, with options taken on a further three machines to be delivered later. These aircraft were to be configured with 400 economy class seats and were to be capable of reaching the Caribbean from the United Kingdom with just one refuelling stop. With this delivery date, Court Line would be the first airline to operate the type outside the USA.

Before a final decision was made, John Young and Ed Posey from Court Line and Tom Gullick and Donald McQueen from Clarksons crossed the Atlantic to visit Lockheed's Burbank and Palmdale sites to see the aircraft 'for real'. On 23 June 1970 the four were shown around the Sales Centre, and a number of mock-ups (including a main cabin section and underfloor galley), before being taken out to Palmdale to see the prototype and early production examples under construction.

A Group Board meeting on 2 July 1970 endorsed the recommendation, and recorded that a letter of intent had been signed accordingly. The price quoted per aircraft was US$ 15,410,274 of which US$420,000 was required as a deposit. The same day a highly

Lockheed offered the L-1011 Tristar with a number of interior configurations as shown here in this first class area mock-up. This included a six-abreast first class cabin that included swivel chairs and cocktail tables between the two wide isles. In standard airline configuration, the aircraft was intended to carry 256 passengers - in Court Line service the plan was to carry 400! [Lockheed Aircraft Corp]

On 23 June 1970 John Young (2nd left) Ed Posey (3rd left) from Court Line and Donald McQueen (1st left) and Tom Gullick (4th left) from Clarksons visited Lockheed-California Company's Burbank and Palmdale facilities, which were involved in the design, construction and sale of their L-101l TriStar design. Here the team are shown around the Sales Centre at Burbank with some of the finer points of the main cabin being pointed out by Lockheed staff [Lockheed]

significant event occurred. Clarksons Holidays signed a five year flying agreement with Court Line Aviation.

The financial package was still being negotiated in February 1971 when engine maker Rolls-Royce was placed in the hands of the Receiver and RB211 development, let alone production, seemed extremely uncertain. Hard on the heels of that problem came persistent rumours that Lockheed's financial position was highly uncertain. This halted L-1011 final assembly and Lockheed investigated the possibility of a US engine supplier, but by then it was considered too late to change.

The UK government agreed to approve a large state subsidy to restart Rolls-Royce operations on condition the U.S. government guarantee repayment of $195 million in bank loans Lockheed needed to complete the L-1011 project. Despite some opposition, not least from the then Governor of California, Ronald Reagan, the US

The interior layout of Court's TriStars - the then highest density ever used on the type.

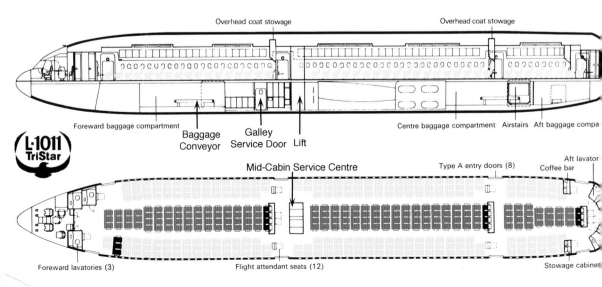

Overhead coat stowage   Overhead coat stowage

Foreward baggage compartment   Baggage Conveyor   Galley Service Door   Lift   Centre baggage compartment   Airstairs   Aft baggage compa

L·1011 TriStar

Mid-Cabin Service Centre   Type A entry doors (8)   Aft lavator   Coffee bar

Foreward lavatories (3)   Flight attendant seats (12)   Stowage cabinet

Here in wonderful downtown
Burbank...

Above (l. to r.): John Young, Tom
Gullick, Ed Posey and Donald
McQueen in what became almost a
standard 'pose' to demonstrate the
width of the main cabin mock-up at
Burbank.

Left: the British team investigate the
underfloor galley mock-up.
[all Lockheed photos].

Ed Posey (standing) and John Young
(seated) discuss aspects of the
L-1011's mock-up interior with
Lockheed salesmen.

The coach cabin mock-up featured
eight-abreast seating with two aisles.
Centre dividers could hold four coats
on hangers. The almost flat ceiling
was nearly eight feet above the floor.

The team from Court Line and Clarksons are dwarfed by the prototype L-1011 TriStar then under construction. [Lockheed photos].

government provided these guarantees. For the rest of the RB211 project, Rolls-Royce remained a government-owned company.

Financial negotiations were suspended, and in the following month a re-evaluation of the overall position occurred. The Aircraft Evaluation Group produced reports in July, August and October 1971, during which it appears that all possible alternatives were considered.

By October the Lockheed and Rolls-Royce financial situations had been favourably resolved and the TriStar and RB211 continued in production, both with an initial reduction in performance and increase in costs.

Court Line Aviation affirmed their choice of the TriStar with a revised letter of intent being signed with Lockheed on 27 October 1971. The letter indicated that the first two machines would now cost US$15,811,126, be subject to escalation factors and would be delivered in February and March 1973. Options on a further three machines were still in hand for 1974/5 delivery. As part of the deal, Lockheed would place US$3 million worth of TriStar spares at Luton Airport at its own expense.

By this time an agreement contained in a letter dated 30 September 1971 for the provision of aircraft capacity was entered into between Clarksons Holidays and Court Line Aviation. This was superceded by a formal agreement dated 29 February 1972 which committed Court to provide Clarksons Holidays with exclusive use of two TriStars for the seven summer months - April to October - for the five years 1973-1977 inclusive. Then, on 27 July Court Line reserved the British registration letters G-BAAA and G-BAAB for the pair of TriStars, the same day incidentally as the next aircraft in the sequence, G-BAAC - though this was for a lowly Cessna 150 - the comparison could not have been more different!

Formal contracts for the first two aircraft were not signed until 17 August 1972 due to further financing difficulties. By now the basic price had increased to US$19.7 million. Both machines would be acquired on long-term lease from Airlease International, a partnership

Sign on the dotted line... Left to Right: Edward Posey, Managing Director of Court Line Aviation; John Young, Managing Director of Court Line Group; Dan Haughton, Chairman Lockheed Aircraft Corp; Lord Cole, Chairman of Rolls-Royce and Robert Sowter, Managing Director of Airlease International, conclude the deal for the lease of a pair of Tristars with options on three more. [Court Collection]

of eleven British banks and financial institutions; The Bank of Scotland, Barclays Bank Ltd, Barclays Bank International Ltd, Brown Shipley & Co Ltd, Kleinwort Benson Ltd, Lazard Brothers & Co Ltd, Lloyds Bank Ltd, Midland Bank Finance Corp. Ltd, Morgan Grenfell & Co Ltd, National Westminster Bank Ltd and the Commerical Union Assurance Co. Ltd.

The first production L-1011 demonstrator aircraft - N305EA, wearing a partial Eastern Airlines colour scheme but with Court Line titling on the port side and the familiar stylised Clarkson 'C' on the starboard and the name '*Halcyon Days*' on the nose - visited Luton airport to acquaint the airline staff, airport management and tour operators with the new equipment.

The demonstrator's imminent arrival was reported in issue 4 of *Court Line News*, the staff newspaper published in April 1972.

After much speculation it has now been confirmed that a Lockheed TriStar will visit Court Line at Luton Airport this summer.

The aircraft will stay for three days en route to the Farnborough Air Show where it will be on general public display. This aircraft will be in the Eastern livery but with our 'Court' insignia. For those of you who wish to view the arrival of the first wide bodied jet into Luton, the ETA will be approximately 1400 hours on Sunday 13th August 1972.

During its three day visit, the aircraft will make several flights in and around the U.K. for Court Line. These movements will take into account evaluation required by various departments who will be concerned with the handling of the TriStar.

During the visit the aircraft will be available for Court Line personnel to inspect. The TriStar will leave Luton on Wednesday evening 16th August 1972.

This 'familiarisation' visit to the airline's base included a celebration dinner in Palma, Majorca, as Doug Bennison of the British Airline Pilots Association, who was one of the guests, recalls:

'The event, billed as the inaugural flight by Lockheed TriStar to Palma, Majorca, was intended to mark the publication of the first Clarkson inclusive tour programme to feature this new

Two 'test birds'. On the left is the structurally complete L-1011 fatigue test rig. On the right is a partially complete TriStar that underwent static testing. (Lockheed Aircraft Corp).

The famous 'first image' of the Court Line TriStar. In fact it's an artwork/model.

aircraft. We were requested to be at a special marquee by the Court offices at Luton Airport by 1530hrs on Monday August 14th 1972, for a 1600hrs departure. The flight out to Palma was aboard the Eastern Airlines aircraft flown by a Lockheed crew under Captain J. D. Wells. Having been wined and dined to perfection, we were back at Luton by 23.30. A better aircraft could not have been chosen, for the demonstrator was only fitted with 230 seats - spaciousness indeed!'

All the guests were invited to inspect every aspect of the new aircraft, including open access to the Flight Deck, where an etched notice on a panel at the Engineers Station was brought to everyone's attention by the flight deck crew. It read *'Achtung alles lookenspeepers! Das machinen is nicht fur gefingerpoken und mitten grabben. Is easy schnappen der springenwerk, bloen fusen, und poppen corken mit spittsensparken. Is nicht fur gewerken by das dummkopfen. Das rubbernecken sightseeren keepen hands in das pockets - relaxen und watch das blinken lights'.*

The TriStar demonstrator also visited other airports around the country; Gatwick, Newcastle, Birmingham, Heathrow and Manchester. The demonstrator then went on to participate in the 1972 Farnborough Air Show. Much was made of Court Line's latest acquisition, as Court Line Chairman The Hon W.S. Phillips CBE said at the time...

'The first two will be delivered in the Spring of 1973 - Court Line expects to fly nearly two million inclusive tour passengers that year - and enter service on 1st April.

They are to be powered by the Rolls Royce RB211, a new

ABOVE: N305EA at Luton, ready for the flight to Palma. (Ed Posey/Autair-Court Collection)

Court Line girls, Eastern Airlines aircraft on Lockheed demonstration work, with BOAC steps - oh, and the location is Manchester! (Ed Posey/Autair-Court Collection)

generation of jet engine specially designed for quiet operation.
   The TriStar will give Court Line more than double the range of its existing fleet. All the major holiday centres in Europe, the East Mediterranean and North Africa will be within the non-stop capabilities of the TriStar and even the Caribbean can be reached with just one refuelling stop in the Azores'

The eventual acquisition of the TriStars was by way of a fifteen year leasing contract entered into with Airlease International Management completed on 22 February 1973, which involved rental payments for both aircraft of some £1,950,000 for the first two years and £2,451,000 for the remaining thirteen. Negotiations for the remaining aircraft on option would take place later.

   The first of the Court Line TriStars - in the yellow scheme - had been christened *'Halcyon Days'* by Michael Heseltine in a ceremony at Lockeed's Palmdale facility on 8 January 1973. A month later - on 9 February - and just twelve days after its first flight, Dennis R.

*Two views of Lockheed's
L-1011 demonstrator as
used for, amongst other
things, the 1972
Farnborough Air Show.*

*N305EA is surrounded
by employees and
invited guests at Luton
as they queue to view its
spacious interior.*

*From Court Line News
comes these two pictures.
Above: The entrance to
the tented Departure
Lounge can be seen on
the left staffed by Marilyn
McConnel, Pauline
Playford and Chriss
Enstone.*

*Below: Arriving for
dinner in Palma.*

Murrin of the Civil Aviation Authority presented the certificate that
permitted operation of the 400-seat in the U.K. to the president of
Lockheed-California, Bob Fuhrman. At the time this was the highest-
capacity TriStar built.

Preparing the ground...

Numerous Court Line personnel had been working hard behind the
scenes to get the TriStars into service; Maurice Rowan became
Projects Director and, although having to retire early from full-time
work, still remained as a consultant. The Evaluation Team now
found more and more people becoming involved. Pilots underwent
training, John Plowman transferred to the Project Office and found
himself undergoing courses on the L-1011 and RB211, followed by
the first of many trips to the USA, this one to visit Eastern Airlines
in Miami to discuss maintenance tooling requirements. Eastern was
expected to be the prime overhaul agency for Court's TriStar
components.

John Allen was out in Palmdale as company representative, with
a number of other personnel - such as Engineer Pete Hart - visiting
on a regular basis. Meanwhile a number of cabin staff visited Eastern
Airlines to train with them to be qualified as Instructors when they
returned to Luton. Six days after the leasing arrangements had been
completed, at 08.09 Pacific Time on 28 February, John Allan, on
behalf of Court Line Aviation took delivery of the first aircraft, hull

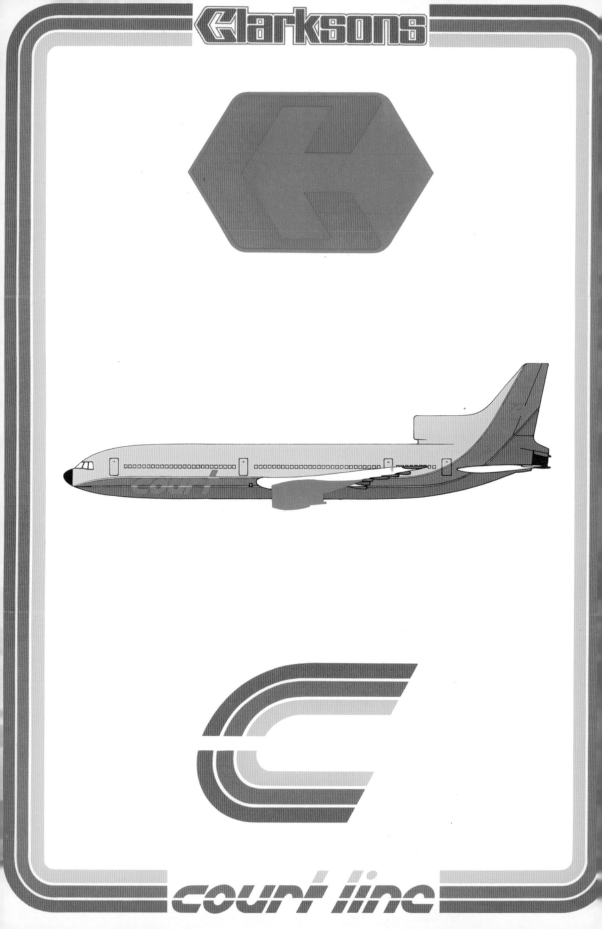

Inaugural
TriStar
flight to
Palma

The Directors of Court Line and Clarksons Holidays invite

E. J. Posey Esq

on the inaugural flight by Lockheed TriStar to Palma, Majorca,
on Monday, August 14th, 1972.
The event marks publication of the first Clarksons
inclusive holiday programme to feature this new Court Line aircraft,
which enters service in the Spring of 1973.

You are requested to be at Luton Airport by 15.30
to enable us to depart for Palma at 16.00.
Boarding will take place from the special marquee
positioned near the Court Line Aviation offices.
We look forward to entertaining you at a celebration dinner in Palma
after which we plan to leave at approximately 21.30
to arrive back at Luton Airport by 23.30.

Flight boarding card and details of special car parking
at Luton and return transport to Central/West London
will be sent following your acceptance on the enclosed card.

RSVP

The fuselage production line at Lockheed Palmdale.

number 1024, registered G-BAAA. The bill of sale was for US$19,771,819.

Now registered G-BAAA, the TriStar arrived at Luton on 5 March 1973 in the hands of Captains Peter Hogg and Len Prudence, having crossed the USA and Atlantic via Bangor, Maine. Welcoming the new machine to Luton, John Young said it was:

> '...a magnificent new aircraft. It has meant over two years of detailed planning and a total investment of approximately $55 million, to reach the stage where we can offer the latest in wide-bodied travel to the British holidaymaker'.

Court Line Aviation Managing Director Ed Posey elected to present a slightly different viewpoint of the TriStar to the public - his comments stressed the environmental and good neighbourly aspects, for nobody could call the One-Elevens quiet:

> 'I am convinced that this aircraft is going to add a new dimension to holiday travel as we know it today. They are going to be the most socially acceptable jets flying anywhere today.
>
> They will cut the number of movements needed to fly 400 passengers because one TriStar is equal to three and a half of our present BAC One-Elevens. In addition, TriStar is powered by Rolls-Royce RB.2-11s, the quietest jet engines in commercial service in the world.
>
> Even with 400 passengers, the TriStar also has a two-inch better seat-pitch than the One-Eleven. People can also walk up one aisle and down the other.

In order to thoroughly test the self-contained airstairs as ordered by Court Line, Lockheed built a fully-functioning test rig at Palmdale even going to the extreme of painting it in Court Line colours!

As can be seen, the system was installed under the main floor, and when required was extended first out, and then moved to the left into position under the door before fully extending outwards. Once in the correct position, the handrails rose upwards. [all Lockheed Aircraft Corp]

PICTURES FROM PALMDALE!

The Paint Shop at Lockheed Palmdale contained a moving platform with eight working positions that allowed the entire fuselage to be sprayed at once after it had been masked off.

The fuselage of Alpha Alpha is moved from the spray-booth back into the assembly shop ready for installation of wings and tail.

The second machine, hull number 1032 and registered G-BAAB, joined the fleet soon after, in time for the summer season. This aircraft cost US$19,857,050.

Alpha Bravo was named '*Halcyon Breeze*' by the airline, although the moment the flight-line crews at Lockheed saw the three-tone pink paint scheme, it was immediately dubbed '*The Pink Lady*'.

The delivery flight of Alpha Alpha from Palmdale to Luton was itself a record. Both aircraft were the first to be equipped with an Advanced Automatic Navigation System (AANS) and an Internal Sensor system (ISS) that allowed an optimum Great Circle Track to be calculated and flown between any two points on the globe.

With the Palmdale to Luton flightplan data stored on the computer, the autopilot automatically flew the aircraft from lift-off to touch-down, the navigation systems continually refering to radio navigation aids, geographic waypoints and the ISS.

According to the TriStar performance book, the flight was technically impossible, for the Series One TriStar should not have the range to fly the 5,500 mile distance non-stop, but Court Line Navigator Dennis White and Systems Operator Bill Ross sat down and figured out a way to beat the numbers.

TriStar Alpha Bravo on the way from the Lockheed Paint Shop - Note the concrete block hanging by shackles to keep the nosewheel on the ground. '1032' is the hull number. [Lockheed Aircraft Corp via Pete Hart]

By using the AANS and ISS to fly an almost perfect Great Circle track and counting on and receiving the normal westerly tailwinds - usually blowing at more than 25 knots - it was easily possible. As Dennis White said upon arrival at Luton:

'It worked out as nicely as you could ask for precisely according to the plan. We covered the distance in 9 hours 46 minutes with fuel remaining for easily another hour's flight'.

Golf Bravo Alpha Alpha Alpha in the Assembly Shop at Lockheed Palmdale. As can be seen, the aircraft could be worked on at many different levels by use of movable staging. [both Lockheed Aircraft Corp via Pete Hart]

Above: 'AB takes its place in the final assembly building. [both Lockheed Aircraft Corp via Pete Hart]

Surrounded by access ladders, Alpha Bravo is readied for hand-over to Court Line at Palmdale in April 1973. [CPC Dibley]

HALCYON DAYS

1024

214

Both Court Line and Lockheed Aircraft made much of the 'launch/christening' of G-BAAA at Palmdale. To quote Lockheed: 'Michael Heseltine, British minister of aerospace and shipping for Her Majesty's Government, crashes a bottle of champagne on first Court Line TriStar at Palmdale January 8. At christening speech he noted that 'wide bodied jets enable holiday firms to offer astonishing value ...an English family of four can spend a fortnight in the Mediterranean area for about $300...'

Later, with Lockheed's Dan Haughton, he inspected one of the Rolls-Royce engines that powers TriStar. The large '1024' on 'Halcyon Days' is the Lockheed Hull Number. The aircraft was formally accepted by Bill Buxton on 28 February.

Two other visitors to Palmdale that made the news were Barbara James, chief training hostess, and Ray Barclay, senior instructor of Court Line, billed as 'Lockheed's newest TriStar customer, inspect L-1011s on assembly line at Palmdale. The British excursion airline recently signed letter of intent for two TriStars, took option on three more.'

Dennis R Murrin, seen here on the left, of the UK Civil Aviation Authority presented the Certificate allowing Court Line's 400-seat TriStars to operate in the UK. Receiving for Lockheed-California is their President, Bob Fuhrman.

Captain Peter Hogg summed up the trip: *'It was an excellent flight, and the navigation system performed perfectly.'*

Both Court Line and Lockheed Aircraft made much of the 'launch/christening' of G-BAAA at Palmdale. The large '1024' is the Lockheed Hull Number.

Court's TriStars were also equipped with another 'first' - an on-board weight and balance system - that would greatly simplify Flight Planning.

The first two aircraft-loads of fare-paying passengers left Luton for Bucharest and Palma in early April. Elizabeth Hutchinson, Ed Posey's secretary recalls that first revenue-earning flight to Palma...

The Aircraft Delivery Certificate of Conformance Export for G-BAAA dated 17 August 1972.

'I was fortunate enough to be on it! There were problems though, for that day we had a baggage handlers strike at Luton and I can still clearly see the four hundred passengers trundling their own luggage out of the terminal and across the

---

LOCKHEED-CALIFORNIA COMPANY
A DIVISION OF LOCKHEED AIRCRAFT CORP.

AIRCRAFT DELIVERY CERTIFICATE OF CONFORMANCE EXPORT	BUYER AIRLEASE INTERNATIONAL	MODEL L-1011-385-1	SERIAL NO. 193K-1024	REGISTRATION NO. G-BAAA

SALES CONTRACT NO. __CLX-216__ DATED __8/17/72 AS AMENDED__

BETWEEN THE LOCKHEED AIRCRAFT CORPORATION, COURT LINE AVIATION LIMITED

AND __AIRLEASE INTERNATIONAL__

ONE EACH, THREE ENGINE AIRPLANE TRANSPORT MODEL L-1011, CONSTRUCTED IN ACCORDANCE WITH CONTRACTORS SPECIFICATION REPORT NUMBER LR20111-_12_ DATED __7/30/71__ REVISED __10/1/72__

AND FURTHER AMENDED BY CERTAIN SPECIFICATION CHANGE STATEMENTS, IS DELIVERED PURSUANT TO CONTRACT NO. CLX-216

THE UNDERSIGNED HEREBY CERTIFY THAT THIS AIRPLANE CONFORMS WITH THE SPECIFICATION AND IS EQUIPPED AS SHOWN ON THIS AIRCRAFT DELIVERY INVENTORY, WITH EXCEPTION AS NOTED ON APPENDIX (A) OF THIS CERTIFICATE OF CONFORMANCE.

Dan Harrison   __2-28-73__
LOCKHEED AIRCRAFT CORP. AUTHORIZED   DATE
QUALITY ASSURANCE REPRESENTATIVE

EXECUTION OF THIS DOCUMENT BY BUYER WILL CONSTITUTE, (1) ACKNOWLEDGEMENT THAT AIRPLANE MANUFACTURING SERIAL NO. __193K-1024__ COVERED BY CONTRACT NO. CLX-_216_ HAS BEEN INSPECTED BY AN AUTHORIZED TECHNICAL
REPRESENTATIVE, OF __COURT LINE AVIATION LIMITED__, AND (2) ACCEPTANCE OF DELIVERY OF SAID AIRPLANE AT PALMDALE, CALIFORNIA.

                                    am PDT
_____   __2-28-73__   __8:09__   pm PST
AUTHORIZED REPRESENTATIVE   DATE   TIME
COURT LINE AVIATION LIMITED

CALX Form 337HN

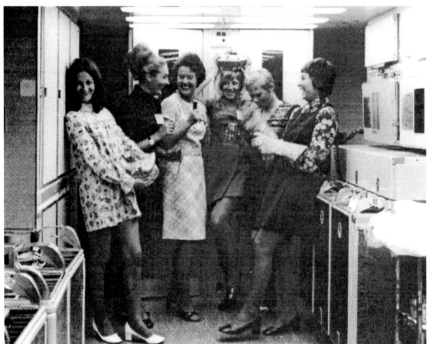

*Eastern Airlines'
Training Instructors
and a number of Court
Line girls in the Eastern
underfloor galley mock-
up in Miami during late
1972. Here Jenny
Ditmus, Kathy Brooks,
Barbra Chapel, Dee
Waringer, Dee Newkirk
and Ding Sadler take a
break from their studies.
[via Ding Sadler]*

*tarmac. I fervently hoped that this aircraft would somehow get
off the ground before we reached the end of the runway...'*

Day Trip To Paris

Court Line was not slow in showing off its new aircraft to the public;
on 18 May 1973 'Alpha Alpha' was demonstrated at the Biggin Hill
Air Fair, and also at the Paris Air Show two weeks later where it
shared duties with G-BAAB, both machines carrying passengers to
and from the show when not on display - shades of using the 748 at
the Farnborough show back in 1966!

Spring Bank Holiday Monday found Luton Airport reeling under
the impact of 400 passengers for the Ian Allan Travel TriStar flight
to Le Bourget. The car parks were incapable of digesting vehicles at
the rate at which they wished to enter and the lounges bulged.
Passenger check-in was efficiently done, however, there being a
number of desks allocated by Court Line exclusively for this
particular flight. Such was the popularity of the Paris Air Show this
year, that the tour organisers found it necessary to put on no fewer
than three TriStar and one BAC One-Eleven flights from Luton, plus
a Northeast Trident and Viscount from Heathrow. The idea for this
type of excursion was conceived some six years previously by Trevor
Bailey, a Director of Ian Allan Travel.

OU4133 was scheduled to depart at 0940 by which time all the
passengers had been transported to the waiting *Halycon Days* and
installed with the minimum of fuss and bother. At this point the
French Air Traffic took command of things which, of course, meant

Delivery! G-BAAA on its way to Luton!

En-route to Luton - the Californian landscape can be seen under the port Rolls-Royce RB-211 and white-painted wing of TriStar G-BAAB as it wings its way eastwards heading for European skies.

a half hour delay. Eventually G-BAAA was allowed to taxi slowly out to Runway 26 for a smooth take off into what had become a murky sky. Most of the passengers by this time were investigating the contents of the cardboard box they had found waiting on each seat, their curiosity if not hunger being satisfied at the sight of some dainty sandwiches and a choc roll. The supplies for the TriStar's round trips weighed two tons, made up with food, drinks and other goods for sale on board which included 150,000 cigarettes.

The captain informed his captive audience that the Paris weather was cloudy and rainy, which proved to be an accurate description! He also mentioned the fact that a fully automatic landing would be made and proceeded to read off heights and speeds, continuing the commentary until reverse thrust was selected and brakes applied. This proved a fascinating experience and was appreciated by his passengers, who were, after all, aviation enthusiasts. No one could be blamed for thinking the arrival of the TriStar surprised the French authorities, since it was some time before one inadequate pair of steps arrived and even longer before a coach materialised. Excited voices called out registrations of airliners seldom seen in the UK until the first batches were allowed to disembark and scatter. Although not open to the public until 1330. Ian Allan Travel had succeeded in acquiring entry tickets to the Show which were issued during the flight by Mrs Jean Dare and her assistant, the two company representatives on board.

As a result of this early admission, the absence of crowds was a great advantage for the photographers. The persistent rain made certain that only the British were paddling around the dripping static exhibits!

During the afternoon the TriStar was demonstrated to the visitors before going off for an hour-long flight for the benefit of a Russian delegation and other VIPs. Apparently the Russians were busy measuring distances between seats while airborne! Certainly, once loaded, those not beside an aisle find it difficult to move. The existence of eight conveniences could be of little comfort to them; although so near they are so far!

Later in the day many of the damp enthusiasts sported one Franc to ascend to the viewing gallery for a final spotting sortie. By the time the party was due to report for the return flight, the rain had ceased. This was fortunate since the long queue from the solitary desk wound its way through a set of automatic doors (which eventually gave up trying to close) and along the outside of the terminal. Mrs Dare and her colleague were trying to keep a check on numbers as their flock filed through Customs-by no means a simple task with 400 people to marshal in one spot at the right time.

Complications arose, such as the odd body who presented himself at Customs minus boarding card, those who couldn't find the right desk etc. A fleet of three buses took the first load off on a tour of the airport to where the TriStar had been parked after its demonstration flight. It took a further five bus loads and fifty-five minutes to get the remainder on board. Were they all present? But no! 399 heads were visible and one empty seat. It was learned then that number 400 had decided to stay!

Back at Luton after an uneventful trip, for the passengers who had travelled from all parts of the UK to make the journey, it meant the end of a most interesting and rewarding day even though marred by the atrocious weather. For the two Ian Allan staff members the end of another successfully completed operation and the thought that it was all to happen again two days later!

The community living around Luton were not slow to appreciate the TriStars. The airport's neighbours whilst not exactly welcoming

The 1973 Le Bourget Air Show is largely remembered for the spectacular crash of the first production Tupolev Tu-144 supersonic transport. After a violent downward manoeuvre the aircraft broke up and dived into the ground, destroyed 15 houses and killed all six persons on board, as well as eight on the ground. Not unnoticed, however, were the first appearance and demonstration of the new Lockheed L-1011 TriStar widebody airliner with two aircraft coming from Court Line, Alpha Alpha seen here taxing back after its display flight.

The Pink Lady taxies in at Le Bourget, while below G-BAAA loads up with passengers for the return flight back to Luton. The number '80' aft of the flight deck-glazing is the so-called 'aircraft type number' that was put on the TriStars so as to aid readers of the Salon international de l'aéronautique et de l'espace brochure. (Ed Posey/Autair-Court Collection)

more aircraft, accepted the new type without any noise protest, so that the night-movement restrictions at that airport could be modified to give preference to the TriStar, which was allowed 340 movements per year before the normal quota was divided up between the airlines flying from the airport - a great commercial advantage for Court.

During that first summer season the TriStars were flown on short-haul European charters for Clarksons Holidays out of Luton Airport. By 30 September some 3,000 flying hours had been completed.

Both TriStars were designed to be operable independent of ground equipment and so were equipped with integral passenger air stairs and baggage conveyors. At the many smaller airports that the airline served it was essential that they were used; being much higher than the narrow-bodied aircraft, many airports simply did not yet have the new ground equipment needed to embark and disembark passengers or their baggage from the larger and much higher TriStars, hence the need for on-board equipment.

A new uniform

At the same time as the TriStar was introduced in 1973, Court Line Aviation asked the famous fashion designer Mary Quant O.B.E. to

design a new range of uniforms for the air hostesses. The result was a stylish, flexible range of more casual garments than had been previously worn. In beige worsted, the basic suit with its tailored jacket offered a choice of skirt with a central inverted pleat, or well-cut flared trousers, along with a natural cotton shirt in three different colours. The striped hat-band and multi-coloured cravats added further touches of colour.

Quant had designed the uniform as a total look from the hat which could be worn brim up or down, to a selection of high boots or plain, mid-brown platform shoes. There was a capacious shoulder bag, and a leather belt for the skirt or trousers. There was a waistcoat for cold weather and a trench-coat that completed the range. Her aim was to give the girls plenty of variations so that they could ring in the changes within the context of a smart uniform that would always be recognisable as Court Line Aviation.

As Mary Quant said at the uniform's launch... *'it's fashionable and practical. The sort of uniform the girls would feel really good in'*.

Barbara James, at the time Court Line's Chief Air Hostess said: *'...the girls like the casual feeling of the new uniform and the freedom of separates. The uniform also works well with the different colourings and is practical for the girls hectic schedule. A particular favourite is the bright pink denim apron the girls use when serving meals'*.

Technical and operational problems...
The expected technical problems of introducing a new aircraft type that was a generation ahead of anything else in service did indeed arise. These were

'The Pink Lady' - AKA 'Halcyon Breeze' departs Luton on another service. Note the high level of security in 1973 - a single chain link fence seperates airside from the street! (author)

Out with the old - in with the new! The outfits Mary Quant was going to replace - Court Line girls - this on the left is the Julia Murdoch-designed uniform, an outfit loved by staff and passengers alike.

Above: All that has survived of the Mary Quant original 'mix n match' concept drawings is this black and white sketch.

Below: From design to reality!

events that generated much negative press attention that was, in many cases, out of all proportion to their inconvenience. For a variety of reasons there were a number of engine failures, the burst tyre incidents at Ibiza and assorted occurrences of the integral air-stairs jamming due to failure of actuators; there was great embarrassment when they failed to appear! For some reason it always seemed that Alpha Bravo was the aircraft that produced the most significant incidents - It was 'AB that burst its tyres at Ibiza, the first major time on 7 August 1973 with Captain Fox in command, when No.1 forward blew at high speed and another one burst when turning off the runway. Less than a week later - on the 10th - it was time for the really big one! Mike Albone was the Flight Engineer aboard...

'With Captain John Nuttall in command and Chris Short as First Officer (or was it John Tank?) we had a multiple blowout on take-off

just before V1 - at 135 kts according to the Flight Recorder trace - the front right hand inner tyre on the main gear blew. The strain on the remaining tyre on the axle was too much, and that also failed. We had no indication on the Flight Deck other than a very loud bang, the aircraft started to decelerate and it required full rudder and nosewheel steering to keep more or less straight. I've never seen John Nuttall work so hard! As we aborted the take-off the aircraft was enveloped in a cloud of white smoke from the tyre bursts and overheating brakes. Parts of tyre and other debris were thrown forwards by the reverse thrust, and some bits got sucked into the number 3 engine, which promptly failed. We came to a halt in a cloud of white smoke, and I honestly could not say other than the bangs and the engine failure what had gone wrong. Stella Clarke (who was Chief Girl) came in and asked if she should evacuate the aircraft. As we had no idea as to the outside conditions, I quickly went to the lower galley and opened the door to see what was going on. By the time I got outside the Spanish firecrews were already dealing with the brake fires, and the rescue services seemed to have everything under control. It was

There was an equally positive reaction when fashion designer Mary Quant created a whole new look for the airline. (Ed Posey/Autair-Court Collection)

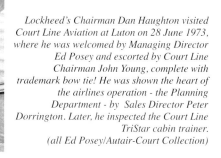

Lockheed's Chairman Dan Haughton visited Court Line Aviation at Luton on 28 June 1973, where he was welcomed by Managing Director Ed Posey and escorted by Court Line Chairman John Young, complete with trademark bow tie! He was shown the heart of the airlines operation - the Planning Department - by Sales Director Peter Dorrington. Later, he inspected the Court Line TriStar cabin trainer.
(all Ed Posey/Autair-Court Collection)

Right: Ed Posey and Dan Haugton in the check-in area that shows 'TriStar Flights Only'.

Below and bottom: Court's Roy Phillips escorts Dan Haughton around the newly completed RB-211 engine test bay, and away from TriStar Alpha Bravo while Ed Posey and John Young discuss the visit off to one side.

A few years later Daniel Haughton and vice chairman and president Carl Kotchian resigned from their posts on February 13, 1976 after becoming embroiled in what became known as the Lockheed bribery scandals....

...These encompassed a series of bribes and contributions made by officials of U.S. aerospace company Lockheed from the late 1950s to the 1970s in the process of negotiating the sale of aircraft. The scandal also played a part in the formulation of the Foreign Corrupt Practices Act which President Jimmy Carter signed into law on 19 December 1977, which made it illegal for American persons and entities to bribe foreign government officials. According to Ben Rich, director of Lockheed's Skunk Works: 'Lockheed executives admitted paying millions in bribes over more than a decade to the Dutch (Prince Bernhard, husband of Queen Juliana, in particular), to key Japanese and West German politicians, to Italian officials and generals, and to other highly placed figures from Hong Kong to Saudi Arabia, in order to get them to buy our airplanes'.

225

LOCATION OF EXTERNAL MARKINGS ON COURT LINE
AVIATION LOCKHEED L-1011 TRISTAR AIRCRAFT
based on Lockheed Drawing No.1560108 'Exterior Marking
Installation - Court Line' prepared by G Lamb.

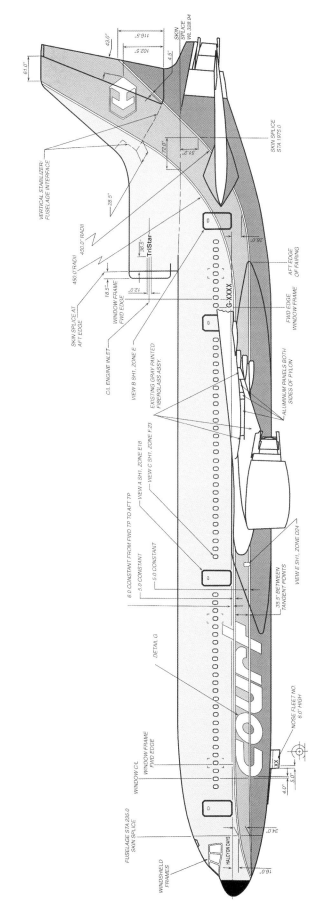

TABLE 'A'

Customer Serial No.	Color 'X'	Color 'Y'	Color 'Z'	Color 'W'	Reg No.	Nose Fleet No.	Aircraft Name
193K001	LAC1241A Orange	LAC1242A Orange	LAC1243A Orange	LAC1354A Light Yellow	G-BAAA	AA	Halcyon Days
	LAC1244A Red	LAC1245A Red	LAC1246 Red	LAC1355A Light Pink			
193K002					G-BAAB	AB	Halcyon Breeze

*decided to wait for the steps, as an aircraft evacuation down
the slides would probably injure some of the passengers.*

*Now that the danger was over it was time to take stock of
the situation. I said to Stella that there must have been some
damage to Duty-Free bottles in the Down Galley bonded store.
She said 'No', so I told her to check again! Sure enough when
she came back, she reported several breakages, three Scotch,
three Gin, three Brandy... As we were going to be forced to
nightstop, we decided to help the company out by disposing of
such breakages in the hotel that evening!*

*The next day we, and our passengers, were ferried back to
LTN in several One-Elevens. To add insult to injury, on arrival
overhead Luton it was fogged out, so after a missed approach,
we went to East Midlands. The perfect end to what should have
been a return day-trip!'*

Alpha Bravo blocked Ibiza's only runway while a team of engineers,
new tyres and brake units were flown out from Luton to a
neighbouring island and shipped across. A total of eight wheels and
a brake unit were changed before the aircraft could be removed from
the runway and prepared for a two-engined ferry flight back to Luton
and more repairs!

It was also soon discovered that there was a more longer-term
difficulty. On a normal short-haul sector flight to the Western
Mediterranean of around one hundred and ten minutes, it was almost
impossible to provide a maximum load of 400 passengers on board
with the service they had come to expect, even with 12 cabin staff!

This was a major problem for the airline, for so tight were the
profit margins that much reliance of TriStar operational profitability
was placed on takings from the Bar Carts!

Court Line had specified some 84 changes in design from Lockheed's
basic aircraft. For example, all eight passenger doors were double-width,
hopefully to speed up entry and exit and the on-board drinking water
system was double capacity to do away with uplifting supplies away
from base with the potential for contamination problems. All seats could
be fitted with alternative headrest sections, so that 'seat-back catering'
could be subsituted on the shorter-haul flights.

The TriStars were fitted with underfloor galleys with one cabin
staff member present there at all times except during the take-off and
landing phases of the flight. Food for many different tastes was
prepared there, then sent up to the main cabin in a lift. In the main
cabin the passengers were looked after by ten cabin staff under the
supervision of a Flight Director; it is interesting to note that every
time a TriStar left Luton it had on board 166 gallons of drinking
water, 425 bottles of assorted spirits, 1000 cans of beer and minerals,
4500 cigars, 150,000 cigarettes, 820 cold meals, 1200 plastic glasses

t's no holiday or Court Line

As one of Britain's biggest clusive holiday airlines, Court ine Aviation expect to carry ome two million passengers 1973.

With up to 119 holidaymakers every Court Line One-Eleven, and 0 in the company's new TriStar, e holiday high season puts cabin aff cheerfulness and patience the test.

It's hard work behind the scenes o. Tight aircraft turn-round times ean a busy summer for the fuelling ews at Luton Airport, where hell supply fuel and lubricants Court Line.

Here, and at other major airports roughout Great Britain, the Shell viation Service works speedily and ficiently. Getting thousands of olidays off to a flying start.

Shell Aviation Service, Shell-Mex House, Strand, London, WC2R 0DX.

Shell

and 32 toilet rolls!

Another problem generated by the TriStars that could not really be laid at the feet of the airline, was that arrival of a TriStar with 400 passengers aboard at a provincial European airport not yet geared up to handling the wide-bodies - especially some of the smaller airports in Spain - caused tremendous congestion and overloading of the passenger and baggage ground handling facilities. Again, the end result was more disgruntled travellers and even more negative press headlines.

Court Line Group Chairman, The Hon W.S. Phillips CBE tried to put on a brave face...

'In April and May 1973 the company introduced its two Lockheed TriStars and since that date, over half a million passengers have been flown in these aircraft. It has proved to be an outstanding aircraft, popular both with passengers and crews and notable for its flexibility and operating economics.

That was for public consumption. Behind the scenes the introductory problems shown up in that first season of intensive operations generated a confidential memo on 13 October 1973 from Mr J.E.E. Blomfield to Edward Posey, pointing out the unreliability and inflexibility of the TriStars.

One incident that could easily have brought much negative press attention occurred at the end - literally - of an early TriStar flight to Almeria in dusty southern Spain. Luckly some nifty lateral thinking avoided any public trouble. On board, apart from the normal flight crew and four hundred passengers, were Lockheed Engineer Bill Garley, and Crispin Maunder from Aviation's Marketing Department, who remembers the incident well...

'Almeria had a very narrow runway and the Captain managed to miss the turn-off so there we were at the end on concrete smaller than the turning circle of the TriStar. The nearest aircraft tug capable of moving us was down in Malaga, so there

G-BAAA departs Luton on another flight to the sun. (Ed Posey/Autair-Court Collection)

G-BAAA climbs away on another flight. (Ed Posey/Autair-Court Collection)

was only one thing for it - do a three-point-turn using reverse thrust!

Bill Garley and myself got out to spot the distances to ensure the Captain stayed on concrete, but the moment the RB211 's on the wings opened up in reverse thrust, they blew dust everywhere, Bill completely disappearing from view in the dust storm.

We managed it, and I am sure most of the passengers never noticed anything out of the ordinary!'

Finding the work - 'Hadjing' with *Halcyon Days '*...

With the end of the summer season, work had to be found for the TriStars. Utilization of aircraft during the quieter winter months could be a problem for any charter airline. With a pair of 400-seat TriStar's to keep busy, the Sales Department was on the look-out for any methods of 'soaking up' the spare capacity. Already a series of 'Hadj' flights (carrying devout Muslim pilgrims to Mecca) had been flown for Royal Air Maroc between Rabat and Jeddah, the airport closest to Mecca. John Begg, who had left Autair in 1968 for Lloyd International at Stansted, returned to Court Line as Sales Executive...

'I was in charge of selling the TriStars for long-haul charters - quite a challenge as they were fitted with short-range tankage! After long negotiations I concluded a deal for a series of charters between Bandar Seri Begawan in Brunei, Singapore and Kuala Lumpur for 'Hadj' pilgrims to Jeddah. On 29 November 1973 G-

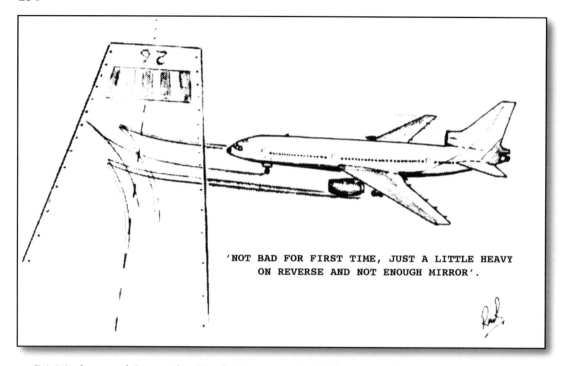

'NOT BAD FOR FIRST TIME, JUST A LITTLE HEAVY
ON REVERSE AND NOT ENOUGH MIRROR'.

A cartoon depicting the TriStar reverse incident as it appeared some time later in the staff newsletter.

BAAA departed Luton for Kuala Lumpur via Dubai, two days earlier than was required for the 'Hadj' flights, for I had been asked by Lockheed if we would go out early so that Lockheed could demonstrate the L-1011 to Malaysian Airline System (MAS). I charged Lockheed $25,000 per day for the two day demonstration, and they agreed without quibbling! It was the easiest and the best charter I ever got for Court Line! Alpha Alpha operated two flights for MAS locally from KUL, and Lockheed put a huge effort into it, including having their President, Carl Kotchian, fly out to meet us from LAX. We then positioned to BSB and were the first widebody to land at Brunei.

Thousands of people turned out to meet us, and we did a low-level pre-landing flypast for them.

Here I was introduced to the Prime Minister of Brunei, and we picked up 200 pax for Jeddah, and a further 200 boarded us at Singapore. That in itself created a bit of a mystery. The TriStar was fitted with Weight and Balance and could weigh itself. As we were preparing to depart Singapore the readout came up that we were about four tons under the estimated weight. Then we realised that our Far Eastern passengers were of much slighter frame than the average European passengers our load charts and calculations were prepared for. The skipper promptly called the fuel tanker back, uplifted extra Jet 1A to put us near max allowable weight and we managed to miss out a tech-stop!'

G-BAAB comes in to land.

The crew of G-BAAA at Kuala Lumpur. Captain Freddie Fox is fifth from the left, Captain Dave Hampson is on the far right. John Begg from Court TriStar Sales is seventh from the left, next but one to a Lockheed Test Pilot. [via John Begg]

On 19 December 1973 a contract was signed between Court Line and Bangladesh Biman for another series of 'Hadj' pilgrim flights from Dacca to Jeddah. At that time few people knew where the recently independent Bangladesh was, let alone what airport facilities it had. The story as to how this came about - and some of the consequences was later told in *CLANG - Court Line Aviation News Guide*, the staff magazine:

On the 18th December, 1973 at 1300 hours, a telex message informed the Sales/Marketing team that the Royal Air Maroc hadj flights between Rabat and Jeddah would cease on the 19th December. It appeared that the anticipated loads were not forthcoming due, it was said, to political reasons. Whatever the

From Court Line News comes these two pictures. Right: Lockheeds TriStar Sales Reception at Kuala Lumpur on 1 December 1973. Left to Right in their posh frocks' are Court Line's Kathy Brooks, Elaine Shorrocks and Sheila Attenburgh, with Lockheed's President Carl Kotchian and Regional Sales Director Bob Wintringer forming the greeting line. [Court Collection]

Below: To work! Lockheed President Carl Kotchian provides a pre-take off briefing to VIP passengers aboard TriStar Alpha Alpha operating as a Malaysian Airlines System demonstration flight. [via John Begg]

cause, some 120 TriStar hours seemed to be slipping down the drain from receipt of that telex. It is part of the Marketing function to collect as many cards as possible - in order that, in certain circumstances, a few fast tricks can be taken. This activity can often be most frustrating because, in the majority of cases, the opportunity to play these cards does not arise, nevertheless, this is a continuous process which, every now and again, can save the day.

It happens that one of the cards stowed away on the 18th December, was labelled Bangladesh Biman and this was played.

The contract was signed at about mid-night on the 18th and the necessary bag of gold changed hands.

Whilst the Marketing elements were so engaged, the Sales team opened up a second front by which, within 24 hours, the Air France subcharter had been contracted. This meant that over 100 flying hours were recovered.

The Bangladesh Biman requirement was for five flights from Dacca to Jeddah to be completed by 30th December and, since we would have to position from the United Kingdom, it was suggested that the outbound flight should operate the Bangladesh Biman scheduled service from Heathrow to Dacca. That is what we did. On the 24th December 1973 the Court Line TriStar G-BAAA operated the first TriStar scheduled service from Heathrow - British Airways PR must love us, for they had been carefully nurturing that privilege for themselves for months!

On board were 184 passengers plus three full Court Line crews. The first Bangladesh 'Hadj' flight began on 26 December with 397 pilgrims aboard. The departure was attended by the Minister of Aviation, the Secretary of State and the Chairman of Bangladesh Biman. Bangladesh Television also put in an appearance, but decided that the pilgrims were actually travelling on a British Airways VC-10 that was on the ground at the same time and shot much footage of that, only realising their error as the TriStar departed!

The runway at Dacca, complete with patched-up bomb craters stood up to the pounding and so by the time 'AA departed on 30 December with the last pilgrims, some 2116 passengers had been carried in 75 hours of flying. With the Bangladesh flights, as with the earlier Singapore/Kuala Lumpur flights, the TriStar behaved perfectly, especially important as no back-up equipment was available.

Capt. Peter Dibley's Voyage Report on the Bangladesh 'Hadj' made interesting reading and spoke very highly of the engineers that kept things going. The report also touched upon other topics...

'First Flight; 397 customers who knew nothing about sanitation and hygiene. At the end of the day the state of the

Christmas Eve 1973 and three complete crews board G-BAAA at London Heathrow for the start of the first ever scheduled service flight operated by TriStar from the airport.
[via John Begg]

aircraft was quite indescribable. Subsequently the Bangladesh Stewards carried did a good job and gave them all a crash course in marksmanship!'

John Begg has the last word...
'It was all the more remarkable when you consider that the only other L-1011 operator in the Far East at that time was All Nippon Airways in Japan, who only had a few examples and were still on their learning curve. There was no back-up, little contingency, no spares, certainly no spare engines, but the aircraft provided 100% reliability throughout, a superb reflection of the dedication of the aircrew and engineers who travelled with the aircraft. The thought of an engine failure was nothing short of terrifying!'

Of course, because everything went as it should, there was no media coverage. But things were very different with another flight...

...and freezing with 'Halcyon Breeze'

Apart from picking up valuable flying hours on the 'Hadj', it was also discovered that there could be good winter business to be had that involved the ethnic potential in the Caribbean. The plan was for a number of outbound pre-Christmas flights with empty return sectors and the reverse in the New Year. As it was, a pair of rotations were flown back from San Juan to Munich which fitted in rather well. For the Caribbean services, the aircraft configuration was changed and a conventional galley meal service installed, with seating capacity

For some reason very few pictures of the interior of the Court TriStars exist. This snapshot is reputedly G-BAAB.
[Hugh Jampton Collection]

reduced to 350 seats at 34 inch seat pitch in order to give the passengers more room for the long flight. It was on one of these long haul flights that possibly the worst and certainly the longest and most difficult of the much publicised 'engine failures' occurred.

On 25 January 1974. G-BAAB was operating Flight No OU4484 from Kingston, Jamaica to Luton. The Series 1 TriStar did not have the range to fly Kingston - Luton direct, so a 'tech' stop to uplift fuel was scheduled at Gander in Newfoundland. The engine 'failures' were not failures in the accepted sense of today; the cause of the whole saga was a combination of idiosyncrasies of the early RB211s coupled with cold-weather operation into a station with minimal L-1011 technical help. It is also a tale of determination, cussedness and fighting against the elements by the engineers of a number of companies to get Alpha Bravo back in the air...

After re-fuelling, Captain Peter Hogg took 'AB out for take-off, but during the early part of the run four loud 'bangs' were heard from the right hand side of the aircraft. With fresh memories of the previous summer's burst tyre incidents Capt Hogg abandoned the run. All eight tyres were inspected and found to be in perfect condition; attention then turned to No. 3 engine.

On board were 350 Caribbean

Three of Ruth Nicholl's snapshots taken at Gander during 'Halcyon Breeze's enforced stop-over. The pictures may be poor quality, and have been electronically enhanced but they do capture the conditions of the time - and after all, cameras do not work well in temperatures of 20 below!

passengers who had been 'home' for Christmas, mostly dressed in tropical attire. Ruth Nicoll was one the crew aboard...

'There were lots of bare arms and the little girls in pretty frilly dresses. On the occasions of leaving the aircraft every blanket was put to good use. I recall the atmosphere was one of resignation - they had been delayed outbound also - and at times party' in spirit. White Caribbean rum played a good part in keeping the adults happy! I have never forgotten a little old lady who would not allow me to empty the 'water' out of her cup to give her tea. She drank neat 'water' for hours with an increasingly happy disposition! '

The passengers were de-planed and taken to hurriedly arranged hotels in sub-zero temperatures whilst Flight Engineers John Paul and Jeff Morris and Ground Engineer Tom Haggerty set about rectifying the engine problems in a temperature of minus 20C. Advice and assistance was also obtained from Steve Thorp, the Rolls Royce Representative on secondment to Air Canada in Montreal, who flew up to Gander in a chartered HS125 and made a boroscope inspection on the internals of Number 3, and also checked the Variable Inlet Guide Vane (VIGV) system, since this was the usual cause of engine surging, now suspected as the cause of the bangs. Number 3 was passed off as satisfactory, but now Number 2 would not start, the cause being that the Pneumatic Isolation Valve would not open. These valves could be manually opened by a spanner, but as Number 2 was high up in the aft fuselage, the only way to gain access was via a cherry picker.

In atrocious weather conditions the engineers were forced to work in five minute relays to find the fault. Outside temperatures were now down to -28C with a 30 knot wind giving a wind chill that brought the effective temperature down to minus 50! After five hours struggling in appalling conditions Steve Thorp had to have oxygen administered

50 BELOW

The Pink Lady taxied out,
fuel`d and set to go,
All eyes on her fading form,
her lights a faintly glow:
She slid forward gathering speed,
a decision made too soon,
For engine surge on No. 2
stopped her take-off . Boom!

Downcast she turned and limped
back to her frozen stand,
Flightdeck conferred, hostesees served,
passengers sat getting canned,
Flight engineers braved the cold
to see what could be done,
But as fate would have it that night,
she had to be left alone.

And so it was that dreaded eve
to Gander and Grand Falls,
Went a black invasion, the lady's load,
350 souls in all.
Clutching blankets to bare arms,
they disappeared into the night,
Followed by crew to 'bridal suite',
to discuss their plight,

The drinks flowed, chilled cheeks glowed
tension slipped away,
The beds were sought, heavy lids
dropped, as the hours began to pay.
Well needed sleep was had by all,
and little did they know
Of what was to come in so few hours,
Oh! lamentation and woe!

Rolls-Royce's man joined the scene
and the engines fired,
The word get round 'all set to go',
Luton then was wired.
So while the Lady stood abandoned
and passengers were gathered,
Old Fate stepped in only to say,
'Oh, engineers you shouldn't have bothered!'

The temperatures dropped, the wind
grew in knots, it was near 50 below,
The engineers in courageous mood
tried again to have a go.
But frozen hands failed and reeling
heads spelled, that there was no way,
And so it was that the Captain P .A'd,
'Sorry, but a further delay'.

Well, it was laugh or cry,
no one could decide,
And again the Arctic snow so
passengers transported far and wide.
The crew just sat feeling quite flat
and the brandy flowed like wine,
While beds were arranged in
Ganders domain, but it all took time.

Eventually some cots were found
and the first bound to a private home,
Then a motel's conference hall for four,
turned out cold as stone.
The Terminal building and an Air Force base
gave space for some,
But for the rest the aircraft was best,
and so it all was done.

When morning dawned the following day,
the crew joined forces once more,
And moved into the warmth of a hotel,
which then could open it's door.
For two days they were to stay,
while efforts were being made
By authority and engineers,
who in Halifax had been delayed.

And so it was, a Tuesday morn
that all systems were go,
Would they see the UK again?
Only God could know.
Said all Gander, 'Fate be kinder',
the Lady taxied out,
At runways end she sat,
was there still a doubt?

The engines roared, Spirits soared,
she moved off eager and willing,
Eyes never blinking, watching, thinking.
the suspense was more than killing.
Then sighs of relief, she tipped her nose
and was Heaven bound.
All stood quite spent as they listened
to her fading sound.

And so from Jamaica, four days later,
at Luton she arrived,
Home to the UK that memorable day,
no one seemed surpised.
Some had doubted, others fretted
at her frozen plight.
But as hostess, I do confess,
I got 'pissed' that night!

Ruth Nicholl's '50 Below' epic poem was written in the style of Robert Service who also waxed lyrical about the Yukon and frozen wastes of Canada!

whilst Tom Haggerty and John Paul suffered frostbite, Tom to his knee through leaning against the -20C metal of the fuselage.

Frantic signals were sent to Luton and Air Canada in Montreal for back-up assistance and further spare components - again accommodation had to be found for the passengers and the weather was still deteriorating.

Ground Engineers Keith Law, John Bradley and John Plowman from Luton along with a spare Pneumatic Isolation Valve and a spare Fuel Flow Regulator (which got 'lost' in Canadian Customs and was not seen for days after the drama was over!), plus engineers from Air Canada could not get any nearer than Halifax, Nova Scotia due to the atrocious freezing fog at Gander.

By mid-day the next day the boys from Luton had arrived and went straight to work on the aircraft, attempting to start No.2 while manually holding open the Isolation Valve. No joy, so the valve was replaced. While this was happening a potential catastrophe was in the making. John Plowman takes up the story...

It was during the valve replacement that someone went into the Flight Station and turned on the cabin heating system. The APU had been running, but the heating system run by hot compressed air was turned off while we removed the valve from the ducting. When the heat was turned on, we in the cherry picker got a big shock and a blast of hot air in our faces.

Luckily no one was injured and there was no damage done to the aircraft and we did not bother finding out the culprit, but we did make sure that no-one turned anything else on in the Flight Station without us knowing! All the effort was wasted, for the valve would still not open when selected from the Flight Station, so all subsequent attempts were made with the valve manually held open.

It was not that the engine would not 'start' as such - it would, but it would not spool up to idling speed without overtemping.

This was not an unusual occurrence during the early days of 211 operations, where the gas turbine temperature would rapidly accelerate up to 600 degrees unless the temp gauge was watched and the fuel shut off before something melted! Finally, after changing some air filters and making some startling fuel scheduling adjustments to the FFR, we finally got everything working as advertised.

We contemplated leaving the engine running until we were ready to depart, but realised that this could be hours, as the pax were billeted in every available hotel and motel on the island of Labrador - it would take hours to round 'em all up. We left the APU running unattended all night and planned a 0600 start for a 0800 departure.

Sure enough, next morning we had overtemping again and it took another six attempts to get No. 2 running!'

It was not until 13.43 hrs on 29 January that 'AB was finally able to leave for Luton where, upon arrival the passengers were met by Representatives from Passenger Relations, who were pleasantly surprised to discover that, generally, the passengers had nothing but praise for the Cabin Staff. Somewhat understandably perhaps, some were not amused with the delay. Shortly afterwards a cartoon appeared around the Court Offices in Luton depicting G-BAAB re-named as 'Halcyon Freeze'!

At peak times the stresses and strains of dealing with passengers problems and complaints - justified and otherwise - could get out of hand if a release could not be somehow found. The usual outlet was humour as this 'letter' that appeared on staff notice boards demonstrates...

Court Line Aviation's 'Safety Card' for the TriStar.

Dear Sir

The Managing Director has asked me to thank you for your most recent letter and I would like to record the concern with which he learned of your dissatisfaction.

Your complaint regarding the inadequacy of the seating arrangements in the first cabin you entered were, I believe, explained by the engineer, at whose insistence you emerged

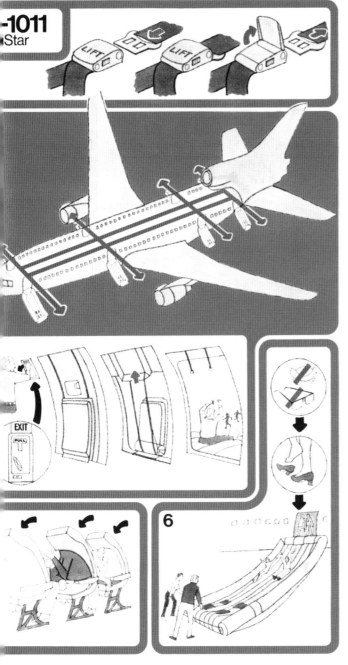

from the baggage hold. Your desire to be the first aboard the aircraft in order to secure a window seat was quite natural but, with respect, your running jump with the inherent miscalculation for drift was ill-advised. You will be interested to learn that, despite the fact that the mini-van was a complete write-off, the Passenger Officer inside was reported to be as well as could be expected in the last bulletin issued by the hospital.

The alleged inadequacy of the toilet arrangements has been fully investigated and it has been clearly established that the first area you entered was, in fact, the flightdeck and not the 'gents' as you somewhat hastily assumed. There is little doubt that the second door you passed through was the forward exit; on reflection you will possibly agree that your subsequent experiences collaborate this view. We must refute your allegation that our airstairs are a little too short and do not therefore require a notice warning to 'Watch the last one, it's a doozie'. The fact that the aircraft was airborne at the time you disembarked is possibly the most likely explanation for the gap you

240

discovered between the bottom step and the ground.

I regret to have to inform you that, by the Terms and Conditions of Carriage, we are excluded from any liability towards the costs associated with the hire of the Mule, Coach, Train, Boat and Underground Fares to which you were committed in the process of your journey from Mont Blanc to Finchley Road.

I sincerely hope that your recent experience will not have prejudiced your future use of our airline, as I do assure you that, subject to adequate notice, I shall be pleased to arrange priority boarding and ensure that necessary modifications are carried out to enable you to remained strapped to the toilet seat throughout the duration of your flight.

Yours sincerely...

The 1974 summer season saw the TriStars employed on regular flights to St Lucia and Antigua as part of the 'Clarksons Go-Caribbean' programme. They were also scheduled to operate a regular weekly ABC (Advance Booking Charter) service to Canada for AirFair, the Group's own marketing organization.

Streakin' rubber!

1974 was also the time for Court to claim another 'first' although it was not something the Public Relations people could be proud of Flight OU1052, a Triple Alpha service from Palma to Luton with Captain Fox in command had been proceeding smoothly. The flight was less than half full - only one hundred and sixty odd passengers, a rather jolly crowd of lads, idly chatting up the stewardesses as they passed by...situation normal. Then came a series of shrieks from the direction of the mid-cabin service centre - Cabin Controller Stella Clarke had been literally stopped in her tracks... there he was, a streaker - stark naked, doing a circuit of the main cabin! Passenger reaction was suitably interesting - a uniform embarrased smirk, obviously they could not decide whether it was 'quaite naice` or not!

Another 'moment' happened on the ground, away from the public gaze. Firestone, the tyre people, came down to Luton to take pictures of TriStar tyres for publicity purposes. It was kind of important that triple Alpha wore Firestone tyres for the pictures but, lo and behold, it was shod in a mixture of Goodyears and Dunlops! As Court had the only Firestone L-1011 tyres in the country, it was time for a trip to the tyre bay for the quickest tyre change in history and triple Alpha was seemingly correctly shod for the photo-shoot!

Off to Moscow!

The appearance of the TriStar - be it a yellow or a pink one - in European skies was still a very novel event - for one to appear at a Soviet air show, deep behind the Iron Curtain was probably regarded by members of the Politburo as a perfect example of Western decadence!

Being a high-profile company - and one with an excellent safety record - it was not surprising therefore that Court Line announced their co-operation on

G-BAAA departs Luton on another flight - and is seen in the hangar. The tail dock was designed by Court Line to their own specification and built by Aero-Docks of Southampton. Constructed in two halves, each can be towed laterally on rails by a standard aircraft tug to allow the aircraft to enter the hangar. The tail dock had six working levels, and when close, completely enclosed the rear of the aircraft. (Ed Posey/Autair-Court Collection)

a Lockheed and Rolls-Royce charter to present the TriStar to the Soviet Union in Moscow, the first time a wide-bodied airliner had been seen in Russian skies.

The task - to show off the aircraft to the best advantage - was planned with military precision, with people gathering in Moscow from all points of the globe. On board 'Halcyon Days' was a delegation of nearly sixty people; including Lockheed personnel, headed by George Prill, President of Lockheed International with their own interpreters; a team from Rolls-Royce; a number of Court support personnel - Michael Bell, Fred Kozo, John Margrave, Kenneth Nicholson and Gordon Wright; and, of course, the Flight Crew.

On the Flight-Deck were Capt. Michael Williams, Capt. Peter Hogg, First Officer David Walker, Flight Engineer Michael Albone and Flight Engineer David 'Danny' Duffain. In the main cabin were Angela Abrahams, Barbara Alexander, Maureen Ashton, Kathleen Atkinson, Patricia Dalgleish, Linda John, Patricia Knights, Ann McNulty and Margaret Royffe.

Alpha Alpha departed Luton, arriving at Moscow at 1637hrs local on 10 March 1974. Whilst there, the aircraft gave demonstration flights to officials from the Soviet Ministry of Aviation Industry, and representatives from Aeroflot, the State airline. The aircraft was also open for inspection on the ground, until departure on 16 March. From all accounts the aircraft had a 'major check' during its stay: the majority of removable parts were removed; the aircraft was photographed from the outside, inside, upside and downside. People were seen scurrying about with pads and pencils on which appeared little diagrams and sketches of ice tongs, trays, seatbelts, food trolleys and oxygen masks.

The questions kept on coming: *'Can you really board in 15 minutes?' 'Can you drop the oxygen masks?' 'Does it really seat 400 people?'*

So successful was the tour, that afterwards George Prill, President of Lockheed International wrote to Edward Posey, Court Line Managing Director...

'On behalf of the Lockheed/ Rolls-Royce team, I wish to express our appreciation for the absolutely outstanding cooperation and assistance rendered by the Court Line personnel during our recent successful flight demonstration of the L-1011 in Moscow.

As you well know, the demonstration of an aircraft is heavily dependant upon the attitude and competence of the crew.

Captain Hogg and Captain Williams and the other members of the

All the staff wore name badges - the Court Line ones produced on visitor badges - with their names in cyrillic Russian. Here is Patricia Knights' badge.

PROCLAMATION

This document proclaims the world's first wide-body jet flight to

the Union of Soviet Socialist Republics.

Be it known by these presents that

P. J. Knights

participated in the flight of the Court Line Lockheed L-1011, Halcyon Days,

from Luton, England to Moscow, Russia in the Soviet Union; said flight

being accomplished at 1637 local time on March 10, 1974.

The Lockheed-California Company wishes to express its admiration and

esteem for this first in the international aerospace world.

In witness whereof, this certificate has been signed on this _____1st_____

day of _____May 1974_____.

flight crew acted as front-line Lockheed salesmen. Their knowledge and competence and their approach obviously had a special effect on the Ministry of Aviation Industry and Aeroflot officials.

The young ladies of the cabin crew, led by Ann McNulty, did particularly valiant work, both during the demonstration flight and the ground displays. They received plaudits not only from the Lockheed /Rolls team, but also from our Soviet guests. The fact that the airplane performed perfectly and all the operations in Moscow went smoothly throughout was testimonial to Michael Bell and his ground crew.

I can make no better comment about the success of the charter from our point of view than to say that if we had to repeat it, we would immediately seek the same charter airline, the same arrangements and the same crew.

I think the Press coverage was good both in the United States and in the UK. In summary, I trust you were as satisfied with the endeavor as we were.'

Midnight in Red Square...

Whilst the trip to Moscow with the TriStar turned out to be highly successful in publicity terms, it very nearly came to the media's

attention for a very different reason, as Patricia Knights, one of the Air Hostesses on the trip recalls...

Some of the Court Line personnel 'off duty' and in civvies outside their hotel in Moscow. Left to right: Kathleen Atkinson, Patricia Knights, Maureen Ashton, the Russian guide and interpreter and possible KGB 'plant', Michael Albone, Angela Abrahams, David Walker and Ann McNulty. (via Patricia Gill)

'...twenty-four of us left our hotel just before midnight to watch the changing of the guards in Red Square - apparently a sight not to be missed. March in Moscow, especially at night saw freezing cold temperatures and so someone had a half-bottle of something to keep the cold at bay.

We were all up at one end of the Square, behind the barriers to keep spectators in their place and I must admit the bottle was being passed around. Then someone dropped it - the sound of the bottle hitting cobbles echoed around the Square like a pistol shot. You could have heard it miles away!

The sound had not even died away when one of the Russian soldiers, arms swinging and legs high-stepping in that unusual manner they have, started

Patricia Knights and Danny Duffain pose for the camera in Red Square, Moscow. In the background can be seen the Kremlin, queues for Lenin's Tomb and, on the left, the spires of the cathedral of St. Basil (via Patricia Gill)

marching over to us. To say it was nerve-wracking was an understatement! Luckily Danny Duffain one of our flight engineers took charge, scooping up the broken pieces of glass and putting them in his pocket, at the same time placating the soldier with sign language and gestures. Where was our guide and interpreter when we needed her - nowhere to be seen!

Needless to say, we did not hang around to watch any more, just thankful to escape!'

As early as April 1973 Court were both singing the praises, whilst at the same time being honest about some of the problems they were experiencing. Ed Posey:

'The aircraft is fitted with Decca/Ambac Mona inertial area navigation equipment and an on-board weight and balance system to simplify flight planning, which has yet to gain CAA approval. A below-deck galley is fitted to allow trolley food service, but the seats have replaceable head-rests so that seat-back catering can be substituted. If required the aircraft will fly with a bonded store of alcohol and tobacco aboard, like a ship.

We are increasing its maintenance staff by about a third to cater for the TriStar - and have bought the ex-RAE Farnborough Beverley to transport spare RB.211s and associated equipment. The RB.211 disc problem is regarded as a nuisance and for the time being will mean pulling fans every five weeks. All Court engines now have the 'B' discs

A nightstop party to end all nightstop parties! During the trip to Russia to promote the TriStar one room was 'invaded' by aircrew, Lockheed, Rolls Royce and other personnel...

And a good time was had by all! (via Michael Albone).

Sandy Keegan (neé Smith) in the underfloor galley on one of the TriStars., so often the location of one of the Court Line traditions - the Reverse Thrust Cocktail!

which are cleared for 300 cycles, and the airline holds three complete spare engines, a fourth broken down into modules and an additional turbine module. One spare engine per aircraft is regarded as normal practice once the aircraft is established in service. Utilisation is to be limited to 72 hours per aircraft per week for this summer, compared with 95 hours per week on the One-Eleven. In the winter we are considering the lease of one aircraft, and to this end our TriStars have been certificated to both CAA and FAA standards.

The installation of our own test cell, which will cut down noise to 95PN dB at 50ft, results from the size of the RB.211 and thus the difficulty of transporting it to Derby, where it would take up to 22 hours even to set it up for tests. We could do module changes, but without a test cell we would have to keep sending the rebuilt engines to Derby for testing before they could be fitted to the aircraft. We are also working closely with British Airways BEA on TriStar and RB.211 introduction and may well come to some agreement on use of flight simulators and on engine overhaul. BEA personnel are regular visitors to Luton to see how we are handling the introduction of the aircraft. We are also in close touch with the other TriStar European inclusive-tour customer - LTU of Dusseldorf.

This item contains two references that is of unconfirmed interest, and they should be regarded as gossip both of which seem to have passed into Court Line legend! The reference to the on board bonded store has been linked to assorted tales that drifted my way, one day a Luton Customs Officer was on duty when he came across a Court Line air hostess crying hysterically. He eventually got the story from some of the other girls that she had not received any pay for that month, in fact she had got an enormous bill from the airline. She had been charged for an amount of missing duty free goods from some of the flights she had worked on as the senior cabin crew member. She had no idea how she was going to pay her rent and other expenses.

As insurance against RB 211 failure 'down the line' Court Line bought Blackburn Beverley XB259/G-AOAI from the Royal Aircraft Establishment in March 1973 to ferry around spare engines. In the event it was never used nor was it ever painted in Court colours and markings... a shame, perhaps, because it would have looked 'pretty in pink'.'

It seems that on the first flight of the day the customs-sealed duty free containers would be loaded into the aircraft; one in the cabin and the remainder in the baggage hold. On landing the containers would be swapped around, full for empty. The customs seals could only be broken when airborne and so the cabin crew didn't have the opportunity before the flight to check the containers against the contents lists.

Following a Special Branch investigation all was revealed. It seems that the duty free warehouse manager would short-fill the containers and they would be subsequently sealed by Customs Officers in on the fraud; the spoils being shared by both. According to legend, there was a court case and the warehouse manager ended up in jail. The Customs department had a huge shake up as quite a few of the officers were involved.

There has also been consistent rumours over the years that Court Line flight crews used to hold

parties in the cabin of the Beverley at the end of the day's flights. The aircraft cleaners used to get very upset as they couldn't get on with their jobs. These parties used to go on for ages during which training and instruction for the various stages of membership of the Mile High Club may have been undertaken. These rumours possibly have origins in what was a well known Court tradition - the Reverse Thrust cocktail, otherwise known as the after-landing drink! It did not matter what alcohol went into it - any bottle that was open would do - as long as it was orange juice based as a disguise! Another favorite was Drambuie and milk, used as a pick-u-up before serving breakfast on a long nightflight.

Despite the undoubted success in using Court's TriStars on this type of promotional campaign, there were numerous complaints and comments relating to the TriStar 'snags' - were these justified?

Without doubt they had tremendous appeal to passengers and crews alike. Court's worked in close co-operation with the manufacturer and Eastern Airlines in the USA, where Frank G. Peterson was Court Line's Project Manager, North America. One person who is well able to cast a professional eye over the aircraft is John Plowman, who offered the following personal technical recollections in 1994:

'The L-1011 now is arguably the most reliable and efficient of the first-generation wide-body jets, but by today's standards, the technical problems experienced with the Court Line L-1011s were appalling - a part of the price of acquiring aircraft

Supposedly designed as a children's competition prizes from this were highly desired by holidaymakers and airline enthusiasts alike! Printed in the in-flight literature, the drawing may have looked normal at first glance, but there are in fact fifteen deliberate mistakes. It shows a TriStar and BAC 1-11 on the ground at Court Line's Luton base. By looking for the mistakes and sending them on a postcard to the company you could be a VIP guest and win a special tour around the airline, sit in a TriStar cockpit. the flight simulator and watch the airport staff in operation behind the scenes. Forty prize positions were to be won - despite looking at this for years, I still cannot find more than fourteen mistakes!.

so early in the production process. After all, the Court TriStars were only the 24th and 32nd models built, were the first in use outside North America, and were a generational leap forward from the BAC 1-1 ls. The most unreliable aspects of the aircraft were the engines, the APU, the Integrated Drive Generators (IDGs), main windshields, main tyres, total loss of hydraulic contents, and many of the avionic components such as the display units for the Inertial Navigation units, and the multiplex ('MUX') boxes for the passenger entertainment system. The failure rates of all these expensive components was atrocious compared with the corresponding components on the 1-11s. The removal rates for engines and APUs seemed to be about 100 hours. Today, l0,000 hours is about average for RB211s and this engine now holds the world record for 'on-wing' life - over 26,000 hours. The APU can now be expected to last 2,500 hours between removals. If new L-1011s were still being sold today, the windshields would be expected to last for about eight years, the engines could be expected to stay installed for 5 years, the IDGs 2 years, and the APU, maybe a year. In the 18 month period that Court Line had the two L-1011s, every engine, APU, main windshield and IDG seemed to have failed at least once. And these were just the major

Court Line

Court Line managing director John Young (left) with CLA chief executive Ed Posey, w will head Court's leisure division, including Clarksons, OSL, Atlas and Court Tra

"I CAN'T think of anything else we'd want to buy at present," said John Young, managing director of Court Line,

●Court Line's shopping spree is over—for the present at any rate. Now, with Clarksons, Atlas and OSL under its belt, the order of the

leisure interests. It is made up as follows:

Court Line Aviation: two TriStars and 10 BAC One-Ele-

Court Line Catering plies meals to airline and industrial and commerc ganisations.

components, the ones that caused flight cancellations, and often resulted in Court Line having to sub-charter other aircraft to carry waiting passengers to their holiday destinations. A sobering sight was seeing a Laker Airways DC-10 arrive in Luton to carry Court Line passengers to their destination in Spain or Italy. Larger fleet sizes, together with spare parts and skilled, L-1011 trained mechanics at every port-of-call, greatly mitigated the technical problems other L-1011 operators had with the TriStar in those early days. For example, in the summer of 1973, Eastern Airlines had 14, TWA 13, Air Canada 4 of these aircraft. Other delay-causing and expensive component failures were the lavatory pumps, passenger door and cargo door actuators, and total loss of hydraulic contents - something that seemed to occur so often, we used a 45 gallon drum on a trolley to top up the L-1011's four hydraulic systems.

Today the reliability of these components is beyond anyone's wildest dreams in 1974'.

The travel trade newspapers started to question Court's leisure divisions's activities as the doubts started to appear.

Court Line's operations were still based mainly around the provision of capacity for Clarksons Holidays. In the race to win the volume holiday market that had been initiated by Tom Gullick's Clarksons a number of casualties were starting to appear.

Chapter Ten

To The Brink - And Beyond!

In 1972 Arrowsmith made a profit of £100,000, with Lord Brothers £40,000 (both these concerns, independent for many years, were now under the operating arm of Freddie Laker). But Vladimir Raitz's Horizon Holidays lost £388,000, Thompsons lost £1,600,000, whilst Clarksons lost a massive £4,800,000!

With losses like that, it is not surprising that in April 1973 Clarksons Holidays were standing at the edge of the abyss of bankruptcy!

Before the crisis became acute, there were a number of times when Clarksons might have been sold. In mid-1970, an American corporation, W. R. Grace and Company offered its parent company, Shipping and Industrial Holdings, £10 million but was rejected because Hambros Bank valued it at £14 million. Two years later American Express came close to taking a 19 per cent stake in Clarksons, but was frightened off by the firm's deepening losses.

G-BAAA departs the terminal area at Luton going 'up the hill' to the runway. This was a favourite spot to shoot aircraft because they passed very close to the road/car-parks and it was possible to get photos entering/leaving the terminal area or on to the runway. [Simon Peters Collection]

The heavy losses sustained by Clarksons in the interest of gaining market share continued throughout the early 1970s. The company seemed to adopt the old joke principle of 'We lose money on every client, but our turnover is enormous!' - but they were taking it seriously! This was very bad news for everyone else in the industry. 1972 and 1973 saw the price war in package tours continue as unabated as ever. A number of smaller operators collapsed. The mighty Thomson Holidays was losing money, but were fortunate to be sustained by their rich parent company, the International Thomson

'Passengers are requested to please board by the central stairs'. The next load board the Pink Lady for another flight to the sun.

Organisation. Horizon Holidays continued to make losses.

In order to trade, each company had to renew its tour operating licence with the Civil Aviation Authority every year, part of which involved submitting year-end accounts - and woe betide any firm that showed a red bottom line!

If this happened, the CAA demanded not only fresh injections of capital but also an increased bond, which was issued either by a bank or an insurance company. This was both difficult and expensive to obtain. Thomson and Clarksons were better positioned in this respect, both of them having 'rich Daddies' in the shape of the International Thompson Organisation of Shipping and Industrial Holdings respectively.

Possibly the most intriguing of these potential take-over deals involved the late Sir James Goldsmith and a plan to merge Thomson Holidays with Clarksons, again with participation by American Express. This scheme was not only the product of Clarksons' worsening plight. By 1972 the Thomson Organisation was also intensely nervous about the future of its package holiday offshoot. To stimulate demand and buy market share, the tour operator had

BAC 1-11 G-AXMH rests between flights. (Simon Peters Collection)

slashed prices by an average of £5 a head - an immense amount at the time. The move banged yet another nail into Clarksons' coffin but it also pushed Thomson Holidays into serious losses.

By mid-1972, Gullick had fallen out with the directors of Shipping and Industrial Holdings and decided to bow out, but was unrepentant:

'I had lost overall control. I had told them they should either develop Clarksons or sell it to another big company who would. They had become frightened by the bad publicity over unfinished hotels and complaints about cruises and they weren't prepared to develop it themselves. If they had stayed in the game it would have been Clarksons' heading the industry - not Thomson.

He departed for Spain, where he capitalized on the great love which had helped launch his extraordinary career off the ground, organizing shooting parties.

Filling the seats...

On 19th April Court Line and Shipping and Industrial Holdings signed Heads of Agreement whereby SIH sold 85% of Clarksons Holidays to Court Line for £1. At that time Court's were told that unless they made the acquisition, Clarksons Holidays - and therefore most of their travel business for the next five years and almost all of that summers TriStar capacity - would be wound up.

Immediately after the acquisition, Court Line attempted to deal with the problems of Clarksons Holidays. A new Managing Director was sent out to Palma to re-organise Servicios del Sol S.A. with the instigation of a new information system reporting profitability and cash flow.

TriStar training! Court's built a TriStar cabin mock-up at Luton for Cabin Staff training. Here Mary Ann and Joy wait their turn as Vicki slides down. [Honor Brooker]

Court Line Aviation were continually on the look-out for ways of securing sales of seats on aircraft. In 1971 a group of operators under the banner of the Associated Travel and Leisure Services (ATLAS) was formed for student and affinity group travel, mainly on the trans-Atlantic air routes, intending to operate a form of Advance Booking Charter (ABC) - the ability of being able to sell seats-only on charter flights as long as they were booked a specific time in advance - marketed under the name of 'Airfair' which brought in a deluge of 40,000 potential passengers when ABC's became legal in April 1973.

This was beyond the capability of ATLAS, and so following negotiations, Court Line obtained ATLAS on 8th May 1973. Court's wanted a set-up similar to this for ABC travel was an expanding sphere, one that the airline wanted to get into, for it could soak-up any spare capacity on the TriStars going to either the USA or the Caribbean. There was also a distinct possiblility that ABC's could soon be made legal in Europe...

Further preventative investment had to

Court Line staff during happier times - (standing left to right) Joanna Petit, Bryn Jones, Colin Garner, Mike Budge, Sally Anne Thompson, Brian Keeler (kneeling) Henry Phyo and Stella Clarke. [via Stella Clarke]

Part of the Court Line BAC 1-11 fleet seen at Luton from under the tail of one of the TriStars. (Ed Posey/Autair-Court Collection)

Eileen Harrison and Kathy Atkinson pose for publicity photographs inside the intake of a RB211.

The Pink Lady almost back on the ground at Luton. (Ed Posey/Autair-Court Collection)

be made in early 1974 when Court Line took over the ailing Horizon Holiday Group; there was still the need to safeguard the income for their large fleet of aircraft. This was one of the longest-established and most respected names in the business and had been founded in 1949 by Vladimir Raitz and Len Koven. The Group operated a number of concerns; Four S Travel, Horizon Midlands, and subsidiaries in Ireland and Scotland. Most of their flying was conducted by British Caledonian Airways, although some use had been made of Court Line over the years.

Raitz approached British Airways, Thomas Cook, Thompsons and others but none were interested. In a meeting with Horizon's biggest creditor, the National Westminster Bank, Court agreed to buy the goodwill of the bankrupt company by paying £1 for every Horizon passenger flown for the next three years. On the surface it looked as if Horizon's holidays were saved, but all that had really happened was that Court's spare capacity had been soaked up.

The moment Court started to divert Horizon passengers from BCal there were vehement objections - so much so, that Court's were forced to replace their own underused One-Elevens with those from BCal. Adam Thompson, Chairman of BCal gave some indication as to the size of the loss of business in his biography 'High Risk':

'British Caledonian was one of Horizon's main charter operators and in a year which was bad enough in any event, the loss of this business - amounting to over £1 million in revenue which could not be quickley replaced - was a body blow. In fact the Horizon collapse left us with three One-Elevens idle.'

External crises

The end of 1973 and the beginning of 1974 saw the western world and the United Kingdom in crisis. In 1973 the Oil Producing and Exporting Countries (OPEC) of the world decided to flex their muscles and use their resources as weapons to control their own destiny. Gone forever were the days of cheap fuel - prices rocketed skywards, trebling in a matter of days - and fuel was under threat of rationing. In the United Kingdom, Peter Walker, the Secretary of State for Trade and Industry announced that deliveries of fuel would be cut by 10% to help conserve supplies - then the Miners announced an overtime ban with threats of an imminent strike followed by cuts in electrical power. This was the era of threats of petrol rationing, Trade Union rule and the three day working week.

It is no wonder that given these external circumstances, Court's suffered poor bookings for the 1974 season which did not help its financial position; the country was suffering a poor overall economic position, a situation that was not helped by massive increases in the cost of fuel. This had discouraged people from booking holidays abroad. Court Line did manage to lease two of the One-Eleven fleet to other operators - Germanair and Cyprus Airways - and flew the Tristars out of Gatwick sooner than Luton.

With the arrival of the 1974 summer Inclusive Tour season, Court Line's financial position should have started to improve, but in June the company announced that unless additional finance could be found immediately, then the whole of the Court Line Group of companies was faced with bankruptcy. The then British Labour Government therefore announced that it it would take over Court Lines shipping interests for £16,000,000 and thus allowed the airlines operations to continue normally until 19.00hrs in the evening of 15 August when the airline ceased all flying and the company was placed into liquidation.

Warnings about the inprudence of Court Line's policy of market share at any price had been coming thick and fast throughout 1974, but had gone unheeded; Clarksons responded publicly to these warnings with a typical quote: *'If you can't stand the heat, get out of the kitchen!'*

Ed Posey explains some of the background goings-on...

'John Bloomfield, who had taken over responsibility for the integration of Clarksons and Horizon under Court ownership was doing a good job, but was attempting to do it in the impossible circumstances of a declining market. The oil crisis and recession were upon us, we had something like £10 million in cash invested in Caribbean hotels which, in the prevailing climate proved to be unsaleable, and the Clarksons revenue, unsupported by SIH was well below budgetted figures. Events moved very quickly and in all divisions we seemed powerless without the cash reserves to 'weather the storm'.

Eventually the debts finally outweighed the income and assets and the banks finally pulled the plug.

Most of the fleet managed to return to Luton later that evening, but One-Elevens G-AYOR was impounded at Cardiff and G-AXMF suffered the same fate at Manchester.

'Sneaking like thieves in the night...'

The final Court Line movement was the arrival at Luton of Tristar G-BAAB at 09.39 hrs on 16 August after returning from the Caribbean with a party of very relieved tourists. This flight, like others during the demise, was full of intrigue and emotion. What arrived back, had to have departed, and the crew that took 'Alpha Bravo out to St Lucia had no idea that their world was about to collapse. Cabin Controller Stella Clarke worked the outbound...

'The inbound flight to St Lucia was long and busy as normal, but no one minded as the week ahead promised to be one of sheer enjoyment full of sun, sea, sand and total relaxation. We handed over G-BAAB to Jaqui Maschera and crew, waved a fond farewell, then headed for the hotel. The cabin crew checked into the main hotel and the flight deck into a bungalow in the grounds. We had all arranged to meet for drinks and to discuss plans for the forthcoming days - we were well into the swing of things when our Flight Engineer Tom Flett was called away to the telephone. As soon as he returned we could tell that something was amiss and after a quick word in Capt. Fox's ear, he suggested that we all adjourn to the bungalow to discuss what had been said on the telephone. The rest of us were still completely in the dark, but how serious could it be, after all, it

TriStar girls in the Caribbean! Identified in Jon Charley's photograph somewhere is Janet Goddard, Anita Holmberg, Helen 0'Connor, Honor Wilson, Sandy Bates, Marilyn Benham, Sue Lawson and Alison Mee.

The second of only two interior pictures of the Court TriStars ever located - this is thought to be inside G-BAAA. The ceiling and sidewall panels were sectionalised into various colours to match the exterior of the aircraft. [Simon Peters Collection]

was only a call from Tom's girlfriend!

Captain Fox broke the news - at midnight that night Court Line ceased to be! This statement obviously had to be verified, so Capt. Fox put in a call to Luton Ops - yes, it was true, and after some hours waiting the final message was delivered. Get yourselves home the best way possible. I cannot describe how we all felt - disbelief, desperation and total despondency that our worlds were falling apart.

Meanwhile, Cabin Controller Jaqui Maschera was aboard G-BAAB heading for home:

'We had a hectic and enjoyable stop-over in St Lucia and somewhat reluctantly the crew got themselves together to take over the incoming aircraft for the journey home. After take-off all the pax (passengers) seemed in a relaxed and happy mood. Nothing appeared amiss until several hours into the flight when a snag around on No.2 engine that forced a divert to and overnight stop at Halifax, Nova Scotia.

Accommodation was arranged for the pax and crew by our handling agent. From the hotel Capt. Hogg spoke directly to Luton Ops., from where he was told about the very serious financial situation of the company and that they were on the point of being declared bankrupt - when that happened we would be stranded with the aircraft impounded against debts.

As a crew we met up privately and talked the situation over, Capt. Hogg spoke to our engineers out at the airport and was advised that 'AB was now repaired and fully fuelled. That did it! We all decided to make a quiet, careful run for it, hoping that the news had not seeped through to Canada yet!

Our handling agent got everyone organised with a pick-up time - when ours came it was a very quiet and sombre crew that travelled out to the airport, not wanting to say a word in case it was overheard and reached the airport authorities. We all boarded through maintenance steps into the lower galley. The flightdeck crew got everything started and we moved across to the terminal to pick up the pax. Obviously there was no catering uplift - it was pick up and go! Most of the pax boarded but there were a few that couldn't be located - they would have to be left.

At last we took off. It had been arranged that everyone would stay seated until we were well away and levelled off, then Capt. Hogg would do a P.A. announcement explaining the somewhat strange situation. He did a brilliant job, telling everyone that the company was bankrupt and that there was not any catering as we did not want to draw attention to ourselves. He explained just what had happened even to the point that the crew could have just got themselves home, leaving the passengers to fend for themselves! I have to admit that I dimmed the cabin lights whilst the Captain was talking as there wasn't a dry eye amongst the crew. When he was finished I made a P.A. to say that all we could offer was the

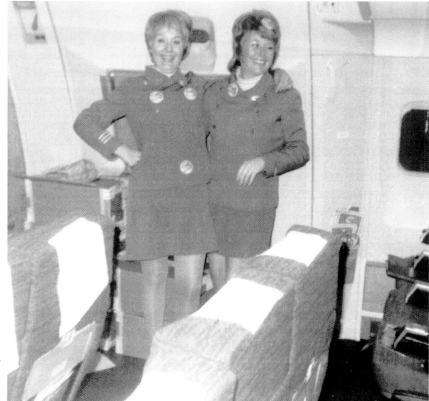

Jaqui Maschera (right) and Kathy Colebrook share a joke during turn-around aboard TriStar 'Halcyon Days'.
[via Stella Clarke]

bar, so two service points would be set up to serve. The cabin crew put one trolley at the mid-service centre and one at the front. It was like the loaves and fishes - we had a box of salted peanut sachets and a few packets of biscuits that were divided out equally.

It was now that the pax realised what we had done in order to get them home and that we were going back to nothing. One pax came up and said that he was a lawyer and that if any of the crew wanted to know where they stood, he would be happy to talk to them. Two guys came up to me and said 'leave serving the drinks to us - you girls sit down'. It was a lovely thought, but the last thing we wanted to do - although the temptation did remain to put your feet up and have a few drinks, after all, we were out of a job! I reminded all the cabin crew that as we didn't know what we were going in to and who, if anyone, would be meeting the aircraft standards were to be maintained. I did not want anyone 'falling off, with hats askew' at Luton. As events turned out, it was a good thing we did not drown our sorrows.

Whatever happened, they would have to go! On 11 July the Board decided that the TriStars would not remain into 1975.

After what seemed a lifetime Capt Hogg announced that we were coming up to Europe and a few minutes later a group of passengers came up to me with one of the girls hats just overflowing with money, saying it was for all the crew with their thanks. I just managed to stammer 'thank you', then fled into the privacy of the flight-deck where I burst into tears. I just sat on the jump-seat and bawled with a lap full of money!

COURT LINE FLYING PROGRAMME - THURSDAY 15 AUGUST 1973							
Charterer	A/C	Flt.No.	Dep.	From	To	Arr.	Remarks
	?	OUposn	0435	Luton	Gatwick	0505	
OSL	?	OU685	0600	Gatwick	Malta	0915	112 pax
OSL	?	OU656	1000	Malta	Gatwick		1315
CLK/Pont	G-BAAB	OU1201	0610	Gander	Gatwick	1045	396 pax
OSL	?	OU665	0645	Gatwick	Malta	1000	112 pax
OSL	?	OU666	1045	Malta	Gatwick		1400
	?	OUposn	0650	Birmingham	Gatwick		0650
MELIA	?	OU4809	0830	Gatwick	Santiago	1025	119 pax
MELIA	?	OU4809	1125	Santiago	Oporto		1205
MELIA	?	OU4808	1310	Oporto	Gatwick		1510
CLK	?	OU767	0700	Luton	Alicante		0925
CLK	?	OU768	1010	Alicante	Luton		1240
SIS	?	OU4790	0715	Luton	Cologne	0845	119 pax
SIS	?	OU4790	0910	Cologne	Birmingham		1025
OSL	G-AXMF	OU681	0800	Manchester	Malta	1120	110 pax
OSL	G-AXMF	OU682	1205	Malta	Manchester		1535
CLK	G-AYOR	OU771	0800	Cardiff	Nice	1030	110 pax
CLK	G-AYOR	OU771	1100	Nice	Corfu		1255
CLK	G-AYOR	OU712	1355	Corfu	Nice		1555
CLK	G-AYOR	OU712	1625	Nice	Cardiff		1850
Horizon	BCAL	OU047	0845	Gatwick	Gerona	1035	114 pax
Horizon	BCAL	OU048	1120	Gerona	Gatwick		1325
OSL	?	OU657	0935	Luton	Malta	1250	110 pax
OSL	?	OU658	1335	Malta	Luton	1650	
OSL	?	OU669	1120	Birmingham	Malta	1440	110 pax
OSL	?	OU670	1525	Malta	Birmingham	1845	
MEON	?	OU137	1410	Luton	Faro	1705	113 pax
MEON	?	OU138	1750	Faro	Luton		2040
Horizon	BCAL	OU049	1500	Gatwick	Naples	1730	114 pax
Horizon	BCAL	OU050	1815	Naples	Gatwick		2050
USIT	?	OU921	1550	Gatwick	Dublin		1705
USIT	?	OU923	1750	Dublin	Le Bourget		1925
USIT	?	OU924	2025	Le Bourget	Dublin	2200	
USIT	?	OU922	2245	Dublin	Gatwick		2355
Horizon	?	OU041	1615	Gatwick	Mahon	1820	114 pax
Horizon	?	OU042	1925	Mahon	Gatwick		2315

Captain Hogg, (right) Jaqui Maschera and First Officer Chris Short deplane from The Pink Lady following the last-ever Court Line Aviation flight.

Relief to be home! Passengers deplane from The Pink Lady at Luton following the collapse of the company. [Ed Posey Collection]

When I got myself together to explain what it was all about there were not too many dry eyes amongst those up the pointy end! Capt. Hogg made another stirring P.A. thanking everyone for their kindness and the money was divided out equally.

As we approached Luton I went onto the flight-deck to advise 'Cabin secured for landing' and to see if anyone had any ideas as to what sort of reception we were likely to get. No-one really knew. We landed, taxied in and on chox. As the stairs came up I opened the door to an amazing scene. There were people all over the tarmac, waving to us. The Press - I later *found my face in the 'Daily Telegraph' - engineers, office workers, Check-In staff - and not just Court Line, but people from Monarch, Britannia...*

Reality came home with a resounding thump when someone rushed up the stairs to slap a notice on the aircraft saying it had been impounded. Customs half-heartedly asked if there was any duty-free bar left to go into bond, which of course there wasn't. The pax disembarked and the crew went to what was left of the crew room. From there on it is history.'

Back on St Lucia, Stella Clarke and the remainder of the crew were facing problems of their own...

'We all knew that at some point we would have to face our passengers - they were staying at the same hotel, so how long would it be before they heard the news? We did not have to wait long - one pax listening to the BBC World Service heard about the collapse and the news spread like wildfire. From

Even though this publicity picture is in black and white, it is a truly stunning image of a Court Line TriStar and the flight crew.
[Ed Posey Collection]

then on we were accosted at every turn and faced a barrage of questions - all of which we could not answer. We spent most of our time hiding out in the bungalow, only showing our faces when we had some facts to pass on. These were few and far between, but we had been told that other airlines would be used to get the passengers home. On the whole they were a great bunch, accepted their plight and made sure that they still enjoyed their holiday.

Eventually - I cannot remember how many days later - we were summoned to another meeting and told that tickets had been obtained for us on a BA flight Barbados - London the following evening. So, off we went to pack for an early getaway. Next day we literally crept out the hotel and flew St Lucia - Barbados courtesy LIAT. Our uniforms were well packed away, we were just a group of 'civilians' travelling home. We checked in for the London flight immediately and faced the prospect of all day at the airport for the LHR flight did not depart until that evening. It then became apparent that there were questions about the validity of the tickets we were holding and so we lived in fear and dread for the next few hours that we may be 'bumped off' the flight. Eventually we boarded, took off and were royally looked after by the BA crew. No one said anything, but I am sure they knew who we were and what we were doing. A coach arrived at Heathrow to take us back to Luton, where we were deposited well away from the operations area. I'm not sure if that was done to keep us away from the press, or because we all looked a little worse for wear!

From there we were left to our own devices and certainly, for me, that was when I realised that my dream had come to a very abrupt end - what else to do but go home and drown our sorrows together.'

This event marked the then worst collapse of any airline in the history of British aviation and bonds valued at £3.5 million were used to pay other operators to bring stranded Court Line passengers back to the UK. At the time the Court Line Group owned Clarksons, Horizon, 4S Travel, Halcyon Holidays, OSL Travel, and Air Fair. 50,000 passengers were left stranded abroad, a further 150,000 lost their holidays and over 1,100 employees lost their jobs. But that was by no means the end of the story, or the implications as to what had happened.

Chapter Eleven

Aftermath

COURT LINE LIMITED
Press Announcement for Immediate Release.

The following statement is issued by the Directors of Court Line Limited.

It was announced earlier this evening that the company has ceased trading and that it is taking steps to go into liquidation in the immediate future. The company will petition the High Court for a winding-up order and application is being made for the appointment of a Provisional Liquidator. As soon as this application has been heard a further announcement will be made.

The immediate consequences for the Group are as follows:-

1. Shipbuilding and Shiprepairing Divisions.
As already made clear in an announcement issued earlier this evening by the Department of Industry, these Divisions will be fully safeguarded and there will be no threat to employment or to the activities of those divisions.

2. Aviation and Leisure Divisions.
It is with deepest regret that the company has had to announce that these divisions, principally Court Line Aviation, Clarksons, Horizon, 4S, 4S Sports and Airfair (but excluding Owners Services Limited, and Horizon Midlands) have had to cease trading with immediate effect.

Check-In Desk Seven at Luton Airport. The sign says it all. [Ruth Mathews]

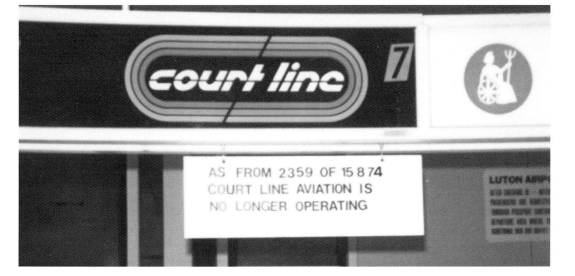

This, the Directors well know, must have a disastrous effect on the holidays, either planned or in progress of more than 100,000 people.

The eventual decision to effect an immediate closure was inevitable for a whole variety of factors, but the root cause was last year's oil crisis and the multiple economic problems which it triggered, both world-wide and within all division of the Group.

Arising out of this situation, discussions were started with the Group's bankers in the Spring and thereafter with the Government.

The Group had also instructed a leading firm of Chartered Accountants to report on the problems of the Aviation and Leisure Divisions.

The company's willingness in June to negotiate with the Government for the sale of the shipbuilding and shiprepairing divisions sprang largely from the wish of both parties to protect the cash flow of the Group, and specifically to enable the Aviation and Leisure Divisions to continue, pending a complete financial investigation.

In the negotiations, it was expressly stated that the Group could not give the Government any assurances that the Aviation and Leisure Divisions could in fact complete their 1974 programmes, although of course it was hoped that the shipbuilding and shiprepairing sale would enable those and subsequent programmes to be carried out.

In the event, the financial pressures on the Group mounted and for several weeks discussions were taking place with the Department of Trade and others. It was hoped that these discussions would lead to the formation and implementation of a rescue plan. This would have been designed not only to enable people already abroad to complete their holidays, but also to enable people who had booked their holidays and paid for all or part of them to have those holidays. The same plan envisaged an orderly wind-sown of the Group's activities generally.

It is sad that the efforts of many people to achieve these objectives failed.

3. Other Divisions.
Steps are being taken to appoint as quickly as possible liquidators or receivers of certain other U.K. operating companies. Wherever practicable, trading is being carried on pending decisions about possible disposals.

It is too early as this stage to forecast what dividends will be payable in the liquidation.

So read the Press Release issued by the company at 2200hrs on 15th August. The news did not hit the media until the next morning - the same day - and in the light of subsequent events this could not be regarded as a coincidence - as the Secretary of State for Industry Anthony Wedgewood-Benn published a White Paper *'The regeneration of British Industry'*. This revealed the Government's plans for greater state

The aircraft were impounded after their last Court Line flight.
[Kurt Lang]

intervention in industry - in other words shipbuilding, aircraft manufacture, North Sea oil and Port industries would be - and to all intents and purposes already had been - nationalised.

In normal times, this would have been the top story, but news of the Court collapse knocked the government from the prime spot, almost certainly as was intended. Luton Airport was invaded by the media and the newspapers were full of banner headlines. Nevertheless, the recently-elected Labour Government did make statements, the first from Anthony Wedgewood-Benn...

'It is the firm intention of the Government to acquire those interests and take whatever action may be necessary in the immediate future to prevent the liquidation of Court Line from causing any disruption in the shipyards, ship repair and engineering facilities owned by its subsidiaries.

Discussions have been taken with the companies concerned and their bankers and the necessary steps will be taken to proceed with the purchase of the shipbuilding and associated interests from the liquidator of Court Line and so complete the transaction as soon as possible'

From the tone of that statement, it is clear where Wedgewood-Benn's thoughts lay. He clearly did not give a damn about the holidaymakers and their travel plans - he was only interested in pursuing with greatest possible speed the Labour dogma of State nationalisation of everything!

It fell to The Department of Trade to explain to the Press that Peter Shore, the Secretary of State for Trade, had held talks with many interests in the hope that at least the holidays of those booked to the end of September could be safeguarded and that hoteliers and others overseas would have their contract honoured. *'But...'*, said the statement

'...unhappily it has become clear that a comprehensive operation of this kind which met the requirements of all parties involved could not be mounted. The Government's immediate concern is to ensure that these holidaymakers now abroad are brought home at the end of the holiday that these have paid for.

The Government have also asked the Civil Aviation Authority and Association of British Travel Agents to explore urgently what can be done for passengers booked with Court Line companies who have not yet left for the holidays'.

The Civil Aviation Authority (CAA) and the Association of British Travel Agents (ABTA) also issued statements at 2200hrs on 15th August; the CAA advising passengers to contact ABTA, and ABTA advising that passengers should not make their way to the airports, but to contact their local ABTA travel agents unless otherwise advised.

A bond of some £2.3 million had previosuly been lodged by Court Line companies under ABTA regulations; this was called in and deposited in a trust fund operated by the Tour Operators Study Group (TOSG), a 'club' made up of twenty or so tour operators. They rapidly organised an airlift under the stewardship of Sidney Perez, the Chief Executive of Halcyon Horizon, one of the Court subsidiaries, to get stranded holidaymakers back to the U.K. It was estimated that it would cost some £1.5 million to repatriate some 50,000 passengers who were overseas - predominently in the Balearic islands or on the Spanish mainland, but also in other resorts throughout Europe, North Africa and the Caribbean - at the time of collapse. The hotel bills incurred by these people after midnight on the 15th would amount to £500,000 and there was a further 150,000 holidaymakers losing their holidays. The first two thousand or so passengers were airlifted back to the UK as early as Friday lunchtime, which created dramatic images for the press to use.

One person with an onerous task was Alan Smith of BAC who, strangely enough, flew with both Autair and Court Line, assisting with the introduction of both the 400 and 500 series machines. Now, on 16th August he had the sad task of flying around the country in a company 125, serving writs on a number of impounded One-Elevens.

Whilst quoting the numbers, one must not forget the eleven hundred plus employees that lost their jobs - all they got on their eventual return to base was a single sheet of paper from Personal Manager, R. J. Glover:

CERTIFICATE OF SERVICE
TO WHOM IT MAY CONCERN
This is to confirm that .... was employed by Court Line Aviation Limited from........ to 17th August 1974.
Due to the sudden collapse of the company, I regret that it has not been possible to provide detailed references that would normally be available, but any future employer can be assured

Peter Murdoch designed a number of promotional items for Court, including this car sticker that advertised their hot-air balloon and the fact that they operated advanced technology 1-11s and TriStars!

We also operate advanced technology Lockheed Tristars and BAC Super 1-11's

For charter information ring
LUTON 31222

that the bearer of this Certificate of Service has given the Company good cause to be grateful for his/her loyalty, integrity reliability and capability as an employee.

Elizabeth Hutchinson, Edward Posey's secretary was one of the few Court Line staff to be retained for a while after the collapse, as she explains:

Mr Posey rang me from the London Office to say that Court Line was about to go into liquidation. It was so sad, not only for the owners and staff, but sad also for the public who had reacted to us in the same way that they had reacted to Freddie Laker. Both companies had really given the public what they wanted - very competitive air fares to exotic destinations and both were very much part of the British rush to find the sun.

Mr Posey asked me to stay on to work for the Receiver, but my first instinct was to refuse. He then pointed out that I might be able to help some of the staff who were having to leave and, as he predicted, I took calls the following weeks from at least a dozen airlines who were all looking for pilots, air hostesses, engineers, administration people… I was able to pass on the addresses and phone numbers of a great many staff. It was a very lonely eight months for me, travelling to the airport every day to a silent Halycon House, with not a multi-coloured aircraft in sight.

The Court Line collapse was set to become a political football and the media were scenting impropiety afoot. If the government of the day thought that they could get away with sneaking out the news of massive nationalisation under the cover of the collapse by *'saving' the shipping and shipbuilding interests of the group'* they were sadly wrong. Michael Heseltine, Opposition spokesman for industry went on the attack in an official statement on 16 August…

At 10.30 yesterday morning Mr Anthony Wedgewood Benn announced the most ambitious plans to involve the state in industry since the nationalisation plans of the 1940s. Within hours a record of deception, amateur misjudgement and almost unbelievable apathy from Wedgewood Benn himself and Mr Peter Shore was revealed.

Thousands of people have lost their money and their holidays which, if the government had done what it said it had done, or acted when it should have done, could in part, at least, have been avoided.

Peter Shore has talked about the growing concern with Court Line since early July. Not a word of warning has been given to anyone who booked after he first knew the facts.

At a stormy press conference Peter Shore faced a barrage of tough questions from journalists. He stated that as the accountants worked through the books, it had become clear that there was a changed situation. Only within the last 48 hours had the position been reached where the company was no longer solvent.

Asked why a full state take-over of the entire Group could not be made, he replied:

> *I had no reason at all on the information that I have received that this was an operation, which even under different management, could hope to thrive in the future and therefore it would have been imprudent to make a takeover of the leisure activities.'*

Both Anthony Wedgewood Benn and Peter Shore's behaviour were beginning to be called into question. Stevenson Pugh, a director of the TOSG in a letter to *'The Times'*...

> *'I was closely involved in the last hours of Court Line and in the rescue operation that followed. The experience has demonstrated the Minister's commercial incompetence certainly, but perhaps more significantly, how tainted and compromised a Minister may become if he steps outside the political area and dabbles in the harsh world of commerce. The extent of which Mr Benn is compromised by having bolstered an ailing company is already a political issue.*
>
> *What of Mr Shore? First there was his performances on television and at a Press conference after the Court Line failure had been announced. That a Minister should bluster and bluff to get himself off the hook is predicable, but that he should speak in manifest ignorance and spread despondency is another matter. Even while we were meeting to decide how best to do our job - to organise the rescue and do it sufficiently economically to have money over for refunds - we had the astonishing experience of switching on the T.V. and seeing Mr Shore suggest that he was organising the rescue and also expressing the alarming fear that the people who had paid but not travelled probably would not get their money back.*
>
> *Perhaps the most serious question of last week is whether Mr Shore was informed immediately he returned to his desk on Tuesday that Court Line was insolvent, and if so, how could he justify any delay in an announcement even if only for 48 hours. It may be justified (marginally) for directors, bankers, suppliers and other creditors to struggle for a limited period to sustain a sinking company in the hope of a constructive outcome; but it surely must be given a different name for an elected holder of public office under the Crown.*

With such lambasting in the media it is not surprising that steps would have to be taken to reveal more - if only for the politicians and Civil Servants to justify their actions.

Court line Aviation

Peter Murdoch also created a number of more general car stickers for the company.

An ocean away...

Meanwhile, out in Antigua LIAT, although not an integral part of Court Line, was legally entangled in the corporate body, and thus faced liquidation along with its parent company.

Following the announcement on 15th August, a mammoth rescue operation was mounted in the Caribbean, not only to get overseas holidaymakers back to their home countries, but also to save LIAT.

Although the airline itself was not yet solvent, despite the shake-up and cost-cutting undertaken by Michael Warwick in January, representations were made through the British Government to the Special Manager of Court Line for dispensation for the continued operation of LIAT, on the basis that:

a. The Governments of the Associated States and Grenada had indicated a positive desire to acquire ownership of LIAT and process required a short period of time to make the necessary legal and financial arrangements.

b. The position of all the company's creditors as at 15th August 1974 would not be worsened by continuation of LIAT's services.

In order for this to happen, the Governments of the Associated States and Grenada made available EC$ 220,000 from already-committed British grants to provide working capital for the airline during this time.

As detailed investigations started, it was thought that a positive offer could be made to the Special Manager of Courts so that LIAT could be obtained as a going concern. Government representatives held a series of meetings, including a Ministerial delegation from Grenada and the Associated States who met with representatives of the British Government in London. Out of these meetings came the provision for a line of credit guaranteed by the Governments of Grenada and the Associated States so that British Aid Funds allocated to the Caribbean could be used. Accountants Coopers and Lybrand were engaged as special advisers to the Caribbean Governments concerned in the negotiations for LIAT's assets and for the formulation of long-term financial and managerial plans for the airline.

Throughout October and November Commonwealth Governments held a series of meetings, which eventually resulted in a new company incorporated under Antiguan law, called LIAT (1974) Ltd that would take over the operations of the old company. This company still trades successfully to this day.

A further statement...

Possibly stung by such hostile comments in the media, on 21 August

Peter Shore issued a lengthy Press Release announcing an enquiry into the affairs of Court Line, and future protection for holidaymakers. This release served to shed further light on the goings-on of the last few months that had only been hinted about in recent press reports...

On Thursday 15th August, Court Line Limited and its major aviation and travel subsidiaries ceased to trade. This has caused widespread loss and distress to many thousands of holidaymakers and employees of the Group.

I have considered the position thoroughly in the light of all the information available to me and recent precedents including the Rolls-Royce collapse of 1971 and have decided;

1. to appoint inspectors under Section 165(b) of the Companies Act 1948 to carry out an investigation into the affairs of Court Line Limited.

2. to reinforce strongly for the future the protection available for individual holidaymakers.

The terms of reference for the Inspectors will include all the circumstances leading up to the failure of the Group and the losses suffered by holidaymakers and other members of the public both here and abroad. They will be able to investigate the affairs of subsidiaries and the Government will be ready to co-operate to the full in the enquiry and to this end will make available to the Inspectors all the information available to the Government at all material times for which they may call. They will be asked to report as soon as possible and where practicable to make interim reports on matters of particular public interest.

The full story of these events will be examined by the Inspectors, but in the light of inaccurate accounts that have already appeared certain points need to be made clear.

First, the statements announcing the Government's decision to purchase Court Shipbuilders made by the Secretary of State for Industry on behalf of the Government on June 26 and July 1, were made on the basis of the best information that the Board of Court Line and their financial and legal advisers were able to provide at that time.

On July 1 the Secretary of State for Industry told Parliament that:'The Board of Court Line Limited has agreed to these arrangements which, it is confident, safeguard its holiday operations' and this statement was agreed with the company and its legal advisers. The Government had no information which might be regarded as being in conflict with the

Anthony Neil Wedgwood 'Tony' Benn (b.3 April 1925 – d. 14 March 2014) He became the 2nd Earl of Stangate on the death of his father, but fought to renounce this hereditory title, which he did in 1963. He was a prominent figure on its left wing and the term 'Bennite' came to be used for someone with radical left-wing politics. Benn was described as 'one of the few UK politicians to have become more left-wing after holding ministerial office.'

Peter David Shore, Baron Shore of Stepney PC (b.20 May 1924 – d. 24 September 2001) was a British Labour politician and Cabinet Minister.

Storm over Government role in Court Line failure as rescue operation begins

As a rescue operation got under way yesterday to bring back spokesman on industry, said thou sands of

Bleak outlook for Court Line creditors as Official Receiver is put in charge

By John Whitmore
As the courts moved rapidly yesterday to appoint an Official

cost could be extremely high. That could well leave very little money left with which to start

made to other Court Line panies.
The question here is whe

Press told airline staff of collapse

The Government also s last night that it had been to believe by Court Line t

Tears and anger as tourists mob offices

By Staff Reporters
Police were called yesterday to the offices of Clarksons, a Court Line company, in Sun

18,000 Court Line holidaymakers flown back to Britain

By Diana Geddes
About 18,000 stranded Court

Mrs Anne Cole, managing director of Holiday and Sports

assurances given by the Board and its advisers.

The purchase by the Government of Courts' shipping interests, which employ 9,000 people in Assisted Areas, would inevitably have had the effect of making a substantial sum available to Court Line for use in the rest of their business. No additional assurances were given to Court Line or indeed asked by them in relation to the conduct of the rest of their business, for which it was clearly understood that Court Line would remain entirely responsible.

As part of the arrangements for the Government's purchase of Courts' shipbuilding interests, Court Line were asked jointly by the Department of Industry and National Westminster Bank to commission Peat Marwick Michell & Co. to undertake a detailed examination of its longer term viability in the light of trading and cash flow projections. The Report, prepared by Peats was to be made available to the Government and the National Westminster Bank and will, of course, now be available to the Inspectors.

On August 1, a report from Peats showed that although Court Line apparently had, on a going concern basis, a surplus of assets over liabilities, its plans at that time for disposals of its leisure activities which would have enabled it to continue to trade while doing so. The Government was in close touch with Court Line about the various attempts being made to solve its problems. On August 13 it became clear to all concerned that these attempts could not succeed. Court Line then asked to see the Secretary of State for Trade.

Throughout August 14 and the morning of August 15, the Secretary of State for Trade personally considered with Court Line and other interests concerned, a scheme to enable companies involved, in the event of their deciding to go into liquidation, to continue to trade during the liquidation to the extent necessary to enable holidaymakers who had booked holidays lasting to the end of September to be provided with them. This would have involved the agreement of the many and varied interests concerned, together with a limited Government guarantee of necessary bank borrowing and a Government indemnity for the liquidator to cover any claims by creditors whose position had been prejudiced by the working of the scheme.

On the afternoon of 15 August, it became clear that it would not be possible to arrange a scheme which would be effective, even if the Government, on behalf of the taxpayer, had been prepared to accept an open-ended and unquantifiable liability. Court Line was informed accordingly.

One of the considerations the Government had to bear in mind as long as there was a reasonable prospect of Court Line being able to fulfil its obligations throughout the holiday season was the danger of provoking an unnecessary collapse by issuing warnings to intending holidaymakers.

Finally, apart from the many proper questions the Inspectors will be addressing themselves, there have been a number of wild and irresponsible statements. It is quite unjustified, for whatever reason, to exploit the anxieties and serious disappointments of tens of thousands of holidaymakers.

It is also necessary to reinforce the protection for individual holidaymakers - and I am determined to do this - in the light of the changed circumstances in the travel trade.

My department had some time ago initiated discussions with the Civil Aviation Authority and the Association of British travel Agents on strengthening the security given to holidaymakers by the bonding arrangements now imposed on the air travel organisers; these

A little known part of the Group was Court Britain, a tour group that promoted holidays in the UK.

discussions are being pursued urgently with the Civil Aviation Authority and the travel industry and will not be limited to any particular method. My objective, in co-operation with the Civil Aviation Authority, will be to secure a comprehensive set of safeguards on a generally accepted basis but, if necessary, I shall not hesitate to seek further powers when Parliament resumes.

...that opens a can of worms.

The statement from Peter Shore provided some signs as to what had been going on behind the scenes; for instance, it indicated that members of the Court Line Group Board met with the Secretary of State for Industry, Anthony Wedgewood-Benn on 26 June and 1 July - but it later transpired that these were by no means the first contact the Court Line Board had had with the Labour Government or officials within the Civil Service. The Secretary of State for Trade's press release failed to reveal just how closely the situation had been monitored by numerous parties with vested interests.

Day-to-day dealings had been ongoing with the Department of Trade and Industry (as it then was) in the context of a £9 million loan to one of the Court Line Group's companies, Sunderland Shipbuilders Ltd. On 19 March the Department of Trade (the Department had spit into two that month) wrote to the Michael Makin, Group financial director, listing information required about the Groups finances; this was one of the conditions of the loan. On 1 April the official called on Mr Makin but was told the information was not ready - the director and his staff were under pressure to prepare for the Group's AGM later that week. It seems that following public criticism after the publication of the 1972/3 accounts it had been decided to re-cast the Groups cash-flow projections to reflect the deteriorating trend in their holiday business, as bookings were well down. The information as required by the Department of Trade would be ready by 10 May. Also in April the Department of Trade received a report from a travel agent about a rumour that was sweeping the industry that Court Line was in financial difficulties. This was passed to the Civil Aviation Authority, who informed the Department that they had recently examined Court Line's accounts and, although pessimistic about the long term survival prospects, were happy in the short term to re-new the company's Air Travel organisers licence for a further year.

The figures provided to the Department on 10th May revealed that the Group had suffered badly from the change of world economic conditions brought about by the fuel crisis. Clarksons alone would probably make a 1973/4 loss of £5 million compared to a forecast of £2 million. The total loss on aviation and tour related business (excluding those in the Caribbean) for 1974 was expected to be £4.7 million . By 1975, following streamlining, they expected to break even. The Group made mention of selling off most of the Court Line ships and the four hotels in the Caribbean - expected to raise £14 million. It was also revealed at this time that, on recommendation of their financial advisers, the group had asked accountants Price Waterhouse to report to them on their aviation and leisure activities in order to ascertain that their (Court Line's) plans and targets were realistic.

A further meeting occurred on 16 May then, on 19 June, Court Line director Mr J. P. Gilfillian and Court Line Financial Director Michael Makin, requested and were granted an urgent meeting with Mr Neville-Jones, Branch Head of the Shipbuilding Policy Division in the Department of Industry. They stated that some disposals had already taken place, others were on-going - however, the monies from this realisation would not be available into September or October. Court's bankers were demanding that in time for a meeting on 20 June that Court Line should receive assurances from the Department of Industry that Government money would become forthcoming in respect to the Sunderland Shipbuilders loan.

The official told the directors that such an assurance was out of the question, but that he would write to the bank stating that the directors had explained the position to the Department and that they were giving the matter it's most urgent attention.

The next day - 20 June - the Permanent Secretary to the Department of Industry met with five Court Line directors, representatives of the Groups principal bankers, their financial advisers and officials from the CAA, Department of Industry and Department of Trade. It seems that at this meeting John Young, the Managing Director of Court Line Group, informed the Permanent Secretary as to their financial position; one that had deteriorated seriously since the forecast at the start of their financial year in October 1973 when they had forecast a profit in 1973/4 of £8 million. Now they were expecting a loss of £3 to 4 million and were facing an immediate and serious cash crisis. He attributed their difficulties on the oil shortage affecting their tanker trading, the three-day working in the ship-repair and ship-building businesses due to external industrial action and a 40 - 50% drop in booking for the IT holiday business. These were, he reported expected to be short-term problems, although the Group did need £3 million in the next three weeks to stay viable. By selling assets they expected to raise £18 million during August and September and that the bank account would be in credit by October, although the following winter they would need a £5 million overdraft .

A representative from the Groups financial advisers told the meeting that the Price Waterhouse report would be available the next week and would forecast a substantial improvement in cash-flow for 1975 and a viable future. But John Young commented that in order for this to happen, not only had to Group to receive cash help, it also needed a strong statement to restore viability in order to overcome a crisis of confidence that had been growing in the past few days.

Officials from the Department of Trade and the CAA asked about the Group's bonding arrangements for safeguarding their package tour

*More Court Line
promotional images.*

customers in the event of a collapse; one of the directors replied that these were for a total of £3.5 million - an amount that he thought was enough to meet the liabilities in such an event, but he undertook to re-check this.

In conclusion of this meeting John Young again re-iterated the need for urgent action. The Permanent Secretary undertook to consult ministers so that a reply could be given by that weekend.

Reports circulated around Westminster with, it seems, all Departments keen to avoid a collapse. From a meeting on 21 June chaired by the Secretary of State for Industry, Anthony Wedgewood Benn and attended by officials from the Departments of Trade, Industry, and the Civil Aviation Authority it was eventually decided that the Government would take a substantial equity stake in Court Line's shipping concerns. This should then give Court's and it's bankers a breathing space to assist the holiday business.

After the meeting the Department of Trade, with agreement from Prime Minister Harold Wilson's office, issued a press release at 1p.m.

'Court Line have approached the Government about their current difficulties. Discussions are proceeding urgently, in conjunction with the company's bankers, to see whether a solution can be found which, among other things, would secure the interest of the work-force in the company's shipyards and of holidaymakers who have arranged holidays with the company.'

Shortly afterwards, and at the request of the Court Line, trading of it's shares was suspended on the Stock Exchange. To give an indication of the size of the loss of confidence, in 1973 the Groups shares stood at £1.70. In March 1974, just before the 1972/3 accounts were published they stood at 38.5 pence. By 20th June they were at 23 pence - after the announcement prices fell to just 6 pence, but recovered to 14 pence.

Further meetings took place at Westminster that day. At one, a representative from one of Court's bankers expressed doubts that the actions proposed may not resolve the crisis. His bank could only consider immediate bridging finance if the Group had some prospect of long-term viability. The proposed Government's acquisition of the shipping interests would deprive the Group of future profits.

Eventually the final meeting adjourned for the Court Line Group Board to consider with their bankers and financial advisers the principal that the Government should purchase either the whole of, or a controlling interest in their ship-building and ship-repair businesses.

Resuming the meeting, John Young said they had decided that it was wisest to proceed on the basis of Governmental purchase of the whole interest. It was agreed that detailed discussions would start at Court's Thayer Street offices the next morning - Saturday - with the intention of presenting detailed proposals for Ministerial consideration the following Monday and Tuesday. Court again stressed the need for public confidence, saying that the company was afraid that the Spanish Government might instruct hoteliers to refuse Court Line customers, unless reassured soon. They were assured that the Department were already acting on this with all speed.

'The Crisis in Court Line Ltd'...

After the weekend meetings, officials met again in the Department of Industry on Monday to discuss progress. During the weekend the leader of the Government team had prepared a paper titled 'The Crisis in Court Line Limited' which described the options open to the government. The first was to refrain from interfering at all and allow the Group to go into receivership and liquidation. There were disadvantages to this, one of which was that *'...a buyer could probably not be found for the holiday business and in any case immediate chaos would be inevitable'*.

The other option was to acquire some of or all of the share capital of Court Shipbuilders Ltd, the weekend negotiations of which had resulted in agreement of a recommended price of £16 million. however, conditions would be imposed; Court should continue to realise assets where possible, the holiday business should be contracted to a point where it was a viable operation and the Government and the National Westminster Bank, the Group's bankers would appoint accountants Peat, Marwick, Michell and Co. to supervise the streamlining operation. Finally, that the company would seek additional equity finance by means of a merger or otherwise.

Ed Posey captures the moment perfectly:

Everything happened at such an alarming rate. Every division of the Court Line Group was doing its best to mitigate the situation. Ralph Parry, the Court Line Group Company Secretary was doing his best to provide helpful links between the Divisions and the parent, but there was great pressure from the Nat West, Court's bankers to sell assets - the most obvious of which were the hotels.

The Permanent Secretary submitted the paper to Anthony Wedgewood Benn the same day, along with a covering memorandum drawing the Secretary of State for Industry's attention to the unemployment and holiday aspects of the situation:

'*It is not part of our primary purpose to save the leisure activities of Court Line. But if our preferred solution (i.e. the purchase of the shipbuilding and related interests) enables us to do so, this is an additional benefit since it should safeguard the deposits on holidays of several hundred thousand holidaymakers this summer...*

...Naturally we would have preferred to have considerably more

A table showing the Group's forecast overdraft level during July and August 1974.

SHORT TERM CASH FLOW TO 30 AUGUST 1974

Forecast overdraft for weeek ending	Forecast 18 June 1974 £M	As prepared 3 July 1974 £M	As revised 12 July 1974 £M
28 June	6.1	5.9	5.9
5 July	6.3	8.0	7.4
12 July	5.1	6.9	6.7
19 July	4.6	6.3	6.6
26 July	4.9	6.4	6.9
2 August	5.1	7.3	7.7
9 August	5.0	7.2	7.7
16 August	5.4	7.6	8.1
23 August	5.4	7.7	8.2
30 August	5.8	8.7	9.5

Benn's big holiday rescue

In the House of Commons yesterday Tony Wedgewood Benn announced that the Government were about to acquire the entire shipping interests of Court Line that would safeguard the holidays

Lifeline for holiday firm

Tony Wedgewood-Benn, the Secretary of State for Industry, last night threw a lifeline to

by deciding to take over the shipbuilders interests of Court Line, the Government have averted the risk of collapse of the Group as a whole.

BENN'S GRAB SAVES TOUR FIRM

time to go into this whole situation. But I believe that, within the constraints imposed upon us, the proposed solution is the best available. We shall be acquiring a profitable shipbuilding and ship-repairing company in advance of nationalisation at a defensible price, thus safeguarding some 9,000 jobs in the assisted areas and a substantial on-going order book which could otherwise be jeopardised. If a lot of the population also gets away on holiday, so much the better'.

Wedgewood-Benn then drew up a draft statement to present to the House of Commons on the afternoon of 26th June:

As the House will know, Court Line, which owns shipyards and Clarksons and Horizon Tours, has approached the Government for assistance to deal with financial difficulties which might have threatened employment in the shipyards and the order book for ships and the many hundreds of thousands of people now booked to go on holiday tours this summer.

*The Government are ready to acquire the entire shipbuilding and ship repairing interests of Court Shipbuilders and consider that this should **release sufficient cash-flow to safeguard the remainder of** Court's interests, including the holidays booked this summer. Further details are being worked out, and I will make a fuller statement as soon as possible'*

The section highlighted is of interest, for it demonstrates how political ambiguity appears. After the draft was circulated to other Ministers and senior officials that part was downgraded in positivity. In the House the phrase '*...stabilise the situation in respect of...*' was substituted.

To go with the statement to be read before the House, Wedgewood-

Benn's officials prepared a number of possible 'questions' and 'answers' for him to use...

Question: *What is the Government's authority for rescuing a group concerned largely with package holidays?*

Answer: *This was not the primary object of the Government's action. We believe that is should be possible for the purchase of Court Shipbuilders to be done under Section 7 of the Industry Act, which is entirely appropriate since all the jobs at stake in that company are in the assisted areas.*

Question: *Will Court Line survive after the hiving off of the shipyards?*

Answer: *The company is in full agreement with the arrangements I have described, and believes it can continue in its operations.*

Question: *Can people who have booked holidays with Court Line be sure of getting them?*

Answer: *The company willingly agreed to these arrangements and would not have done so if it did not believe it could continue operations. Obviously I cannot give guarantees about an independent commercial operation, but certainly people's prospects of getting their holidays have been greatly improved by the Government's action.*

Two further references were made by Wedgewood-Benn in the House that afternoon. In reply to the member for Henley, he said:

It was thought right that holidaymakers who had holidays booked this summer should have some reasonable security, and the Government were anxious to help them....

Prime Minister James Harold Wilson, Baron Wilson of Rievaulx, KG, OBE, FRS, FSS, PC (b. 11 March 1916 –d. 24 May 1995)

...What we are proposing to do is to bring into public ownership some sixteen companies that are owned by Court Shipbuilders in a form that is completely agreeable to the firm thus saving the jobs of 9,000 workers and safeguarding the holidaymakers...

and in reply to the Member for Sunderland South he said...

...the statement I made today is a holding statement designed mainly to reassure my Hon. Friends, constituents and other shipyard workers and holidaymakers...

This statement (and supplementary questions and answers) was the first of a pair of statements from the Secretary of State for Industry that was to cause much furore following the collapse; simply put, could the above statement mislead holidaymakers into thinking that they could confidently complete, or enter into new holiday arrangements with Court Line or any of their subsidiaries? Read them again - even the down-graded version without the questions and answers seems to imply that all was well for at least that year!

Urgent investigations....

The next day Court's bankers formally appointed Peat, Marwick, Michell and Co. They were asked to consider four things:
i.   The future viability of the residual Court Line Company, taking account of its capital position and financing requirement.
ii. The borrowing and bond requirements and how these could best be arranged to safeguard the position of lenders.
iii. The adequacy and practicality of the asset realisations proposed.
iv. The extent and practicality of merger possibilities.

John Young was still very concerned about the absence of a definitive statement about the financial arrangements for the purchase of Court Shipbuilders and the continuing lack of confidence within the travel trade regarding Clarksons and other Court Line holidays. Eventually, on 1st July further details of the financial arrangements between the Court Line Group board and the Government were revealed in a written statement by Wedgewood Benn to the House:

> '...the board of Court Line Ltd has agreed to these arrangements which, it is confident, safeguard its holiday operations.
>
> The Government's primary concern in these arrangements has been to safeguard the employment of nearly 9,000 people employed in the assisted areas by Court Shipbuilders and its subsidiaries. Existing management will remain.

On 3 July John Bloomfield, director of Court Line Leisure Division (who joined Court Line from Shipping and Industrial Holdings when the Court Group acquired Clarksons Holidays and was appointed a director of Court's on 1 March 1974) issued an upbeat circular letter to travel agents, referring to Wedgewood-Benn's statement two days earlier...

> 'Dear Agent
> The Court Line Leisure Division is in a positive on-going situation with all its tour companies operating normally, taking bookings for this and next year, and completing its programme arrangements for 1975.
>
> This is the clear and constructive message I can give you following the recent period of newspaper speculation which must have left you, and some of your clients, in an uncertain mood.
>
> As businessmen you will know that cash flow problems are affecting many aspects of British Industry. In our case these problems are by no means insuperable, but a newspaper report some two weeks ago started stock market speculation which in

turn, resulted in further exaggerated press reports.

These reports created a degree of uncertainty which necessitated Court Line Ltd. taking action to protect its many interests. Talks were immediately instituted with the Department of Industry resulting in the Government's announcement in the Hose of Commons on Monday (1st July).

In essence this said that the Court Shipbuilding Division would be sold into public ownership at a sum approximating to the book value of the assets. This sale means that Court Line is now in a position to maintain and develop its Aviation and Leisure interests with the necessary financing and backing to support an on-going operation.

All companies in the Leisure Division - that's Clarksons, Horizon, Air Fair, OSL, 4S, Far Horizons, 4S Sports, Court Travel, Cristalotel - as well as the Aviation Division are therefore secure. All bonding and financial arrangements are continuing and our relationships with overseas governments, hoteliers and other suppliers are strong and healthy.

I would like to take this opportunity of thanking those of you who have given us support during this recent difficult period. Because we are involved in negotiations with the Government it has been impossible for me to give relevant details until this time, though you have my assurance that ABTA was kept fully informed of the situation at all stages.

Company humour - 1
A cartoon by an unknown artist sent by Ed Posey to John Young not long after Court Line acquired the company back in 1966...

We at Court Leisure are confident that our plans for the future will keep us in the forefront of inclusive holiday operations.

We have the products. We have the management. We have the necessary financing.

Our plans for the future involve you, in fact depend on you. Our researches say that in partnership we will succeed'

A few days later ABTA followed this up with a letter of their own, reproducing an extract from a letter Court Line sent to them after a meeting confirming *'the major assurances and undertakings'* that ABTA had been given. These included statements that Aviation and Leisure Divisions were operating normally and that agents need have no fears when taking bookings for their programmes; the airline and hotel arrangements were secure.

The accountants report...

On 5 July three things happened. Detailed discussions started on preparation of the legal documents for the sale of Court Shipbuilders; a committee was established and met to monitor the residual activities of Court Line and Price Waterhouse completed their report and this was considered by the Department of Industry.

Price Waterhouse were concerned as to the accuracy of their own 'report', for they had been obliged to work with inadequate accounting information and it failed to include information about the Group's trading activities in the Caribbean at Court's request. Price Waterhouse felt that the extent of any financing arrangements needed by the Leisure Division had not yet been established and until that had been done, no final conclusions should be drawn as to the viability of these activities.

Some decisions relating to the streamlining of the Group were beginning to be taken - on Thursday 11 July it was noted that the Board had decided that the two Lockheed L-1011 TriStars would cease operations 'next year' and that a meeting would be arranged for the following day at Luton so that staff could be informed. As far as can be ascertained, this staff meeting never took place, certainly the information does not appear to have reached employees below Manager level. It does seem however, that some information seeped out, for rumours circulated that there was a possiblity that the airline would 'downsize' and operate just six One-Elevens.

Pressure was on the Board to consider a mryiad of items, coming at them from different directions - decisions for the immediate and longer term. For instance, the Summer 1975 holiday brochures were due for publication and a decision had to be made around this time to prepare, publish, print and distribute - it could not be delayed much longer. The cost of this would be around £1.5 million - money that was just not there. To publish was to advertise for customers for 1975 - not to publish would be to publicly concede that Clarksons - and therefore Court Line - was no longer in the holiday business. They hung on, and in the end it was not even ordered.

The first of four interim reports from Peat, Marwick and Michell - this one dealing with the company's short term position - was presented on 12 July. It dealt with cash flow to 30 August 1974 a pro forma balance sheet to the end of the following month, level of indebtedness at 30 June 1974 and the asset realisation programme. This report forecast a trading loss for the year to 30 September 1974 of some £11 million, although actual results could differ greatly if some of the accounting assumptions made in preparation of the report were incorrect. It was thought however, that if the sell-off of Court Shipbuilders was completed before 30 August there would be enough funds to continue. This PM&M report offered four broad options for the Court Line board to consider:

i.   to continue trading at the levels currently forecast.
ii   to contract the leisure operations to a more controllable and profitable size.
iii to merge with another entity in the leisure industry.
iv   to dispose of its trading activities.

PM&M warned they they thought that at this time the Board did not have the financial information available to consider these alternatives.

The monitoring committee met on 19 July, expressing thoughts that it was '...*difficult to see a future for the Group as present constituted for any long period ahead*'. Mr Lippitt from the Department of Industry wrote to John Young on 22 July, expressing that the committee wanted to make clear that it was the Group's management's responsibility to tackle its problems with the energy that was clearly necessary. John Young replied on the 24th that the board were well aware of the problems facing them, but that he thought that the company did not have the resources to tackle them on its own. He asked the Department to assist.

By the latter part of July Court Line's major creditors were beginning to press for hard information about the present and future prospects.

On 26 July PM&M's second report was submitted. It set out details of the Groups assets and their disposal of which required consideration. The monitoring committee met the same day with Court Line directors and representatives from their bank to discuss the cash-flow position, the need for improvements in administration and the directors proposals. Plans were suggested to lease some aircraft to other users, sell off some ships and hotels and that it was desirable to dispose of the loss-making LIAT in the Caribbean.

Three days later - on 29 July - the Department of Trade convened a meeting with representatives of the Department of Industry and the Civil Aviation Authority to discuss Court Line's future in the light of PM&M's first report. Clearly the Group could not continue trading at the present levels, and this meeting considered that a merger or sell-offs were not hopeful prospects.

John Young met with the Departments of Trade and Industry on 31 July, where it was agreed that the company would continue to investigate merger possibilities, but that PM&M would advise on the practicality of an orderly running down of the company's trading activities.

The next day Prime Minister Harold Wilson was informed of the Group's continuing difficulties, that the Department of Trade was in daily touch with them so that if events took a turn, jeopardising holiday plans of tourists before the end of the summer, the Government would be in a position to set in operation a rescue plan by other tour operators. Harold Wilson asked to be kept in touch with developments.

This point appears to be the end of the beginning of the crisis within the Court Line Group. It appears that by now, although other options had not been discarded, all interested parties were in favour of an orderly winding down of Court Line with a view to it ceasing trading, but at the same time avoiding liquidation before the end of the 1974 season. However, prospects for such a course of action were not good, so preliminary steps for a rescue operation in the event of an uncontrolled collapse were put into place.

*Company humour - 2
A memo from John Bloomfield to Ed Posey dated 29 June 1973 with a Maddocks cartoon that depicted some of the 'misconceptions' of IT...*

The beginning of the end.

On 1 August PM&M issued their third report, this one examining the longer-term prospects for the group. It appeared that the Court Line Group had, as a going concern, a surplus of assets over liabilities at least up to 30 September 1974 - the end of their trading year. However, from that point onwards there would be a need for substantial extra borrowing to see the Group through the lean winter months. PM&M recommended immediate consideration be given to a merger and that firm proposals be put forward within six weeks.

The next day the Department of Industry asked the accountants to prepare two contingency plans:

i.   a plan for the complete, orderly winding-up of the Group that included an appraisal of the best time to implement such a scheme.

ii. a plan for the company to continue operations on a much reduced scale, including the elimination of major loss-making elements such as Clarksons and Horizon.

Two meetings of the monitoring committee took place on 2 August. At the first it was noted that the accountants were now suggesting an overdraft peak in November of £11.4 million and that the company were pursuing a number of merger possibilities, although prospects were poor. At the second meeting, this one attended by Court Line Directors, the Department of Trade expressed concern about deposits received by the company from holidaymakers travelling after the end of the 1974 season. Court supplied figures that showed that some £520,000 had already been received from 65,000 customers in respect of holidays after 30 September 1974. This worked out at £8 per head deposit, the standard amount for Clarksons clients. Furthermore, it was expected that bookings would continue to be made at the rate of 8,000 per week, bringing in £64,000 every seven days. Some of this was available to Court's, although much of it was held by the travel agents and accounted for.

By 7 August it was beginning to appear that the Group may have to go into liquidation within the next fourteen days, although everyone was working hard to avoid this. That afternoon Court Lione advised the Department of Industry that their attempts to arrange a merger had been unsuccessful. The next day the CAA were called to an urgent meeting with the Department of Trade over anxiety of passengers possibly being stranded abroad. They informed the Department that in the absence of any serious prospect of a merger, by the beginning of the next week they would have to give 21 days notice of revoking Court Line's Air Operator's Licence under Section 23 of the Civil Aviation Act 1971, for it was their duty to revoke or suspend licences if they were not satisfied that the operator in question had adequate financial resources and arrangements to discharge its actual and potential obligations. The Prime Minister was then informed.

British Airways involvement?

That same day - 8 August - British Airways (BA) informed the Department of Trade that they were not interested in taking over Court's Airline or Leisure Divisions then or at all. There had been speculation in some quarters that deals were about to be done with British Airways and that they might take parts or all of the Court Line Group over. It seems that these stemmed from the early part of 1974, when BA introduced package tours of their own under the banner of Sovereign Holidays flown on their scheduled services and Enterprise holidays flown with their recently-formed Airtours operation at Gatwick. Commercially, BA were duty bound to consider any possibility open to them, so when Horizon became 'available' early in 1974 they looked at acquiring it from the viewpoint of a take-over.

However, by the summer of 1974 BA were encountering the same down-turn in trade that the remainder of the airline industry was experiencing, and were having to look long and hard at their own position. Court's Leisure and Airline Divisions offered BA no real benefit through acquisition.

BA was approached however by the Department of Trade with two enquiries - what passenger capacity would BA have available to bring holidaymakers back if Court Line Aviation collapsed, and whether BA could take over part or all of Court Line's 1974 Summer programme.

With regards to capacity, BA made calculations and informed the Department of what they could do in that eventuality. As it transpired they were needed, and brought back some 7,000 passengers to the U.K. Taking over the programme was a different matter altogether.

Enormous problems would have to be overcome, both operationally, legally and financially. Although investigated, it is understandable that nothing came of it.

The Court Line Aviation Headquarters building at Luton.

Without doubt there are on-the-surface comparisons that can be drawn between the collapse of Court Line and that of Dan-Air Services Ltd some eighteen years later, with British Airways as the potential purchaser of both. However, there are a number of fundamental differences between the two events that clearly demonstrate why Dan-Air's Chairman David James had some success in interesting BA in it, but why John Young could not interest them in Court Line.

In mid-1990's terms Dan-Air actually 'went down' for considerably less than Court Line. Dan-Air 'went' for around £37 million, Court for £11.4 million in 1974, that is equivalent to over £51 million in the mid-1990s! The Court Line Group at the end (having already effectively lost the shipping aspects of it's business) was a pure charter airline with strong associated leisure interests - holiday companies and hotels. Dan-Air Services and Davies and Newman were predominantly a scheduled service and charter airline with a series of passenger-handling concerns and small holiday interests. BA obtained Dan-Air for two basic reasons; movement 'slots' at a number of airports that BA already operated from and a number of scheduled service routes to Europe - both reasons fitting in well with BA's plans for global domination. Everything else they junked as soon as they could. Court Line, unfortunately, had nothing like that to offer BA. But, back to August 1974...

The start of the slippery slope...
On the surface, things appeared normal - holidays were being booked, tourists were getting away and aircraft were coming and going. On 9 August John Young was asked what it would take to keep the Group going - he declined to give a figure, but Michael Sayers of Brandts, one of Court's bankers suggested £12 million [£54.84m]. John Young agreed that it could not be less than this, plus a guarantee of continued bonding. This would, of course mean that the CAA would call off its threat of suspending Court's licences. The Parliamentary Under-Secretary for

Companies, Civil Aviation and Shipping sent a minute to Harold Wilson, the Prime Minister, to the effect that the Court Line Group would almost inevitably go into liquidation during the next seven days.

Over the weekend of 10th and 11th August all was quiet, but on 12 August, the Department of Trade asked the Association of British Travel Agents (ABTA) and the CAA to produce a contingency rescue plan by mid-day of the 13th. That day Mr Lippitt of the Department of Industry called a meeting with most of the interested parties. Here it was again revealed that British Airways were not interested in obtaining the Group. At this meeting, and at their request, the Court Line directors agreed to meet with the Secretary of State for Trade during the afternoon of 14 August, with Mr Shore cutting short his overseas mission and returning home for that purpose.

By now it had become apparent to those involved that if there was to be any help for the Court Line Group it would have to come from the Government with the help of public funds. Meetings with Peter Shore during the afternoon and evening of 14 August further investigated every possible avenue. At 1730hrs on the 14th Peter Shore met with Court Line representatives to ascertain the views of the Board. John Young and Michael Sayers thought that the whole matter was so urgent now that a definite decision would have to be made within the next two days. It seems there were still two options; an orderly shut-down or immediate termination of business followed by implementation of the rescue plan. Court's view was that there was no real alternative to the repatriation of the 40,000 people currently abroad. Peter Shore promised the final Government answer by Friday 16th August. At 1800 hrs he then met with the aircraft lessors, banks and others concerned with the Court Line Group and put them in the picture.

Attempts to find a way to enable the holiday companies to continue to trade in one form or another if the Group was to go into liquidation were still being sought during the morning of 15 August - not an easy option, for it would have required agreement from a number of differing interests and an indemnity from the Government to cover any liquidator against claims by creditors whose position had worsened during the continued trading. By the afternoon it became clear that it was not possible to arrange a suitable scheme. The Court Line Group Board Members were told of this and the Group then finally ceased trading. For many who had worked so hard to save the Group, it was all over bar the rescue operation.

Shock, disbelief, then anger.
Although Secretary of State for Trade Peter Shore's statement of 21st August explained in detail what had happened over the last few months, it did little if anything to calm tempers. Thousands of holidaymakers were understandably upset about the loss of their holidays, their money or both. Some were philosophical, others were not. A number contacted

The delgation from the Court Line Action Group outside Number 10 Downing Street. From left to right: Reg Law, Mr. V W Mat, Mr M Keene and Louise Symonds.

their
Member of Parliament. Others had
their loss disclosed in the newspapers, both local and national.

Anthony Adams from Exeter lost £462 on a cruise starting from Athens, William Fox of Billingshurst lost £225 on a fortnight in Greece, Eric and Elizabeth Joy and four friends lost £650 on a holiday in Minorca, Marie and Alex Ogilvie should have been on honeymoon in Tenerife, but lost their £211... the list went on.

Many thought that they had been misled by the Government into thinking that their holidays were secure. One such holidaymaker who was to figure large in the events that followed was Reg Law of St Albans. Reg and his wife had lost £137.11 on a 5-night holiday to Norway. They should have departed on Flight OU517 from Luton on 27 August. Instead Reg found himself appearing on the Jimmy Young Radio Show as a spokesman for the fledgling Court Line Action Group. Events then snowballed.

By 4 September Reg and other members of the Group were outside 10 Downing Street, handing in to Prime Minister Harold Wilson a petition stating that the Group felt that the Government had a moral responsibility to reimburse the money through the Association of British Travel Agents' (ABTA) bond.

Unfortunately people who had booked and paid a deposit or the total cost of their holiday in full were unable to get their money back - even the funds that had been paid to Travel Agents and were not yet passed on to Court Line!

This money had been frozen by the Receiver. Eventually, after much discussion and political wrangling as to how an acceptable formula for repayment could be arrived at, funds were released so that the holidaymakers could get their money back from the Tour Operators Study Group fund - and payments started to be made in August 1975, one year after the collapse.

For months after the collapse there was a 'feeding frenzy' within the Press. Some pretty vindictive things were written and it got nasty for a while. It all started up again when the Interim and Final Reports into the collapse were published, both of which have been called upon to recall events mentioned in this chapter. No single reason for the collapse was found.

The curtain falls...
But that was not quite the end of the story. As a direct result of lobbying by Reg Law, the Court Line Action Group and others, the Air Travel Reserve Fund Act 1975 came into being. This protected the payments made by clients of an air travel organiser that financially failed. Some good at least came out of the debacle.

The One-Elevens quickly moved to other operators, but the pair of TriStars languished at Luton for 12 months...

It all seems an age ago now.

Chapter Twelve

Time Marches On

Twenty years after the collapse of Court Line I started writing this story... much had happened and yet nothing much had changed. In 1997 when the hardback book came out, holiday companies were still offering deals at ridiculously low prices, losing money and get taken over, charter airlines were appear on the scene in lurid colours, and a Labour Government is back in power.

By the time of the 40th Anniversary of the collapse rolled round the travel trade and leasure airline industry had changed almost out of all recognition. Now travel brochures were hardly ever printed, with holiday sales happening almost totally online, with all sorts of protection in place. Airlines were now not only 'low cost', but also 'no frills', and Inclusive Tours had become 'All Inclusive'.

It may be of interest here to bring the reader 'up to date' as it were... Of the Court Line Group little-to-nothing tangible survives, although many of the constituent companies are still around - indeed, some are thriving.

Many of the employees found jobs elsewhere in the industry, others experienced a career change. By 1994 some thought that enough water had passed under the bridge so it was time for a reunion. Jaqui Maschera and Geoff Tong got together, and sent out hundreds of aviation chain letters wich resulted in a highly successful reunion at Brighton on 22 October 1994. From that event evolved the Court Line Staff Association.

Over the years since the first version of this book came out I have often been asked numerous questions by many people about the collapse. These questions fall into three categories:

1. Who was to blame?
2. Why did the Group fail?
3. Could it have been avoided?

Question One has no value; it had none at the time, when it was asked by those in the media searching for an easy headline and a 'scapegoat' - it certainly has no relevance now. Questions Two and Three however, are valid.

From a newspaper cutting - the 1997 Reunion.

Back row, L to R: John Nuttall, Phil Bowles, Dee and Mike Rudge, Paula Parke, Angela Constantinou, Dee Newkirk.

4th Row: Clive Barton, Mike Albone, Chrispin Maunder, Chris Carver, Mike 'M.G.' Williams, Barry Elliott, Graham Anderson

3rd Row: Kurt Lang, Sheena Carver, John Purdon, Mrs Jon Charley, Mrs John Nuttsall, Dennise Truner Iona Peck, Hellen Connolly, Pauline Lord, Carol Barford, Stella Elliott, Geoff Tong, Ed Posey.

2nd Row: Vanya Anderson, Susie Bernard, Chris Penny, Rosie Boorman, Jaqui Maschira, Sandy Keegan, Gavin Keegan, Chistobel Reiche West, Linda Hills, Elizabeth Hutchinson.

Front Row: Jenny Berryman, Jon Charley, Anne Baggott, Ding Sadler, Sue Farr, Yvonne Ovey, Carol Odegaard.

Better minds than mine have studied all the evidence in great detail and I am forced to agree in the main with them. It must be made clear from the onset, both the Interim and the Final Report into the collapse found that there had been no fraudulent trading, that the Directors had conducted their business in the correct and proper manner and that 15 August 1974 was indeed the right date to cease trading.

Court's expanded rapidly in many directions, some of which were justifiable and logical, others were not. With the benefit of hindsight - which is always 20:20 vision - the management structure was not supported by as good a financial control system as was needed. This meant that the more the Group expanded, the more vulnerable it became to setbacks.

Without a doubt up to September 1973 the Aviation Division of the Court Line Group of companies was a strong, vigorous and prosperous business. When a serious set-back did occur - the 1973 oil crisis - it immediately affected the Shipping, Leisure and Aviation Divisions. All cash resources and reserves had already been 'locked up' for the medium term in the Caribbean, leaving no scope for support, which meant that the position progressively deteriorated and collapse was inevitable.

Court Line Aviation Managing Director and Court Line Group Director Edward Posey was probably the one person in the best position to offer an insight into the demise. The oil crisis undoubtably was the trigger, but there was one other 'oversight' - involving the 'time charter' concept - that had been made much earlier and was lying dormant waiting for circumstances to trigger it off, as Ed Posey explains...

'We learned about time charters from our Court Line colleagues steeped in their shipping experience. It was an ideal way of us doing business, even with the benefit of hindsight. There is, however, one caveat and that is that both parties involved must be able to back up their side financially as well as operationally.

Aviation fulfilled its side of the bargain by providing an excellent service with the latest equipment. Clarksons, however, were unable to fulfil their side of the contracts because of declining passenger loads.

They were contracted to pay for our service whether the aircraft were full or empty. We never obtained a guarantee from their parent company, Shipping and Industrial Holdings (SIH). John Young, who knew the SIH Board well, always believed they would stand by their own 100% owned subsidiary, Clarksons Holidays. In the event they did not and would have put the company into liquidation had not Court Line taken it over. Here, unfortunately, Court Line had no option because SIH did not stand by the undertakings of their subsidiary.

I must reiterate, it was not the concept of time charters that was at fault, but in this case it was the contract for not having, on Clarksons' side, a guarantee of substance'.

This was put into stark relief by the arrangements for financing and operating the pair of TriStars. Acquisition of them it seems, stemmed from market appraisals put forward by Clarksons. Sadly the continued expansion of the market peaked with the oil crisis and Court Line Aviation found themselves with seating capacity to spare. This problem was compounded by the virtual collapse of Horizon and Clarksons Holidays which forced Court Line Group to acquire these concerns in an effort to keep the aircraft utilised. One TriStar may have been capable of carrying over three One-Eleven loads, but that is only of benefit if over three One-Eleven loads of passengers all want to go to the same destination at the same time! All appears elsewhere, but it deserves repeating here, profit margins were such that costings had been worked out on full aircraft - Courts 'icing on the cake' profits came from Bar and Duty-free sales, and that could mount up to many hundreds of thousands of pounds in a year!

Acquisition of Clarksons took the Group outside their normal sphere of operations and outside its 'comfort zone', forcing a change from being just 'operators' to becoming 'charterers' with all that entailed. Legal requirements forced onto the Group by British Caledonian Airways to use a pair of their One-Elevens following the takeover of Horizon did nothing to ease the spare capacity or cash flow within the Court Group.

The approach by the company to the Labour Government of the day provided opportunistic politicians with an easy back-door method of 'nationalising' the Group's shipping interests under the guise of saving around 9,000 jobs - at the same time sucking up to their Trade Union Council masters. Straightforward, open and honest State acquisition of the industry would have been a far harder prospect to sell to the nation!

In late June/early July of 1974 this generated much praise and column-inches in the Press - little thought seems to have been given to those jobs in danger in the airline or to the fact that those holding the very jobs they were 'saving' had probably booked their holidays with Court Line!

I tried long and hard to find the last tangible aspect of the Court Line saga: eventually the very last fragments in the story surfaced. Court Line Limited (In Liquidation) continued in existence for many years. The shipbuilding interests could be finalised in a reasonably short period of time; not so the other marine matters, insurance claims and the sale of the Caribbean hotels.

At the commencement of liquidation the shares in subsidiary companies had a book value of £19m and were estimated by the directors that they would realise £1m - in the event they raised £336,000. Loans and advances to other subsidiary companies had a book value of £21m and were estimated to realise a value of £4m - in the event they realised over £11m.

Overall a nett fund amounting to £29,749,000 became available for distribution to creditors of the company in the following manner:

Secured creditors		£13,283,000
Preferential creditors (paid in full)		£159,000
Unsecured creditors (£62,418,335)		
in nine dividends	26.125p	16,307,000
		29,749,000

The date the liquidators were released?... 26th October 1989!

Appendix One

Area of operations for Autair helicopters

Autair Helicopters operated all over the World, for numerous clients. Although the scope of this operation is outside the main thrust of this book, there is a relevance within the overall story, and so has been included here in chart form.

LOCATION	CLIENT	OPERATION
ANTARCTIC	Falkland Islands Dependencies Survey	Shipborne expedition moving land survey teams.
ARCTIC	Nordmine Ltd	Mineral resources expedition.
ARGENTINA	U.N.DevelopmentProgramme	High altitude geological surveys of the Andes Mountains.
ASSAM	Burma Oil Co. & Agip	Pipeline route survey and construction.
ATLANTIC - North	*M.V. Willem Barendsz*	Shipborne fishing reconnaissance.
ATLANTIC -South	Shell, BP & Esso Tanker companies	Shore-to-ship services ex-South Africa.
AUSTRALIA	Continental Oil & other survey co.	Oil & specialist surveys of West Australia & Northern Territories.
AUSTRIA	Malta Valley — Alpine Hydro—Electric	Lifting work teams and construction materials.
BANGLADESH	Shell Oil Co.	Offshore rig support services.
CAMEROON	Utah International	Uranium survey team support.
CANADA	Government & Commercial clients	N.Eastern area surveys & support services.
CRETE	Greek Government	Olive crop surveys and treatment.
DUBAI	Various major clients	Oil exploration support services.
EGYPT	Government	Agricultural control & spraying services.
ENGLAND	Hunting Surveys Ltd	Tellumetersurveys.
	British Gas	Pipeline security patrols.
ETHIOPIA	Hunting Surveys Ltd	Support of field survey teams.
FERNANDO PO	Gulf Oil Co.	Offshore rig support.
FRANCE	Paramount Film Contractors	Aerial cine photography.
GERMANY	Emts Ludt. K.G.	Agricultural spraying and dusting.
GREECE	United Nations	Pre-investment forestry surveys.
HIMALAYAS	Everest Expedition (Sir Edmund Hillary)	High-altitude operation at Nepal/Tibet border.
INDIA	Standard VacuumOil	West Bengal seismic survey and mobiledrill rig support.
INDONESIA	French Atomic Energy Commission	Uranium surveys in East Borneo.
IRAN	Bechtel Corp/US Mapping	Terrain surveys.
	Agip Mineraria	Offshore oil exploration.
IRAQ	Iraq Petroleum Co.	Services to offshore tanker terminal Khor-Al-Amaya.
KENYA	Somiren & Associates	Field surveys and transport.
LIBERIA	Liberian International American Corp.	Mineral exploration and lifting operations.
LIBYA	Government Departments	Transport Senior Officials.
LUXEMBURG	C.E.A.	Agricultural spraying operations.

MADAGASCAR	United Nations	Special fund operations technical assistance.
MALAWI	McPhar Geophysics Ltd.	Airborne geophysical surveys.
MALI	United Nations F.A.O.	Locust control operations.
MALTA	Home Oil Ltd.	Offshore oil exploration.
MOZAMBIQUE	Gulf Oil Co.	Oil exploration support.
	Aero Service Ltd	Airborne gravity survey.
MYANMAR	Louis Berger Associates	Highway route surveys.
NAMIBIA	Anglo American & Marine Diamond Corp	Offshore diamond dredger services
NEPAL	Cook Electric Co. & U.S.O.M.	Communication equipment location surveys.
NIGERIA	United Nations	Maiduguri survey services.
OMAN	Petroleum Development Ltd and E.L.F./E.R.A.P.	Oil exploration support.
PAKISTAN	Sun Oil Co.	Oil exploration coastal areas.
PHILLIPINES	American Overseas Petroleum/Texaco	Oil exploration services.
SAUDI ARABIA	United States Geological Survey	Government oil exploration support.
SCOTLAND	Forestry Commission	Survey, lifting & fertiliser spreading.
SIERRA LEONE	Sierra Leone Selection Trust Ltd.	Security control diamond mining areas.
SOMALIA	Nucleare S.P.A. & Ministry of Mining	Airborne & geophysical uranium surveys.
SOUTH AFRICA	Kruger National Park	Game control.
	Electricity Commission	Power line patrol.
SPANISH SAHARA	Richfield Sahara Petroleum	Transport geophysical survey crews.
SPITZBERGEN	Government Concessions	Survey team support.
SUDAN	United Nations — F.A.O.	Land and water surveys Jebel Marra.
SWAZILAND	United Nations/Lockwood	Magnetometer surveys.
TANZANIA	Snam Progetti - Agip	Tazama pipeline survey & construction.
TUNISIA	Mineragip	Seismic surveys Borma Desert region.
UGANDA	Interior Ministry	Flight training & advisory services.
ZAIRE	Union Miniere & Bureau de Recherches Geologiques.	Field support mineral survey teams
ZAMBIA	R.S.T. Ltd	Geological surveys.
	Snam/Agip	Pipeline patrol.
ZIMBABWE	Electric Power Board	Power line patrols.

Appendix Two

Fleet Lists

Throughout the company's history a number of different aircraft types were operated. In order to make this proliferation of types, sub-types and variants easier to understand (and put their use into some form of perspective) a full as possible fleet list is provided.

AUTAIR/AUTAIR INTERNATIONAL/COURT LINE AVIATION

Registration	Type	c/n	Remarks
Douglas C-47 Dakota			
G-AGHJ	A	9413	Obtained 2.62 from Jersey Airlines. Wfu Luton 8.65.
G-AGYX	A	12472	Obtained 21.4.61 from BEA. To Martin's Luchtvervoer Maatschappij NV 23.7.65 as PH-MAG.
G-AJIC	A	9487	Obtained 39.3.61 from BEA. Last known to be derelict, Libya 1966.
G-ALTT	A	12000	Obtained 13.11.62 from BEA. To Iceland 8.63 as TF-FIS
G-AMGD	A	9628	Obtained 8.4.60. from BEA. To Southern Rhodesia 12.61 as VP-YTT for Autair (Rhodesia) Ltd. To Rhodesian Air Services Ltd.
G-AMNV	D/B	16833	Obtained from Spain 2.65. Leased to Sweden as SE-EDI 5.65-10.65. To Bechuanaland 11.65 as VQ-ZEA.
G-APPO	A	20453	Obtained 10.66. Wfu at Luton 8.67.
Vickers Viking			
G-AGRW	639	115	Obtained from Overseas Airways Ltd following collapse in 8.61 entered service 1.62. Wfu 7.68.
G-AHOY	499	128	Obtained from Pegasus Airways Ltd following collapse in 11.61. Entered service 5.63. To Invicta Airways 3.65.
G-AHPB	639	132	Obtained from Overseas Airways Ltd following collapse in 8.61. Entered service 3.63. Wfu at Luton 5.68.
G-AHPJ	614	147	Obtained from Overseas Airways Ltd following collapse in 8.61. Entered service 1.62. To Aero Sahara 6.65.

G-AHPL	610	149	Obtained from Pegasus Airways Ltd following collapse 11.61. Entered service 3.63. To Invicta Airways 1.65.
G-AHPS	610	167	Obtained 5.64, ex-D-ABOM, D-BORA. Used as spares, then scrapped.
G-ASBE	634	214	Obtained 6.62. Used for spares - never entered service.
G-AJBT	245		Obtained from Pegasus Airways Ltd following collapse in 11.61. Scrapped at Luton 1962.

Bristol 170 Freighter

| G-AIFS | 21 | 12778 | Obtained 2.66 from Aviacion y Comercio, Scrapped at Luton 1.68. |

Airspeed A.S.57 Ambassador

G-ALZS	2	5215	Obtained 11.63 from Globe Air. Damaged beyond repair at Luton 14.9.67.
G-ALZV	-	5218	Obtained 12.63 from Globe Air. Scrapped at
G-ALZZ	-	5222	Obtained 8.63 from Globe Air. Scrapped at Luton 5.69.

Douglas C-54 Skymaster

| G-ASZT | D | 10640 | Obtained 1.65. To Air trans-Africa as VP-YYR 8.65 |

Handley Page Herald

G-APWA	100	149	Leased from Handley Page Ltd. 4.63. Returned off lease 8.63.
G-APWB	101	150	Obtained from Handley Page Ltd 11.66. Disposed of to Linease Aereas la Uracca, Colombia as HK-178 11.70
G-APWC	101	151	Obtained from Handley Page Ltd 11.66. Disposed of to Linease Aereas la Uracca, Colombia as HK-175 11.70.
G-APWD	101	152	Obtained from Handley Page Ltd 11.66. Disposed of to Linease Aereas la Uracca, Colombia as HK-721 11.70
G-ASSK	211	161	Leased from Handley Page Ltd 8.63. Returned off lease 12.63.

Avro 748

| G-ATMI | 225 | 1592 | Obtained 30.3.66. Leased to Leeward Islands Air Transport 13.11.67. as VP-LIU to 14.5.68. Wore name *Halcyon Breeze* in LIAT service. Leased to Skyways 14.5.68 to 1.10.68 and 15.3.69 to 11.11.69. Leased to Leeward |

Islands Air Transport 11.11.69 to 4.70. Leased to SATA 5.70 to 5.10.70. Leased to BAF 4.71 to 11.71. Disposed of 12.71 to Leewards Islands Air Transport.

G-ATMJ 225 1593 Obtained 20.4.66. Leased to Jamaica Air Services. as 6Y-JFJ 15.1.68 to 2.4.69. Later leased to Leeward Islands Air Transport 11.71 to 4.72 as VP-LAJ. Leased to Rousseau Aviation 4.72 to 6.72. Leased to Leeward Islands Air Transport 7.72 to 10.72 Disposed of 10.72 to Civil Aviation Flying Unit.

British Aircraft Corporation One-Eleven - Four Hundred Series

G-AVGP 408EF 114 Obtained 13.12.68 on lease from BAC. Painted in full Autair colours, but only leased at weekends, in week used by BAC for crew training. Full time lease commenced 4.2.69. Named *Halcyon Cloud*. Returned off lease to BAC Weybridge 10.2.70.

G-AVOE 416EK 129 Obtained 19.3.68. Named *Halcyon Days*. Disposed of 12.69 to Cambrian Airways Ltd.

G-AVOF 416EK 131 Obtained 8.2.68. Named *Halcyon Breeze*. Disposed of 10.12.69 to Cambrian Airways Ltd.

G-AWBL 416EK 132 Obtained 1.5.68. Named *Halcyon Dawn*. To Court Line Aviation 5.12.69. (turquoise). Disposed of 20.1.71 to Cambrian Airways Ltd.

G-AWXJ 416EK 166 Obtained on lease 20.3.69 from BAC. Named *Halcyon Sun*. Returned off lease 11.69.

British Aircraft Corporation One-Eleven - Five Hundred Series

G-AXLM 523FJ 199 Obtained 24.9.73, on lease from British Midland Airways. Returned off lease 4.2.74.

G-AXLN 523FJ 211 Obtained 29.2.72, on lease from British Midland Airways. Returned off lease 25.9.73.

G-AXMF 518FG 200 Obtained 5.12.69. Named *Halcyon Breeze* (pink). In service at time of collapse. Ferried from Manchester to Hurn 29.8.74. To PT-TYX 12.74,

G-AXMG 518FG 201 Obtained 18.12.69. Named *Halcyon Sky* (turquoise). Leased to Cyprus Airways 15.5.74 as 5B-DAF. Stranded at Nicosia after Turkish invasion 22.7.74. Still there at time of collapse. Returned to Hurn 11.12.75.

G-AXMH 518FG 202 Obtained 11.2.70. Named *Halcyon Sun* (orange). In service at time of collapse. Ferried

a **court line** flight guide for you...

			to Hurn 11.9.74. Re-registered as G-BDAS 2.75 for Dan-Air Services Ltd.
G-AXMI	518FG	203	Obtained 24.3.70. Named *Halcyon Days* (pink). In service at time of collapse. Ferried to Hurn 11.9.74. Re-registered as G-BDAE 2.75 for Dan- Air Services Ltd.
G-AXMJ	518FG	204	Obtained 12.3.70. Named *Halcyon Nights* (turquoise). Collided with Piper Aztec G-AYDE 18.4.74. Repaired, back in service 11.5.74. In service at time of collapse. Ferried to Hurn 11.9.74. Re-registered as G-BCWG 2.75 for Monarch Airways. Ltd.
G-AXMK	518FG	205	Obtained 17.4.70. Named *Halcyon Star* (turquoise, but re-painted orange during that summer). Leased to Aviateca Guatemala as TG- ARA, arriving Guatemala City 23.11.70 Returned off lease 6.4.71. Leased to Leeward Islands Air Transport as VP-LAK 22.11.71. Returned off lease 5.7.72. Leased to Germanair Bedarfsluftfahrt 21.5.74. In service at time of collapse. Lease continued until 30.10.74. Re- registered as G-BCWA 2.75 for Dan-Air Services Ltd.
G-AXML	518FG	206	Obtained 30.4.70. Named *Halcyon Cloud* (pink). Leased to LANICA 22.12.71 as AN -BHJ. Returned off lease 28.3.72. In service at time of collapse. Ferried to Hurn 11.9.74. To BAC Ltd.
G-AYOP	518FG	233	Obtained 26.3.71 on lease from BCAL. (orange) Named *Halcyon Beach*. Returned to British Caledonian Airways 8.12.72.
G-AYOR	518FG	232	Obtained 5.2.71. (orange) Named *Halcyon Dawn*. Ferried from Cardiff to Hurn 21.8.74. Re-registered G-BDAT 2.75 for Dan-Air Services.
G-AYWB	531FS	237	Registered to Court Line 14.4.71 although built to British Caledonian Airways order for CourtLine to lease to LACSA. Registration not used.
G-AYSC	518FG	235	Registered to Court Line 4.2.71, but order not finalised and cancelled 30.3.71

Opposite page
The front cover of the Summer 1971 Inflight Magazine, designed and produced by Murdoch Design Associates Ltd. It shows BAC 1-11 G-AGMH banking away from the camera during a publicity flight over the south coast of England.

G-AYXB	521FH	192	Obtained 22.4.71 on lease from Austral. Wore hybrid colour scheme. Named *Halcyon Bay.* Returned off lease 8.10.71.
G-AZEB	517FE	188	Obtained 9.71. Named *Halcyon Bay* (lilac). Leased to Leeward Islands Air Transport as VP-LAP 1.12.72. Returned off lease 7.3.74. In service at time of collapse. Ferried to Hurn 11.9.74.
G-AZEC	517FE	189	Obtained 28.9.71. Named *Halcyon Cove* (lilac). Leased to Leeward Islands Air Transport 1.12.73 as VP-LAR. Returned off lease 26.3.74. In service at time of collapse. Ferried to Hurn 11.9.74.
G-BCCV	517FE	198	Obtained 20.6.72 for use by LIAT. Named *Halcyon Beach* (lilac).Leased 24.6.72 to LIAT. Returned off lease 25.5.74. In service at time of collapse. Ferried to Hurn 11.9.74. Re-registered G BCXR 2.75 for Monarch Airlines.

Lockheed L.101l TriStar

G-BAAA	1	1024	Obtained 3.73. Named *Halcyon Days* (orange). In service at time of collapse. To CathayPacific Airways Ltd. as VR-HHV 3.77.
G-BAAB	1	1032	Obtained 5.73. Named *Halcyon Breeze* (pink). In service at time of collapse. To Cathay Pacific Airways Ltd. as VR-HHW 3.77.

Hawker Siddeley 125

G-AVRG	3A	25144	Obtained 11.71. Named *Halcyon Days* (orange). In service at time of collapse.

Bell 206 JetRanger

G-AXMM	A	405	Obtained 8.69. In service at time of collapse.

Piper PE31 Navajo

G-AYEI	P300	31-631	Obtained 6.70. Disposed of 11.72

Blackburn Beverley

G-AOAI	C. 1	1002	Obtained from RAE 3.73. Moved to Luton, but never entered commercial service.

Opposite page
'Court Line fly ahead with the the world's most advanced airliner. TriStar powered by Rolls-Royce's new generation RB 2-11 fan jets'. So said the cover details for the 1973 Inflight Magazine, designed and produced by Murdoch Design Associates Ltd.

LEEWARD ISLAND AIR TRANSPORT

As Leeward Island Air Transport became a fully owned subsidiary of Court Line Aviation, their fleet (as far as is known for the period of Court Line Ownership) is shown below, along with earlier aircraft leased from Autair.

Avro748

VP-LAA	217	1670	Obtained 8.10.69. Originally ordered as 9Y-TDH for BWIA.
VP-LAJ	225	1593	Obtained 11.71. Leased from Court Line. Returned off lease 4.72. 7.72 until 10.72 Leased from Court Line.
VP-LII	101	1537	Obtained on lease from Dan-Air. Services Ltd 1966. Returned off lease 1967.
VP-LIK	217	1583	Obtained new 21.5.65.
VP-LIN	222	1586	Leased from Channel Airways 4.12.65. Returned from lease 16.5.66.
VP-LIO	101	1535	Obtained on lease from Dan-Air. Services Ltd 1966. Returned from lease 1967.
VP-LIP	217	1584	Obtained new 16.8.65.
VP-LIU	225	1592	Leased from Autair 13.11.67. Returned from lease 14.5.68. Leased from Autair 11.11.69 Returned from lease 4.70. Leased from Court Line 3.71. Transferred to LIAT 16.11.71.
VP-LIV	222	1588	Obtained from Channel Airways 16.5.68.
VP-LIW	222	1585	Obtained from Channel Airways 4.68

Britain-Norman Islander

VP-LAC	2A	80	Obtained from USA, ex-N854JA.
VP-LAD	2A	153	Obtained 4.70. Believed obtained new.
VP-LAE	2A	160	Obtained 2.70. Believed obtained new.
VP-LAF	2A	161	Obtained 2.70. Believed obtained new.
VP-LAG	2A	163	Obtained 4.70. Believed obtained new.

British Aircraft Corporation One-Eleven 500 Series

VP-LAK	518FG	205	Obtained on lease from Court Line, arriving Antigua 24.11.71. Named *Halcyon Star*. Returned to Luton, arriving 2.7.72.
VP-LAN	517FE	198	Obtained from Court Line on lease, arriving Antigua 24.6.72. Named *Halcyon Beach*. Flew last service for LIAT 29.4.74. Returned to Luton 30.4.74.
VP-LAP	517FE	188	Obtained from Court Line on lease 28.11.72. Named *Halcyon Bay*. Returned off lease 7.3.74.
VP-LAR	517FE	189	Obtained on lease from Court Line 1.12.73. Named *Halcyon Cove*. Returned off lease 26.3.74.

Appendix Three

Important Dates

1905	Court Line founded by P. E. Haldenstein.
1911	Haldenstein teams up with H. R. Phillips.
1915	Chairman of Court Line changes name to Haldin due to anti-German feeling sweeping the UK due to the Great War.
1922	Haldin and Phillips Co. formed.
1929	Haldin and Phillips takes over Court Line. Company placed into liquidation and disposed of to United British Steamship Co. Ltd. (UBSC)
1936	Court Line name resurrected by UBSC.
1943	Cory & Strick (Steamers Ltd) Ltd acquired by UBSC and re-named British Steamship Co. Ltd (BSC).
1946	BSC takes over Court Line and Court name disappears for a second time.
1953	William H. ('Bill') Armstrong founds Autair Helicopters working in co-operation with R. M. Myhill's Overseas Motors Ltd.
1955	Autair gain contract to provide helicopter support for survey of Antarctic region.
	Autair provide helicopters for Arctic mineral survey.
	Bill Armstrong negotiates first contract for helicopter operations in Central Africa.
1956 - December	Autair provide helicopters for second Antarctic survey.
	Frank Delisle forms Leeward Islands Air Transport.
1957 - 1 February	Edward Posey joins Autair.
1960	Autair (Luton) Ltd founded. First aircraft, a C-47 obtained from BEA.
1961	Two more C-47's acquired.
- October	Pegasus Aviation goes bust - Autair obtain their Vikings.
- 25 October	John Young joins the board of Court Line Group.
	Aircraft handling company Lutair Handling Services formed.
	Small base at Berlin established by Autair.
1962	Two Vickers Viking aircraft placed into service.
1963	John Young appointed the Managing Director of the Court Line Group.
	Two Herald aircraft leased.
- 1 October	Scheduled Blackpool -Luton service inaugurated.
	Airspeed Ambassadors acquired from Globe Air.
1964 - 23 September	Proving flight made by Ambassador G-ALZZ to Maderia.
	Helicopters South Africa formed.
	Group takes over Rhodesian Air Services and re-names it Air Trans-Africa.

1965	- 15 April	Court Line Group acquire Autair International Airways.
		Bill Armstrong's Autair Group founds Bechuanaland National Airways.
		Court Line acquire Appledore shipyard.
	- November	Two Avro 748's ordered.
1966	- March	Ist 748 arrives.
	- April	Ed Posey and Gerry Threlfall appointed joint Managing Directors of Autair International.
		Autair granted Hull-Luton scheduled service.
	- 16 May	Proving flight to Dundee using 748.
	- 24 May	Liverpool service extended to Glasgow.
		Obtains Handley Page Heralds from BEA
		Durrant House Hotel acquired.
		Autair Obtains contract to operate Libyan Government VIP flight.
1967	- 1 January	Autair takes over BKS Teesside - London service.
	- January	Autair expressed interest in obtaining BAC One-Elevens.
	- February	Autair orders two BAC One-Eleven 400s.
		Dundee - Jersey, Dundee - Isle of Man, Dundee - Luton licences granted.
	- July 11th	Teeside - Amsterdam service started.
	- 23 December	Capt Dryhurst and F/O Boothman killed in HS 125 crash.
1968		Court Line board members and Clarksons representative visit Caribbean on fact-finding tour.
	- 8 February	First BAC One-Eleven 400 delivered.
	- 1 April	Scheduled services move from Luton to London Heathrow.
	- 31 July	Autair announces closure of all scheduled services.
	- 11 September	Autair launches name change and new image at London's Savoy hotel.
	- 1 November	Scheduled services stops.
		Seagate Hotel acquired.
1969		Two hotel sites in St Lucia acquired.
		Eleven BAC One-Eleven 500 series aircraft ordered.
	- November	Airline announce change of image and name.
1970	- January	Court Line Aviation appears to the public for the first time.
	- 23 June	Court Line board members and representatives from Clarksons visit Lockheed Aircraft Corp to view their new wide-bodied L-1011 TriStar.
	- 2 July	Court board sign letter of intent to obtain two L-1011s with options on a further three.
		Court Line acquire Autair Helicopters South Africa.
		First hotel in St Lucia opens for business.
1971		Second hotel in St. Lucia opens for business.
	- 1 October	Court Line acquire 75% share of Leeward Islands Air Transport (LIAT)
1972	- May	Court Line acquire Eastern Caribbean Airways Ltd.

COURT LINE AVIATION NEWS GUIDE — 1st APRIL 1974

COURTKORDSKI
Our Russian Subsidary – by MICHOVSKI BELISCOVITCH.

Amidst the white snow our Orange Ambassador (thought it was a TriStar) landed at Moscow Airport on Sunday 10th March. A great event indeed. Once again, Court Line had the privilege of operating a first with the Tri-Star – only this time with perhaps more significance than ever before.

A last minute rush to obtain clearance on Saturday resulted in our American friends at the Embassy and our Russian colleagues at the Ministry passing official dispatches in the dead of night!!!

All was well – the aircraft was met by senior officials of the Ministry, Airport and Aeroflot. Amidst great handshaking and back slapping, Mr. Prill and colleagues of Lockheed were driven to a VIP meeting to finalise the events of the next three days.

From the accounts received from Lockheed and Court Line people, it would appear that our aircraft had a major check during its stay. The majority of removable parts were removed; the aircraft was photographed from the ground, the air, inside, outside, upside and downside. People were seen scurrying about with pads and pencils on which appeared little diagrams of ice tongs, trays, seat belts, food trolleys and oxygen masks.

Questions flowed like water: "Can you really board in 15 minutes?", "Can you inflate a life raft please?", "Can you drop the oxygen masks please?", "Does it really carry 400 people?".

I heard that all the crew and engineers are going on a refresher course – I wont say that their brains were picked clean, but daylight was visible!

Our Russian Ministry friends invited us all to a farewell reception on Tuesday evening. The dangers of Vodka, Russian style, were feared by all, but after three or four – or was it five or six – our fears were allayed.

Unfortunately, I wonder for who, the next day after carefully checking our aircraft and passengers, we departed for the UK.

During our stay, assistance and helpfulness were plentiful – when a piece of equipment is not available and the Russian ground staff produce it freshly tooled who can complain? One again, all Court Line personnel were a credit to the Company.

Certainly this demonstration can only help any future Lockheed or Court Line activities in Russia.   M.J.B.

THE ART OF COURSE COURT RUGBY
Court Cougars v. Cambrian Dragons
(With apologies to Michael Green, from our Court Correspondant)

In the wee small hours of the 16th February, a small band of experienced rugby players gathered at the Luton Terminal at various intervals for an ETD of 0600. True to form for a scratch fifteen (or was it fourteen) we departed on time 45 minutes later. Ably led by Bruce (Pressgang) Smith we made a quick stop at Caddington to raise our erst while Admin Manager from the land of nod – unsuccessfully, and due to the heavy coach crew made a rapid coach trip in 4½ hours to Cardiff in Welsh Walès.

After changing into a set of fifteenth hand – well ventilated shirts at the Barry Sports Centre (why do Welshmen name their towns after their star rugby players), we adjoined to a soccer pitch at Rhoose Airport to await the arrival of our opponents. The time was spent in practicing handling using an empty Coke can. Tony Mack of OSL chatted up the referee and managed to borrow his boots. John the coach, not the team trainer, appeared on the pitch in his brown cuban heeled boots, more as a result of Bruce Smith's appeals to his patriotism than his desire to play rugby – you can't keep a Welshman from his rugby though.

Fifty minutes later and gasping for a well earned pint, sober discussions took place on the final score – could we have lost by 28 to nil? After all our star team had players in it who had not been on a rugby pitch for period that ranged from last week up to 2, 10 and 18 years ago. Nevertheless the game was played in a very friendly spirit.

Lunch was prepared by Cambrian and served in brown paper bags with vague familiarity to all airline personnel and eaten on the coach that took us to Cardiff Arms Park to see the Wales v France International.

The morning match at the airport was however only a foretaste of the scrummaging and rucking enjoyed by your actual Welsh supporter on the West Terraces. At times the spectators seemed keen enough to take their game into the French half of the pitch. The final score was appropriately a draw with 16 points each.

After a few jars of ale and being serenaded by a band from La Pays Basque, the team and several supporters retired to watch the recorded highlights on the TV in a near at hand hotel room. By this time the team were back in hard training and the density of cigarette smoke was sufficient to trigger off the hotel's fire alarm system.

Several people were by now experiencing hunger pangs and the highlight of the evening was a visit to a nearby steak bar where, serenaded by vociferous supporters in the adjacent bar. The Cougars practised ordering a meal in Welsh from the naturalised Spanish waitress in residence – shades of Egon Ronay. After many false starts and a detour to the Waters Edge Hotel, Barry, thanks for the vino girls!, a tired and triumphant bunch of chaps arrived back at Luton early on Sunday morning.

Anybody who wishes to repeat the experience at a future date should ensure that Brucy Baby doesn't hear about it first.   DWR

CIRCULATION RESTRICTED TO COURT LINE AVIATION STAFF

CLANG for July 1974 - Staff News just before the collapse.

Court Line
Behind the Scenes

Court Line Behind the Scenes
It takes a great deal of detailed and experienced work to keep Court Line's aircraft running absolutely smoothly. Behind the scenes there is a large and highly proficient organisation operating Britain's most go-ahead airline.

Aircraft Maintenance

Court Line's Engineering Department consists of 300 fully qualified and experienced engineering staff who service not only the TriStars and BAC 1-11s, but also many other types of aircraft.

In addition to Court Line's own staff, there are many special experts at Luton from Lockheed, the British Aircraft Corporation, Rolls Royce etc. All these people ensure that the aircraft are in tip top condition before every flight.

Training

All Court Line personnel undergo a very full training period before joining the Airline's operations.

Pilots spend three weeks in the classroom, 28 hours on the Flight Simulator and 6 hours on the actual aircraft, followed by 30 hours training on commercial flights, before becoming fully qualified.

Court Line's 300 Air Hostesses (only one girl in ten interviewed is chosen) have spent 5 weeks training in First Aid, emergency procedure, bar and cabin service, etc. At Luton a full-size cabin mock up of the TriStar, the first in Britain, is used for the final training period on these aircraft. This mock up consists of an entire centre section of the TriStar with fully working lifts, under floor galley, passenger seats with space for lectures and films.

Court Line Catering

Court Line Catering is not just an airline catering service. It is a company that provides bulk meals to industry, large offices, motorway service stations and to hotels. It operates from a large and fully equipped catering centre capable of producing over 20,000 meals a day.

So when Court Line Catering supplies its meals for airliners it can call on the know how and imagination that it applies when feeding the most demanding of customers. And because it is part of Court Line, it knows how to look after air passengers best.

Court Line Coaches

If you came to the airport on a special Court Line Coach, you were travelling with one of Britain's largest coach companies. 56 coaches are operated by the company to make sure that the good service you receive on board the aircraft is extended while you are travelling by road to and from the airport. The coach Company does not just carry airline passengers. A large amount of its work is carrying private parties, special groups and even taking people to work.

So Court Line keep their aircraft operating efficiently by taking other activities very seriously. It's the kind of thinking that makes it a pleasure to have the Court Line working for you.

North London Air Terminal

Luton Airport, Court Line Offices

Flight Simulator Map

Flight Planning Office

Mary Quant Styles for Hostesses

Court Line Coaches

TriStar in Maintenance Hangar

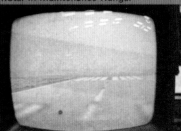
Telescreen Flight Simulator

Court Line Catering

Interior of a Court BAC 1-11

		One hotel on Antigua acquired.
		One hotel on Nassau acquired.
		Court Line Group market Caribbean hotels in the UK.
	- August	Court Line announce leasing of a pair of Lockheed L.1011 TriStars.
	- October	Court Line acquire remaining shares in LIAT.
1973		Mary Quant-designed uniform introduced.
	- 28 February	First TriStar G-BAAA) accepted by Court Line.
	- 3 March	First TriStar arrives at Luton.
	- 19 April	Court Line acquire 85% of Clarksons Holidays.
1974	- 10 March	TriStar G-BAAA visits Moscow on sales trip.
	- April/May	Series of meetings held with Government about financial status of Group.
	- 21 June	Announcement made that Government was to take a substantial interest in Court Line Shipping. Shares suspended on Stock Exchange.
	- 26 June	Anthony Wedgwood Benn makes statement in House of Commons announcing nationalisation of Court Shipping interests.
	- 11 July	Board decide to cease TriStar operations in 1975.
	- 8 August	British Airways inform Department of Trade that they were not interested in taking over Court Line Aviation.
	- 15 August	2200hrs: Announcement made that the Court Line Group will cease trading at midnight.
	- 16 August	0939hrs Last Court Line Aviation flight - NoOU1201, TriStar G-BAAB returns to Luton.
1975	- 21 July	Interim report into collapse published.
	- August	Holidaymakers start to get money back from Tour Operators Study Group.
1989	- 26 October	Official Liquidators finally 'wind-up' the remains of the Court Line Group.

Acknowledgements

With a project as large as this it is usually very difficult to know exactly where to begin with my thanks - normally it is unfair to single any one individual out, but without doubt, this title is different.

I think it is safe to say that there would not have been a *Colours in the Sky* — an absolutely brilliant title for the book which was suggested and must be credited to Court Line Air Hostess Honor Brooker - without the drive and determination of Jaqui Maschera, for without her the story would not have been told! Thanks Jaqui, from everyone in Autair and Court Line!

Thanks must go - in no particular order - to Reg Law; Maureen Campbell and all at the Civil Aviation Authority Library, LGW; Gina Alexander of the British Airline Pilots Association; Aileeen Price; Anthony Nice; W. ('Bill') Armstrong and his wife Doreen for starting it all and keeping all the papers and photos; Mike Stanbrook, BAe Airbus Division, Filton for lots of One Eleven data; John Young, Editor *Shipping Today and Yesterday* ; Roy Fenton for information on things that float; John Clarkson; Maurice and Pamela Rowan; Elizabeth Overbury; C.P.C. ('Pete') Dibley; Susan Aldridge; Kathy Moran; Mike Finlay; Stella Elliott; Melanie Henry, LIAT (1974) Ltd; Peter Hart; John Allan; Mark Strzesiewski, Sue Farr; Kurt Lang; John Young, (Chairman and Managing Director Court Line Group); Simon Peters for collecting so much airline 'junk' over the years; Mike Ellis; Mike Tyrrell; Mike and Rosie James; Mike and Dee Budge; Mike Willis; Martin Clough; Audrey Potton; Jon Charley; John McLean-Hall; Doug White; Sally Thomas; Tom Crawford, Lockheed-Martin Aeronautical Systems Support Co. Marietta for so much L-1011 material; Anne Baggott; Velia Dobinson; Ann Harrington; Edward J ('Ed') Posey, (Director Court Line, Managing Director, Court Line Aviation); Marilyn Benham; John Allen; Maureen Graham; Peter and Julia Murdoch for much original material; Rosie Boorman; Chris Penny; Pamela Guess, British Aerospace Farnborough for some One-Eleven photos; Dee Newkirk; Jenny Berryman; Pauline Lord; Helen Connolly; Ann McNulty; Carol Barford; John Hepworth; Sandy Keegan; Cristabel Reiche West; John Plowman; Ruth Matthews; Mike Albone; John Webb; Shirley Sosnick; Peter V. Clegg and David Leefor proof-reading... and everyone else who worked at any time for the Autair group of companies and the Court Line Group.

Index